D1233691

The Wars of Alexander's Successors

323–281 BC

The Wars of Alexander's Successors

323–281 BC

VOLUME 2: Armies, Tactics and Battles

Bob Bennett & Mike Roberts

Pen & Sword
MILITARY

First published in Great Britain in 2009 by
Pen & Sword Aviation
an imprint of
Pen & Sword Books Ltd
47 Church Street
Barnsley
South Yorkshire
S70 2AS

ISBN 978-1-84415-924-6

The right of R. Bennett and M. Roberts to be identified as Author of this
Work has been asserted by them in accordance with the Copyright,
Designs and Patents Act 1988.

A CIP catalogue record for this book is available from the British Library.

Typeset in 11.5pt Ehrhardt by
Mac Style, Beverley, E. Yorkshire

Printed and bound in the UK by the MPG Books Group

Pen & Sword Books Ltd incorporates the imprints of Pen & Sword
Aviation, Pen & Sword Maritime, Pen & Sword Military, Wharncliffe
Local History, Pen and Sword Select, Pen and Sword Military Classics and
Leo Cooper.

For a complete list of Pen & Sword titles please contact
PEN & SWORD BOOKS LIMITED
47 Church Street, Barnsley, South Yorkshire, S70 2AS, England
E-mail: enquiries@pen-and-sword.co.uk
Website: www.pen-and-sword.co.uk

Pen & Sword
November 2009

Contents

Acknowledgements vii
List of Plates viii
List of Maps ix
Introduction xiii

1. Soldiers and Armies 1

2. The Lamian War 27

3. Eumenes' War 41

4. Gabene and Paraetacene 55

5. Battle of Gaza 89

6. Battle of Ipsus 101

7. Siege Warfare 115

8. Naval Warfare 137

9. Border Wars 157

10. Conclusion 171

Notes 179
Bibliography 191
Index 195

Acknowledgements

As with our first volume, our thanks go out to the late Mr Polack (Bob's old teacher) for his translation of Polynaeus and to Jeff Champion without whom we would not have appeared in print. More specifically for this volume, we would like to thank again Phil Sidnell, our editor, who has been an invaluable source of help and guidance in both the planning and gestation of this book.

Since the publication of Volume 1 we have been touched and gratified by the support of our friends and work colleagues who have not only bought the book but appear to have actually read it and said many complimentary things as well. Finally our thanks go again to our wives Janet and Sue and children Katie, Joe, Philip and Stephen. After publication of Volume 1 they have been at last forced to take us seriously and their interest has concomitantly increased from the intermittent to the almost frequent.

List of Plates

Artist's impression of a Macedonian heavy cavalryman (copyright J Yosri)
Artist's impression of a typical phalangite (copyright J Yosri)
Bust of a Macedonian soldier of the late fourth century BC, Naples Archaeological Museum (author's photograph)
Artist's impression of a light infantryman or peltast (copyright J Yosri)
Artist's impression of a war elephant (copyright J Yosri)
Artist's impression of an Iranian light cavalryman (copyright J Yosri)
Details from 'Issus Mosaic', Naples Archaeological Museum (author's photograph)
Artist's impression of a Hellenistic *lithobolos* (stone thrower), after Jeff Burn (copyright J Yosri)
Hellenistic walls (author's photograph)
Salamis port (author's photograph)
The reconstructed Greek trireme *Olympias* (courtesy of www.hellenicnavy.gr)

List of Maps

The World of the Successors x
Leonnatus' Battle, 322 BC 34
Battle of Crannon, 322 BC 38
Battle of the Hellespont, 321 BC 53
Battle of Paraetacene, 317 BC, initial deployments 67
Battle of Paraetacene, 317 BC, phase 1 69
Battle of Paraetacene, 317 BC, phase 2 70
Battle of Paraetacene, 317 BC, phase 3 72
Battle of Gabene, 316 BC, initial deployments 80
Battle of Gabene, 316 BC, phase 1 82
Battle of Gabene, 316 BC, phase 2 87
Battle of Gaza, 312 BC 98
Battle of Salamis, 306 BC 151

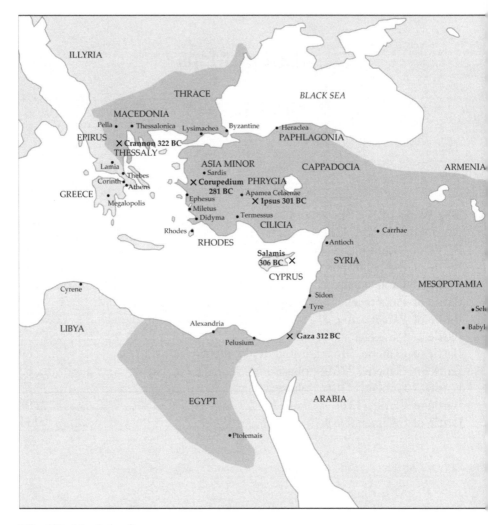

The World of the Successors.

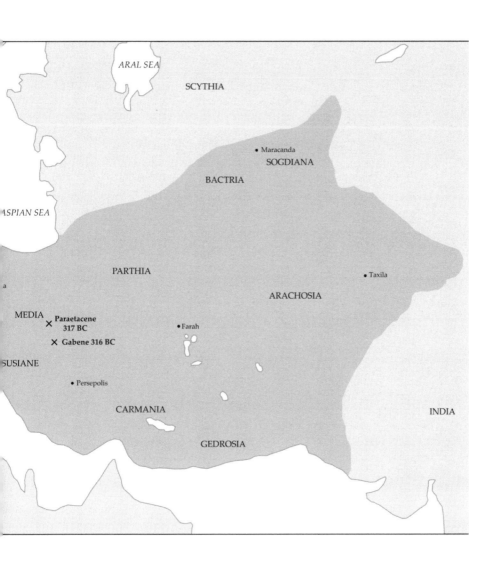

ARAL SEA

SCYTHIA

• Maracanda

SOGDIANA

BACTRIA

CASPIAN SEA

PARTHIA

• Taxila

ARACHOSIA

MEDIA

Paraetacene
317 BC

× Gabene 316 BC

• Farah

SUSIANE

• Persepolis

CARMANIA

INDIA

GEDROSIA

Introduction

Military equipment and organization did not hurry to change in the pre-modern world; in fact, lack of change may be amongst the very definitions of the difference between then and the modern era. But, this did not mean that the people of the time did not think deeply about and modify the military institutions they had grown up with. The cerebral inclination and technological sophistication of the ancient Greeks remains one of the constant surprises of scholarship. The group of generals, rulers and kings who are studied in the following pages were very much amongst those who thought and adapted. Anti-elephant traps, great siege machines, and fire pots for attacking enemy warships just begin to show off their capacity to move and develop with the new. In the first volume of *The Wars of Alexander's Successors* we have suggested that in political motivation, policy and vision the *Diadochi* were understandable to a twenty-first century mind in a way that Alexander himself was not and, in the same way, how they functioned in their martial careers shows they were familiar with what we consider modern principles of war and their tactical and strategic decision making is not at all outlandish to us.

Despite the generally slow pace of change in the ancient era, in some ways the fourth century BC could be claimed as a period of real martial development when compared to the several centuries before it. Battles in the Greek world went from just a hoplite scrum to something very different indeed, with many more sorts of warriors deployed to many different kinds of tactical and strategic blueprints. The scale of warfare, too, expanded in this period, the size of armies increased markedly as did the extent of the territory over which campaigns were fought. And the *Diadochi*, heirs of Alexander, being men born in that century, were children of change, yet still a change that was really an adjustment not a revolution, taking place within a limited range. So, these heroes of our story are still actors working within centuries of distilled military tradition.

The story of ancient warfare is a generally pretty well-ploughed acre and has been for a long time, whether it is coffee table volumes with sumptuous colour illustrations, well-drafted maps and photographs of relevant terrain or more obviously-intellectual efforts that eschew visual extravagance, but make more of an effort to place military matters deep within the culture in which it grew and that reflected the warrior *zeitgeist* of the time. But, in all these works, many of which are exceptionally worthwhile, the martial world of Alexander's Successors gets fairly short shrift. A thin chapter, at best, is all that's vouchsafed to the reader who is more likely to find a few paragraphs attached to the chapter devoted to Alexander, or a section referencing the epoch only as a sort of introduction to the rise of Rome.

This is perhaps not a surprise if, as is often suggested, even by the Emperor Hadrian's time the ancient world already had its greatest 'historical hits'.[1] That most literate people in the Graeco-Roman world in the second century AD already saw Herodotus' Persian Wars, Periclean Athens, the periods of Alexander's conquests and Ciceronian Rome as the times when civilizations had peaked and when the talents and qualities of the Greeks or their Roman heirs had hit the high notes. Suggesting that it was not just that these were the periods from which the sources survived but perhaps that these were where the sources reflected the periods of high culture and civilization and because of this very fact they were the ones that survived.

In any event, what is certain is that the forty years after Alexander's death never has been seen as, and still is not seen as, a period to compare with these other 'epochs'. Though, as with most good and interesting analysis, it is always possible to point to something that does not fit the pattern. So, here it should be noted that Cicero showed great interest in Demetrius of Phalerum, the ruler of Athens under Cassander's sponsorship, and later the polymath at the Ptolemaic court, who is mentioned on numerous occasions in the great man's writings.

If the military world of the Hellenistic states is dealt with at all, it is usually the later period when the collision with the nascent might of Rome was in the wind. This, again, is no surprise as the well-respected Polybius gives credible evidence to tell this part of the story, while the chroniclers who describe the life and times of the *Diadochi* are frequently second division in both literary quality and factual dependability. Indeed, the main one could be dismissed as simply a plagiarist ripping off earlier chroniclers and offering little from his own thought process. But, if much is stylistically dubious, fragmentary and, in the case of Plutarch, disinterested in military matters the epoch is not as badly attested as some; at least until 301 BC, when the main continuous source peters out leaving us very little military meat on the bone for the second half of most of the Successors' careers. Yet, before the century turns we have good material with few major gaps and details of terrific colour for the great campaigns and even for more peripheral events like the Cyrenean wars of Ptolemy or the Nabataean campaign of Antigonus and Demetrius.

Diodorus, who is our main guide, takes much from Hieronymus, who was there as a captain under Eumenes, possibly his kinsman and certainly a Cardian compatriot, and then for the Antigonids, father, son and grandson. And, in a long life, he stood always near the centres of power and thus the sources of information. The kind of numbers that Diodorus gives are always credible and, particularly in battles like Paraetacene and Gabene, the details of troop types and deployment suggest a source that had not just seen the battle arrays *in situ* but, in the first case in particular, had access to the battle plans drawn up in the command tent. More than this, Hieronymus seems to have stayed clear of the kind of fanciful and rhetorical embellishment that mars many of our other sources for these years. Seldom do we hear of 'myriads of men' that reflect a desire to boost the home side's achievements rather than the facts. From the pages of Diodorus army size and details of military types and casualties are almost always convincing. Even when huge armies are described in the field the wealth and power of their sponsors makes this credible. Particularly as armed forces of this kind of magnitude are well and convincingly attested under Alexander (the invasion of India was an affair of over 100,000 men) once he had gained the resources of Darius' Empire in order to mobilize them.

Yet, though the sources exist, few modern writers seem inclined to look in detail at the period. All that is often allowed for the era is a kind of 'freak show' element; an inclination to gigantism, shown in the use of elephants, in the building of monster siege engines and battleships with huge numbers of oarsmen and dimensions, that put them a world away from the triremes and quadriremes that were the typical warship of the line even in Alexander's day. This bloated condition is declared as decadence much like the art forms of the period, that are frequently taken to be a decline from the Classical heights of the fifth century. Like all such generalizations this does not tell us everything, but still there is something in it. Demetrius, Antigonus' son, clearly revelled in his reputation as a great besieger of cities and in each of his sieges he seemed to compete with himself to build bigger and bigger engines of war, with no apparent concurrent increase in performance. Yet, to accept wholesale this picture is certainly unfair to many of the leaders who came to the fore in the wake of Alexander's demise.

The story of the Successor wars is also a tale of subtlety and subterfuge as well as raw might. Intelligence is much prized in commanders and often is shown to win the day; Damis with his elephant traps at Megalopolis is an early example. But if Odysseus was much admired, still Achilles appealed not just to Alexander but to many who came after him and nor were the two exemplars at all contradictory. Eumenes was probably regarded as the most cunning of all, yet he also famously fought and slew his deep and poisonous enemy, Neoptolemus, in a duel in the middle of a great battle at the very beginning of the Macedonian world wars. Pyrrhus, too, was admired for a reflective approach to military matters. He is claimed to be the first to institutionalize the use of the defended marching camp while on campaign, but, just as much, he was lauded for his duel with Demetrius Poliorcetes' bravest captain, Pantauchus, during a battle in Aetolia in 289 BC. Plutarch informs us that 'Pantauchus was by general consent the best fighting man of Demetrius' generals' but the young Epirote bested him in truly Homeric fashion, first throwing a spear then with close quarter swordplay.[2]

We have already dealt with the chronological narrative of the Successors in our first volume. It is now our intention to deal with military strategy and tactics in a more detailed and thematic fashion. However, historical context must still be given particularly in view of the fact that their military development was rooted in the reforms of Alexander and his father Philip.

Alexander, in thirteen years as king of Macedonia (from the death of his father, Philip, to his own at Babylon in 323 BC) first re-imposed the hegemony his forebear had battened on the north Balkans and Greece. He then battled in Illyria, met Celts by the Danube, razed the ancient city of Thebes to the ground before starting on the great project of his life. Then, a few years saw him crush the vast but fragile Persian Empire where the army created by Philip, and still mostly commanded by his old officers, showed itself in battle to be able to take on any odds that could be thrown at it. The army and its leader faced all kinds of military challenges, from satrapal forces of Greek mercenaries and Iranian and Anatolian cavalry to huge armies of all arms led by Darius, the Great King himself, to the kind of mobile force of nomad horse archers that would puzzle almost any conventional army, however well-equipped and intelligently led, until the advent of effective firearms. Then they faced down monsters in India as Porus fielded hundreds of elephants against Alexander, which terrified his men in a way nothing had before. He won at Hydaspes but at a terrible price, even if his foot guards eventually hamstrung enough of the huge beasts or drove them from the field by hacking off their trunks. The rest of the army the Indian ruler fielded was not so formidable but the pachyderms had done their worst. Not long after the battle, Alexander's Macedonians finally refused to follow him any further. Weeks of rotting clothes and snake bites in the monsoon had been important but it was the talk of the kingdom on the Ganges River possessing 4,000 war elephants that finally turned the table. A shrine was left by the waters of the Beas to show how far they had come but, even so, it was far less than the great conqueror would have liked.

Eventually, the extraordinary adventure finally ended on the banks of the Euphrates in 323 BC when Alexander's officers were left with the conundrum of what to do in a situation of contested succession that Alexander had made little attempt to clarify. Great officers argued at Babylon and some would become considerable players in history. Ptolemy would take over the legacy of the Pharaohs; Seleucus would create the nearest thing to a new Persian Empire. Antigonus' progeny would hold greater Macedonia. Others like Lysimachus and Cassander, after playing a game hand, would leave nothing with their name on it to posterity. Perdiccas, Craterus, Leonnatus, Eumenes, Pithon, Asander, Cleitus and Peucestas would, from fine starts, fall all too quickly, leaving in the long haul hardly a trace, but still each would be a major player in the military story that occupied the years after Alexander's death.

At the start, this pool of men was of mixed background and generation. Some were Greeks from cities as far apart as the Thracian Chersonese or the Peloponnese, others were from other Balkan kingdoms like Epirus. Some were of advancing years like Polyperchon or Antigonus, while Antipater, at least, was very ancient indeed. But most of them were Macedonians and most of roughly the same generation of Alexander himself. Others were a bit older, Craterus and Eumenes and perhaps Perdiccas (we can assume from service under Philip) were probably in early middle age but full of vigour and health. A core had even been playmates and school comrades of Alexander, so we know they too were 30 years old or so when Alexander died. Most had left Europe when young and their experiences of young manhood had been all to do with marching, fighting and ruling, with a fair leavening of intriguing as well. Aristotle had sent his nephew to keep his old pupils company, but to what extent Callisthenes sustained a philosophical dimension in the conquering cavalcade is arguable. The men who began to shape the world they found in their control in 323 BC, whether they were stationed in Macedonia, Phrygia, the Punjab or Babylon at the time of the epochal event, were soldiers.

The first chapter of this volume will describe the arms and armies of the main contestants and the military culture in the years after Alexander's death. A culture that they had developed from Macedonian tactical arrangements that were, themselves to a large degree, a synthesis of Greek and Persian ways of making war. A mixing of strong infantry and heavy horse to force victory at the point had been what Philip II had devised and Alexander perfected. And this admixture the *Diadochi* themselves might be seen to personify. They, too, grew to manhood in the Greek world, all be it on the margins, but then spent their often-long adult lives in an extra-European world where perspectives, influences, interests and opportunities could be very different.

At the commencement of our period, the armed forces the Successors fielded were much alike in nationality, cultural inclinations and training.

Many had been brothers in arms till a few years before. But, equally, there were differences of emphasis brought on by geography, resources and personal style that need to be recognized. Alexander's army did not break down into neat sections and then begin to attack each other. From the beginning, the armies fielded by rival *Diadochi* could be different in composition and this only increased as time went on. In 322 BC, the army Seleucus marched with (under Perdiccas' supreme command) to Cappadocia and on to the invasion of Egypt had many similarities to the one brought to Asia by Alexander from Macedonia. But by the Battle of Ipsus, twenty-one years later, the host Seleucus led across half the known world was very different from the army Cassander sent from Europe to aid his ally, Lysimachus, in Anatolia, yet ended fighting in the same climactic battle. These changes need to be recognized and clarified if the reasons the wars developed as they did are to be understood.

From this starting point, the main battles will be detailed from the Lamian War, through to the campaigns where the great rivals clashed: Eumenes versus Neoptolemus and Craterus, Antigonus versus Eumenes, and the other major contests that we have good sources for, culminating in Ipsus in 301 BC. Then we will look at the separate specialisms, siege and naval warfare. Few were the *Diadochi* wars where a siege or naval encounter was not crucial to the outcome and sometimes these encounters are well enough sourced to tell us much about the nature of conflict in the society that was evolving from the death of Alexander.

Finally, we will consider the periphery; Cassander spent more of his time struggling in Illyria, Acarnania and Epirus than he ever did directly confronting the Antigonids. It was a constant hazard for any ruler at Pella; the need to anticipate tribal incursions from the north. Lysimachus' career may have hit its high spot at Ipsus, but it was Getae, Scythians, Thracians and truculent Black Sea Greeks whose eruptions usually filled his nightmares. Even the Antigonids took on and indeed were bested by desert tribesmen. Ptolemy had to handle Libyan charioteers at times and Seleucus grappled with Indians from the Punjab and the steppe tribes of central Asia.

Chapter One

Soldiers and Armies

As with so many discussions involving the *Diadochi* everything seems to drag us back to Alexander one way and forward to the era of Rome on the other. We are drawn to the origin and the nemesis. To try and understand the armies the Successors deployed in their many wars, we must first try and understand the army that Alexander brought to Asia, because both were, by and large, Macedonian organizations. Changed certainly by experiences in Anatolia, Mesopotamia, Iran, Bactria, Sogdia and India, but subsequently only in the case of Seleucus' armies were the changes probably more than skin-deep. Elephants, chariots and light troops seemed to dominate in his armed forces, as they marched west from the borders of India towards the climactic Battle of Ipsus in 301 BC, in a manner that was quite different from his rivals. The military establishments that we have good details for, fighting the great battles of 323 to 312 BC, performed as Macedonians in a manner that would have been all too familiar to Alexander and even Philip, his father. The armies and the *Diadochi's* use of them was rooted in the invading host that Alexander led over the Hellespont in 334 BC and how that organization was used and developed in the years of conquest. What changes there were, between 323 and 281 BC, as the Hellenistic kingdoms shook themselves out, had more to do with the military problems the generals faced over those years, rather than any inherently different attitudes or approaches amongst the leaders and soldiers involved.

The core of both Alexander's armies and those of his Successors was the infantry phalanx, not always the battle winner but always the backbone. We know much of these units, not just from descriptions of their role in the creation of the Macedonian Empire but also because this formation exerted a fascination on generations to come, that stretched even down to Europe of the sixteenth and seventeenth centuries AD. If Machiavelli saw the Roman legion as the exemplar of his Florentine militia at the beginning of the sixteenth century, the cousins William Louis and Maurice of Nassau at the end of that century reformed the Dutch army based on ideas from Aelian's

Tactica, a work from the age of Trajan which discussed the place of the phalanx in the Macedonian war machine.

There had been military manuals written before Aelian, some even predate the rise of the Macedonian Empire. Aeneas Tacticus and Xenophon both wrote in the first half of the fourth century BC. Aeneas apparently penned a number of treatises on war but unfortunately only the one, *How to Survive under Siege*, remains. As for Xenophon, he produced a copious output, most of which is extant; however, his interest in military matters was mainly confined to his beloved horses. The material we do have on Alexander and his Successors' war machine dates from considerably later. Asclepiodotus in the first century BC wrote an account of the Greek phalanx, though it is more a philosophical treatise than a book of tactics designed for generals. Arrian (like Aelian, from the second century AD), usually regarded as the most reliable source for Alexander, was a Roman provincial governor and military man. He also wrote a *Tactica*, of which only the part on cavalry survives, though he has much useful military information in his life of Alexander. Both Arrian and Aelian may well have based much of their work on Polybius who, we know, wrote a *Tactica* in the second century BC, less than 200 years after the *Diadochi* era. Indeed, Arrian specifically cites the work which, again, is now lost. Polybius himself, though a Greek, knew some of the greatest Roman military figures of his age.

But, even if some of these ancient descriptions of the phalanx were anachronistic, describing a military organization which had long been defunct and was now surpassed by the Roman legion, their content still had strong resonance for its audience. Just as in much the same way Alexander's career always retained a special place throughout ancient history as the archetype of the conqueror. He retained this kudos even in comparison to other greats like Hannibal, Scipio Africanus and Julius Caesar; even though, it could be argued, he had an easier task than these later generals. They all fought enemies with comparable fighting qualities to themselves whereas those Alexander had to deal with were, by and large, peoples and tribes unused to fighting together and thus easier prey for the Macedonian military machine. But, whatever judgement is (or was) made, the fact remains that the Romans and their emperors, in particular, were 'suckers' for his glamour.

Nero, in 66 AD, apparently organized a new (all–Italian) force he styled as the 'phalanx of Alexander the Great' in order to conquer Parthia, though in the event it was never used. Caracalla took this hero worship of Alexander one step further and in 214 AD also organized a phalanx, but this time the soldiers were to be all Macedonian and the officers were instructed to adopt the names of Alexander's generals. And, less than twenty years later, the emperor, Alexander Severus, created a unit called the Silver Shields, named after Alexander's guardsmen who had such a major influence on the

Diadochi era. Many of the original members of the elite unit lived for several generations and their reputation and aura was such that units in Antiochus the Great's army in the 190s BC were still being called the Silver Shields. As for their Roman equivalents, both Nero's and Alexander Severus' units fought in the traditional Roman fashion. However, it is possible that Caracalla really did train his phalanx to fight in the 'Macedonian style' and certainly the unit was 16,000 strong as recommended in most military treatises.

This military formation that exerted such an attraction to so many was a real invention that had sprung fully-grown from the head of that extraordinary monarch Philip II of Macedonia. A man whose reputation only suffers eclipse by the inevitable comparison with the son he sired. Macedonia may have been out on the fringes of the Hellenic world when his career began but Philip had known that world from within. He had been exiled in Thebes as a youth of 15 years and stayed with a man called Pammanes, a soldier and a great friend of Epaminondas, and had seen there the cutting edge of Greek military evolution. It must have been here that Philip absorbed the idea of a deeper, weightier phalanx like the ones handled so successfully by Epaminondas at Leuctra in 371 BC and Mantinea in 362 BC, when the Thebans dispelled for ever the threat of Spartan hegemony that had lain like a black cloud over the Greek mainland since the triumph of those reactionaries in the Peloponnesian War.

The longer spears of his phalanx came from somewhere else. Philip, here, may have been influenced by Iphicrates of Athens who in the first half of the fourth century BC toured the ancient world from Thrace to Egypt commanding mercenary armies in the service of a number of employers. Cornelius Nepos even claims Iphicrates as Philip's protector at one stage: 'Eurydice the mother of Perdiccas and Philip fled with these two boys, after the death of Amyntas, to Iphicrates and was secure under his power'; and if this is true Philip would have known of his reforms first hand.[1] Some such closeness to these tactical reformers is required to explain the radical military thinking that Philip so quickly put into practice in his relatively backward country. Iphicrates armed his hoplites with a smaller shield and longer spear as well as a particularly sturdy boot that took his name.

Philip's kingdom was not a land of city states which, since time immemorial, had provided citizen spearmen and foot soldiers equipped to fight in the heart of the battle line, whose social status was intrinsically bound up with this function. Macedonia was famous for its aristocratic horsemen, if anything, and if the commonality fought at all it was as javelin-armed light troops. But the reforming king changed all that; he levied the peasantry and mobilized them around a core of infantry guards who had traditionally protected the king when he fought on foot. The social environment helped to grease the wheels of change. There was no dead hand of tradition dictating how infantry should fight as there was in the cities to the south. In Greece, in many places, it was generations before the military establishments changed their formations to Macedonian-style phalanxes, even though these 'new model' soldiers had already comprehensively seen off old-style hoplites in their own backyard on key occasions, from Chaeronea in 338 BC to Megalopolis in 331 BC.

The name of the original royal guards or foot companions was *pezhetairoi*, and, from then on, this was used as the designation for the whole of the new infantry arm. The men were now equipped with a small round shield (*pelte*) made of a bronze facing over a leather and wood core about 2 feet across, rimless and less concave than the traditional large round shield (*aspis*) of the classical hoplite. The shield was slung from the soldier's left shoulder on a baldric, to free up both his hands to wield an 18-foot pike (*sarissa*) that made the phalanx so formidable. This was in two pieces, weighed about 15 pounds with its front end sheathed with a 20-inch point and its butt similarly covered, so it acted to balance the great bulk of the pike held out in front and also could be used offensively if the weapon broke in combat. In this the phalangite differed from the citizen hoplite who held his *aspis* by a grip in the middle and used one hand to brandish his 8 to 9-foot spear. Helmets, body armour and greaves were worn by some of the men, probably at least the front-rankers, from the beginning and, with Alexander's success and with the resources available to his Successors, defensive equipment became more elaborate and complete over the years. If it is likely that some of the peasants that Philip conscripted made do with just helmet and shield, by a generation or two later they would have been very well armoured indeed.

These warriors were deployed in files usually 16 ranks deep, but this could be cut down to 8 or doubled to 32 as appropriate. The formation was not as deep as the weighty 48-man-deep Theban phalanx, but twice the depth of the typical 8-man file of the Classical era. Individual phalangites usually had 3 feet of frontage in battle formation, though in locked shields defensive formation this space reduced by a half. The smallest tactical unit was the 256-man *syntagma* comprising 16 files (*lochoi*) of 16 men. In overall command was the *syntagmatarch* and each file had an officer at the front, a *lochagos*, and one at the back, the *lochagos*' second in command, the *ouragos*, whose function was to encourage the men from the rear. The *syntagma* was also subdivided into two *taxeis* of 128 men, each under a *taxiarch* and then a *tetrarchia* (four files of 16 men) and a *dilochia* (two files of 16 men). How many *syntagmai* were in the main regimental infantry formation of Alexander (somewhat confusingly called a *taxis*) has caused much ink to be spilt by military historians of the ancient world. Some consider them to be 1,500 strong whilst others think 2,000 a more likely number. It will be noted that this is the approximate equivalent of either six *syntagmai* (1,500) or eight (2,000). But later *Diadochi* formations are described as either 1,000 or 2,000 men strong.

In the case of a 2,000 man *taxis*, when deployed 16 deep, there would have been 125 *lochoi* with a consequent frontage of 125 yards. Thus, at Paraetacene in 317 BC, where we have specific information, we can calculate that for Eumenes, who had 17,000 in his phalanx (and allowing for small gaps between the units), a complete frontage of roughly 1,100 yards. For Antigonus, the equivalent calculation at Paraetacene would give a frontage of about 1,800 yards or more. At Gaza in 312 BC, where the phalanxes were smaller, Demetrius' 11,000 infantry would have had a frontage of about 800 yards and Ptolemy with 18,000 men would have spread to 1,200 yards or so. Presumably, although we are not told, the general with the smaller phalanx would make it less deep, or have greater intervals between units, to avoid being outflanked by his opponent.

But what is sure is that, as in any army, these theoretical divisions and the numbers in them would not have long survived the attrition of campaigning. The phalanx units, like any other formations, would have gradually decreased in numbers until it was possible to get replacements. How this was achieved under those generals whose power base was far from Macedonia is very unclear. We have details of replacements coming from Macedonia to flesh out Alexander's depleted phalanxes but, after his death, activity of this sort is less recorded and also was practically much more difficult with no centrally-controlled state to organize and push them on their way. The tendency for those commanders who had no access to the manpower pool of Macedonia must have been to find replacements locally, but our sources for the *Diadochi* years are pretty specific about the nationality of the make up of the front line phalangites. They are recorded as either Macedonians or of mixed nationality or as mercenaries equipped to fight like Macedonians. This probably means that for some time most of those phalangites described as Macedonians were originally from that country and if they did include replacements from elsewhere, these were few in number.

The warriors that Philip had levied were well-drilled and had, even by Alexander's time, become far more expert soldiers than the citizen militia of classical Greece. Philip's thousands of recruits were trained into near professionals, to a high standard of fitness. They could march with very little baggage, only had one servant for every ten men and could even campaign in winter when most citizen hoplites would demand to go home to their farms. By the time of the Successors, the new essence of this soldiery was typified by the Silver Shields, who epitomize the more notorious and unfortunate qualities of the mercenary. These rootless men were dominated by the cash nexus, with all they owned and cared for in the wagons and tents of their camp. Their loyalty to the original Macedonian state, if not to the memory of Alexander, had been eroded by years away from home and, if they could be kept paid and loyal, they showed they might win an empire for their commanders. Yet, if these veteran professionals were necessary to found a dynasty, any ruler, so established, must eventually return at least a proportion of the men back to the land to become the progenitors of another generation of soldiers, something each of the Hellenistic dynasts strove to do once the campaigns that won them their kingdoms had been accomplished. Military colonies had been the martial bedrock of great states since records began and the Macedonian elites who took control, whether in Europe, Asia or Africa, were no exception.

Whether they were the old sweats from Philip's reign, or the new recruits that had been brought to Asia during the great conquests of Alexander, how many soldiers it amounted to who took the road to Persia is problematic. Diodorus describes 12,000 Macedonian foot crossing to Asia and 3,000 were probably already there, having been sent as an advance guard under Parmenion in 336/335 BC. In the winter of 334/333 BC, some of Alexander's officers took the married Macedonians back home (no detail of figures is given) with instructions to recruit more men. These were most likely those that are recorded as having arrived at Gordium, 3,000 foot and 300 horse in all. Another 5,000 foot and 800 horse could have arrived before Cilicia was invaded in 333 BC, but the evidence is somewhat confused (taken from Quintus Curtius and Polybius) and how many were actually Macedonians is a very moot point. In Babylonia in 331 BC, Alexander received 6,000 Macedonian foot and 500 Macedonian horse. It has been suggested that altogether between 9,000 and 12,000 Macedonian infantry came as replacements between the years 334 and 331 BC and this seems as credible a ball-park number as it is possible to get.[2] Two years later, Antipater sent 8,000 replacements who arrived in Bactria, but they are called Greeks, and in 326 BC Diodorus claims reinforcements of 30,000 foot and 600 horse, but again they are described as allies and Greek mercenaries. It is possible some of these were Macedonians but probably not many. Thus something over 20,000 Macedonians were available in the main army near the end of Alexander's life just before he dismissed the 10,000 veterans who Craterus was to lead back home to Europe. This suggests that 10,000-odd remained at Babylon when the world changed. However, these figures are far from certain.[3] It must also be remembered that some of Craterus' 10,000 veterans remained in Asia as he took only 6,000 Macedonians back to fight in Greece.

In addition to all these Macedonians over the Hellespont, when their king died there was a further new levy that Antipater and Craterus brought over to fight Perdiccas in the First Macedonian Civil War, following their successful prosecution of the Lamian War. Neither group had sustained many casualties in their particular theatres of the war of 321/320 BC and consequently there may have been, all told, between 30 and 40,000 warriors split between the various generals. With attrition, the understandable desire to go home by some of the forces, and the leakage of some to rebels such as Eumenes, there would have been a comparatively small number of troops to be divided between the legitimist officers. Furthermore, all the *Diadochi*, except whoever ruled at Pella, faced the same problem of how to get replacements for these troops and, regardless of whatever other troops they might have under arms, nobody was able to play at the high table of regal ambition unless they could deploy a Macedonian-style phalanx of some description.

The result was that soon, as well as the original Macedonian phalangites who conquered the world under Alexander, many ersatz versions were armed and drilled to fill the gap. Other troop types were re-equipped, trained and armed so they could stand in the main phalanx with their Macedonian comrades. Some of these would have been Greek citizen hoplites who had previously carried the old big shield and short spear that remained for many years the standard military equipment in Greece. Others originally would have been armed as peltasts (versatile unarmoured infantry, taking their name from the *pelta*, a kind of light shield). These, at least, would have had some experience of hand-to-hand combat so could be more easily retrained in contrast to bowmen, javelinmen or slingers who were used to fighting only from afar. What is clear is that the option Alexander considered of fleshing out his Macedonians with young men from the Iranian provinces, equipped as bowmen and javelineers, was not considered by his Successors. The reason almost certainly is that when Alexander had proposed this mixed phalanx he knew that, against the enemies he expected to encounter, it would be useful to have a missile component in the middle of the files between pikemen at the front and back. But when his Successors found themselves confronted by enemy phalanxes, the only answer was to fight fire with fire, to face *sarissa*-armed phalanx with *sarissa*-armed phalanx.

But the changing complexion of the rest of the army had become clear by the time of the conflict between Antigonus and Eumenes. When the satraps who were later to join forces with Eumenes assembled at Susa, Peucestas, the satrap of Persia, had '3,000 men of every origin equipped for service in the Macedonian array'.[4] In battle at Paraetacene, a few months later, Diodorus describes Eumenes' infantry line up on the left as 6,000 and more mercenaries, then after them 'five thousand men who had been equipped in the Macedonian fashion' but were not Macedonian nationals.[5]

On the other side in that combat, the Antigonid set up was described as (again starting on the left) 9,000 mercenaries, then 3,000 Lycians and Pamphylians, '8,000 mixed troops in Macedonian equipment' and finally nearly 8,000 Macedonian phalangites.[6] Again, the first two groups would have been largely hoplites while the rest were *sarissa*-wielding pikemen. At Gabene, in the winter, not much seemed to have changed except that Antigonus had lost men in the previous battle. All that is noted is that Antigonus had 22,000 foot in his phalanx, while Eumenes, although fielding essentially the same units, changed his formation and placed his best infantry on the left side, the hypaspists first (literally 'shield-bearers', an elite infantry unit), then the Silver Shields and after them the mercenaries and non-Macedonians armed as phalangites.

What is clear from all this is that, on both sides, half or more of the phalangites were now non-Macedonians. Except for the special case of Europe, where Macedonians could be easily recruited by the incumbent powers, the proportion of foreigners was bound to increase. Men described as mixed, of all races or of every origin were almost certainly from the Iranian satrapies. If they had been Balkan or Anatolian their region of origin would in all probability have been given in the sources. Thus, for instance, we have Lycians, Pamphylians, Greeks and Thracians all mentioned by name. The inexactitude in reporting the homelands of these other warriors was essentially a function of ignorance. Diodorus and his sources were just not as familiar with Iranian geography as they were of those regions nearer to home, which had long been well within the Greek ken.

Under Alexander, and, certainly under his Successors, these well-drilled infantry, whether ethnic Macedonians of the old or new levy or new recruits from the non-European world were the very heart of the battle line. They would have been an awesome sight as they approached the enemy with pikes raised, lowering them only at the charge when the *paean* (battle song) was raised. Macedonians usually cried '*alalalai*', a cry to their war god, but other nations, no doubt, had their own savage yells. And leading at the cutting edge of that most daunting of phalanxes were the Silver Shields (*Argyraspids*). These, it is generally agreed, were the same units as the hypaspists of Philip's and Alexander's army. The Silver Shields were divided into three *chiliarchies* of 1,000 soldiers each; men raised nationally, not regionally like the rest of the phalanx, in order to reinforce loyalty to the king. They normally fought on the right of the phalanx, in the place of honour, as befitted their status, but if their existence and history is fairly well attested there has been much debate over their equipment. Because they so frequently fought in rough terrain and were at the forefront in attacking towns and forts, it is claimed they were not pikemen. In these circumstances an 18-foot spear would be a great hindrance, so it is conjectured that they were some sort of hoplite or peltast. Further evidence for this claim is adduced from the Alexander Sarcophagus, where the foot soldiers (generally assumed to be guardsmen) are shown in hoplite panoply with *aspis* shield and not the pikeman's smaller *pelte*. The most probable explanation is that they would have equipped themselves depending on the task in hand; such high-status troops would have had access to whatever size of spear and shield was required. But what is most certainly the case is that when we hear of them in the age of the *Diadochi* they fought as pikemen in the heart of the phalanx and, in fact, were the very best of them.

These hypaspists had been built around the royal foot *agema* (guard) who defended the king when he fought on foot as the royal squadron (*ile basilike*) of the Companions did when he led from horseback. They also provided his guard in camp.[7] These units were beautified by Alexander with new silver plating on their shields before they took the road to India in 327 BC, which gave rise to their new name. They also had had an interesting career, post-Alexander, before hooking up with Eumenes. Their leader, Antigenes, had been involved in the murder of Perdiccas during the Egyptian campaign, where these men certainly fought. At the Battle of the Camel Fort, Diodorus mentions shield bearers fighting with the elephants in the attempt to assault Ptolemy's Nile defences. Then, after the settlement at Triparadeisus they were sent on punishment duty to Susa, perhaps because of their involvement in the near mutiny against Antipater. But it has been contended by at least one scholar that the Silver Shields were a new unit different from the hypaspists and created at Triparadeisus from 3,000 disgruntled veterans.[8] Whoever these violent old fellows really were, they brought the Persian treasure from Susa back to Cyinda where they were recruited by Eumenes in 317 BC.

If the question of who the Silver Shields were is open to debate, other information adds further confusion. This is that the Silver Shields were bracketed, in Diodorus' account of the battles of Paraetacene and Gabene, with another body of 3,000 men who are themselves described as hypaspists. They are not attested before Eumenes got to Persia. When he winters in Mesopotamia, only the Silver Shields are mentioned and this is also the case at Peucestas' great entertainment at Persepolis. The first mention of these hypaspists is at the Battle of Paraetacene, when they are placed on the extreme right of the phalanx on the right side of the Silver Shields. The 3,000 men were in the position of highest honour. So who were these, the most prestigious infantry in the whole army, who again at Gabene held the position of honour, next to the Silver Shields (this time on the left)? Not only are they not noticed before the two great battles, neither are they mentioned in the course of the fighting or the negotiations that led to Eumenes' downfall. Again, it is the Silver Shields who receive all the attention of our sources. This is a mystery of great interest as it is difficult to credit any reasonable explanation. It is unlikely to be a mistake or misunderstanding as Diodorus is quite clear about the two units and their position in both battles. It does not seem possible that he would mistake them or double them up. But when he obviously recognizes they are the most prestigious unit, why does he not mention what they did in battle? They are as numerous as the Silver Shields and presumably as effective so why do they not demand the same attention? As they are not mentioned before Eumenes got to Persia, they must have been made up of men who were in the armies of the Iranian governors, perhaps veterans who had remained on garrison duty in the provinces and were recruited by Eumenes as an infantry guard. But the evidence is not there and to compound the mystery further they are never heard of again. It is even possible they were remnants of the well-born Persian warriors, who Alexander, in his later years, ordered to be drilled into *sarissa*-bearing phalangites. They may have remained in the east with satraps like Peucestas. Indeed, perhaps, they are the ones referred to as in the Persian satrap's retinue when Eumenes joined him and his allies in Susiane.[9] A proposition made more probable by the fact they, too, were reported as 3,000 in number.

The Macedonian phalanx that fascinated so many for so long was early on described by the historian Polybius, a Greek general from Megalopolis, who was exiled for many years in Rome. His description of the Macedonian-style phalanx (in *The Histories*, not his lost *Tactica*) has the great advantage that he was contemporary with its use. He may have commanded, would surely have seen, these units drilling and fighting and would have talked to people who had experienced battles both where phalanx fought phalanx and where phalanx fought other sorts of national armies. The other great benefit is that he was, as far as it is possible to be, objective, as he had a foot in both the Greek and Roman camps. He lived from 203 to 120 BC, was a member of the Arcadian ruling class, but from 168 BC spent seventeen years as hostage in Rome where he was closely associated with the great Scipio family who included Aemilius Paullus who triumphed in the Third Macedonian War and Scipio Aemilianus who ploughed Carthage into the sand and finally subdued the brave Celtiberians of Numantia.

Polybius states his intention was to explain to his Greek compatriots why the Roman legion overcame the Macedonian phalanx, as they apparently found this success 'incredible'. He describes the phalanx as invincible 'face to face' when closed, each man occupying a space of three feet square and with every man wielding the *sarissa*, 18 feet long. He describes the first five ranks as showing a great pincushion to the front while the rest kept their weapons upright to both ensure they did not wound their comrades and also to ward off any missiles that might be rained down on them. This is not the only use of the men at the back; they gave a crucial psychological feeling of depth and support and more practically ensure that, even if they wanted to, the men at the front are pushed forward and cannot turn and flee. A very different formation from the one adopted by the Roman legionary who needed greater space to wield shield and sword and who was not pressed on by those behind him.

The Macedonian phalanx, Polybius contends, was a slow and cumbersome formation that could be easily avoided if it could not be stood against. Despite its irresistibility on flat, even ground, the slightest disruption caused by change in terrain was fatal to the Macedonian system; 'ditches, gullies, depressions, ridges and water-courses, all of which are sufficient to hinder and dislocate such a formation.'[10] If the phalanx had to travel any distance there was an irresistible tendency to bunch up or spread out that was not shared by a looser Roman formation that could adjust more easily. The Battle of Pydna in 168 BC showed a classic example of this defect. As the phalanx pushed forward the ground became more uneven with the result that it lost its cohesion, enabling the Roman legion to exploit the resultant gaps. And, to further compound this fragility, the phalanx had another great disadvantage when facing the Roman system. Though each legionary would be facing at least two phalangites as well as ten spear points, the legion and maniple (subdivision of 120 men) with its separate lines meant there were always men kept in reserve. The Roman military organization had institutionalized a reserve of two lines. The front two lines were respectively the *hastati* and *principes* who could reinforce or interchange with each other when necessary. The third line, the *triari*, was able to reinforce the front two lines and could always, in the end, act as protective rearguard if all had gone wrong in front of it. Thus, when the phalanx became disrupted (either after a successful or unsuccessful attack), the Romans had warriors in hand to get under their spears and into the phalanx's formation, where their Spanish swords could do their lethal work.

So Polybius' view was that the phalanx could only stay on clear ground, as if it found itself elsewhere it would become very vulnerable. More than this, it was difficult to split it into small parts, thus only being really of optimum use for great set-piece battles. A Roman legionary, by contrast, was a soldier and fighter either alone or in formation, while the phalangites were only effective in strict mass formation. Furthermore, the legion had the added advantage of a higher proportion of junior officers and NCOs enabling a greater degree of flexibility and use of local initiative.

The phalanx's fragility, which Polybius described, can be seen in the era of Alexander and his Successors, but it is far from the dominant motif. At the Battle of Megalopolis in 331 BC, fought between Antipater and Agis III, king of Sparta, when the Macedonian phalangites were led onto rough ground by the Spartan hoplites falling back, they were certainly less effective, but this did not stop them winning the battle. Equally at Issus in

333 BC, when the phalanx crossed the river in the face of Darius' Greek mercenaries, they had real trouble.

> The Macedonian centre was much slower off the mark; in a number of places, moreover, the steep banks of the stream prevented them from maintaining a regular and unbroken front, and the result was that Darius' Greek mercenaries attacked precisely at the point in the line where the gap was widest.[11]

The phalanx had to suffer the indignity of being rescued by Alexander and his Companions but they then cut the mercenaries to pieces and helped win a famous victory.

By and large, we search in vain for examples of the phalanx losing formation and suffering defeat for it during the *Diadochi* wars. In the Lamian War, at the battle where Leonnatus died, a green phalanx purposely moved to high, rougher ground where they retained formation to keep the rampant enemy cavalry at bay. More than this, veteran phalangites, at times, showed that they could be very manoeuvrable and extremely able to react to circumstances. At Gabene, when Eumenes' phalangites were threatened in the rear by Pithon's cavalry, they swiftly formed a square to a show a bristling wall of spear points all round to their enemies. Yet, the facts of later wars do bear out Polybius' contention; not just at Pydna, but also at Cynoscephalae in 197 BC and Magnesia in 190 BC where exposed flanks and disruption caused by missile fire allowed the legionaries to get in and tear the phalanx apart. It seems almost as if the Roman infantry had a particular quality that tested the Macedonian steamroller. Indeed, Polybius goes on to suggest Pyrrhus was so struck by the usefulness of the Roman way of war that when he came to Italy he adjusted his tactics and mixed maniples of his Italian allies in with his own Epirote phalangites.

Though certainly receiving the most attention, these pikemen were far from the only men who made a mark in the years of Macedonian world hegemony. Diodorus describes 7,000 Greek allies and 5,000 Greek mercenaries as being in Alexander's army at the Hellespont and many thousands more of these came east as replacements over the years. Over 38,000 men described as allies and Greeks arrived when the army was away in Bactria and further east. Furthermore, many mercenaries who had fought either for Darius or his satraps would have been incorporated in Alexander's army as the Persian Empire gradually fell to the newcomers. How these men were equipped and how they fought is open to question. Many of the Greek allies, we know, were hoplites and could have stood shoulder to shoulder with the Macedonian phalanx. That Alexander used them in reserve, as camp guards or on garrison duty was more because of dubious loyalty than equipment.

Some of these mercenaries and allies would have been peltasts. Originally these were Thracian javelineers who got the name because of their characteristic crescent shaped shield the *pelte*. Peltasts were the defining troops of the Thracian peoples, they were lightly armoured and skirmishing was their forte, but they could also fight it out face-to-face if necessary. Well before the Macedonian world era began, the term peltasts had come to mean something far beyond just a specific type of Thracian warrior. It had become a generic term for warriors who became the favoured type of mercenary, that almost all Greek states came to depend on later in the fifth and in the fourth centuries. The designation 'peltast' had come to mean a troop type, something between the frontline hoplite or phalangite, and the specifically light missile infantry using javelins, bows and slings. These soldiers certainly were skirmishers; indeed the Thracians had been brought in as such. They could keep out of the hoplites' way and wear them down as at Corinth against a Spartan *mora* (battalion) in 390 BC.

By our period peltasts seemed to have become a kind of medium infantry but unfortunately the sources for Alexander and his Successors virtually never use the term itself. One of the very few occasions the term is used is when Antigonus 'selected the finest of the peltasts' with light infantry to guard his long military caravan as it wound through the Cossaean hills in the face of a dangerous local enemy.[12] They are clearly seen as an integral part of the war machine. Asclepiodotus describes them, with other light troops, as able to close up in ranks eight deep but they are also described as fighting in open order. Certainly, they are not the men who usually fight at the very front of battle, but are used for crucial but routine duties, like garrisoning towns and other line of communication duties.

It has frequently been assumed that the term 'mercenary' when it refers to Greek or Anatolian soldiers usually means a peltast. This is often the case but certainly not in all circumstances as we know the mercenaries who fought for Darius were hoplites and they fought as hoplites when they went home to fight against their Macedonian foes in the Lamian War. Whether the troops who are described in the *Diadochi* battle line as mercenaries were peltasts or hoplites is open to question. The fact that they are mentioned in the main body next to phalangites suggest they are hoplites but this is not absolute as it is possible medium troops like peltasts could have been deployed as a hinge between the cavalry and main phalanx, as was the case in many of the battles Alexander fought. They subsequently occupied the same role at Raphia in 217 BC, when Antiochus III took on Ptolemy IV, and at Magnesia in 190 BC, where the Romans defeated the same Antiochus' army.

Specialists light troops had been employed by Alexander in his conquering army and many continued to do duty under his Successors. According to Diodorus, 'Odrysians, Triballians and Illyrians accompanied him to the number of seven thousand; and of archers and the so called Agrianians one thousand'.[13] The first two of these were Thracian peoples who would have, by and large, provided light infantry, but also, perhaps, some better armoured aristocrats who doubled as hostages for a people who had recently fought against Alexander. Whether they fought as officers for their own men or on horseback with the Companions is not known. The Agrianians were a Paeonian people supplied by their king, Langarus, and were elite javelin men who, under Alexander, usually worked in tandem with the archers, who seemed to have been either Cretan or Macedonian. These two units were always at the heart of things, whether in battle or in rough country skirmishing, but after Alexander's death we hear nothing of what became of them.

Certain geographical regions were associated with particular light infantry skills. Rhodians were renowned as slingers, who fought by hurling lead shot and neither wore armour nor carried a shield, having just a knife for use in the last extremity. There was never any intention that they should fight hand-to-hand but their lightness would allow them to stay out of harm's way and, like snipers, try to pick off enemies. They are seldom mentioned in the battle line, though they might have been part of any group that are mentioned guarding elephants and sometimes skirmishing in front of the phalanx. These warriors were also of particular use in sieges and it is in these circumstances that we find the telltale lead shot left by them, often with curses or quips like 'take that' incised on the bullet. Of course, not all Rhodians were slingers and certainly not all slingers were Rhodians. They usually came from hilly regions where poor ill-equipped people might use the weapon to protect themselves and their domestic animals from predators. Achaea, Acarnania and Elis in Greece were also well known for their slingers.

Similarly the island of Crete was renowned for its archers, and, more than this, it was generally famous for its fighters for hire. The petty cities of the island were always at each other's throats and this ensured skills in warfare were acquired that made them attractive employees for the rulers of the dissolving Macedonian Empire. The economic imperative that made many turn to this trade also meant many others turned to piracy to make a living. These Cretan bowmen were also without any body armour and with only a knife for protection. They used a recurved composite bow with usually bronze-headed, but sometimes iron-capped, arrows. Like slingers, they were at their best in sieges and it is from the detritus of these events we often find the evidence that allows them to be so described.

Javelineers, like slingers, came mainly from poorer mountainous areas, in Greece particularly from Aetolia, Acarnania and Arcadia, and from other Balkan peoples like the Agrianians. But any place could produce this most easily equipped of soldiers from amongst their own poorer classes. Often even servants might be so armed, anybody indeed who could not provide themselves with adequate arms to stand up in the battle line. These javelinmen could carry shields and even a sword but usually a lack of defensive body armour prohibited them from hand to hand fighting in the front line. Yet, nothing was absolute, as certainly Alexander armed javelin men and others with axes to hamstring elephants at the Battle of Hydaspes. As Quintus Curtius observed, 'The Macedonians began to use axes – they had equipped themselves with such implements in advance – to hack off the elephants' feet'.[14]

But what was central to these troop types was the ability on one hand to hit at long range and on the other an inability to fight in the main line of battle. Their light equipment meant they could get out of the way of most enemies, except of course cavalry to whom they were very vulnerable. Only in rough country could they stand against horsemen. Here cover meant they could escape the enemy's swords and spears and pick them of with arrow, slingshot or javelins.

In the battle lines of the great combats, these light infantry (*psiloi*) are seldom mentioned except as the guards for the elephants who could be very vulnerable to light nimble soldiers who could get out of the beasts' way and drive them into panic by a pinprick rain of missiles. This is well exampled at the assault on Megalopolis in 318 BC when Polyperchon's elephants were halted by planks with nails in them. 'At the same time some of the mahouts were killed by the missiles of all kinds that poured upon them from the flanks. The elephants, suffering great pain because of the clouds of missiles.'[15]

Gaza, in 312 BC, is another dramatic example; Ptolemy's preparations are reported by Diodorus, 'they also stationed their light armed units, ordering the javelin-men and archers to shoot without ceasing at the elephants and at those who were mounted upon them.'[16] Once the attacking beasts had also been stopped by planks studded with nails, these light troops finished the job of routing them back into their own men, thus effectively ending the struggle.

The other occasion upon which missile men had a decisive impact in a major battle was at Ipsus in 301 BC. Here, when Antigonus' phalanx was exposed as Demetrius galloped away with the cavalry, it was the weapons shot and thrown at the phalangites' unprotected right side that drained their morale and led to mass desertion. And, indeed, it was missile men who either from horseback or on foot let fly the javelins that cut down the grand old man himself.

These men had, in general, a considerably lower status than their comrades who stood up in the phalanx and due to this they are less noticed in our sources. Because these light armed troops were easily recruited in almost any region, the *Diadochi* would have recruited them where they found them but their land of birth was seldom of interest to the historians of the time. The only type that tends to be regionally designated with any frequency is Persian bowmen and sometimes slingers. They are mentioned in the army Craterus took back to help Antipater and they are recorded as recruited by Peucestas, to the number of 10,000, to help in the guarding of Eumenes' Pasitigris line. Later in the same campaign they are mentioned as being recruited when the satrapal army made its way to Persepolis in 317 BC, after Antigonus had moved north through the mountains of the Cossaeans.

Now, to turn to the arm of decision; to consider the horsemen, who behind their warrior king, Alexander, won all the battles in the conquest of Persia and who in the era of the *Diadochi* often seemed to have the final say. At the apex of both status and effectiveness in the Macedonian royal array were the 2,000-odd Companions who, with neither stirrups nor saddle but with boots and saddle cloth, were amongst the most formidable of cavalry. For protection they mainly wore an open Boeotian helmet, to allow good vision, and usually a cuirass comprised of linen reinforced with metal plates or a muscle cuirass of bronze. Their main offensive weapon was the 12-foot spear (*xyston*), made of tough cornel wood sheathed in metal at both ends, backed up with a short sword.

The Companions were organized into eight squadrons (*ilai*) of 200 each in Alexander's day, with a separate royal *agema* of 300 or 400 men. They were later reorganized into 500-strong *hipparchies*, each of two *ilai* of 250 troopers, which remained the usual formation in the Successor years. When the Successors established themselves they usually went into battle with a guard of 300 of the best cavalry. The Companion cavalry seem to have been originally regionally recruited, just like their compatriots in the phalanx. There are units described as being from Bottiaea, Amphipolis and Apollonia. The horsemen in the battles of the Successors who are described as Companions were undoubtedly the same sort of troops (if not the same men) as those who had ridden over with Alexander. And, in the battles where their presence is mentioned, they are always on the flank, intended to carry out the decisive strike and always led by an officer of the highest status.

Of the originals who filled the ranks at Granicus, Issus and Gaugamela, some, like their infantry counterparts, would have gone home after Alexander's death but possibly not many, as later kings of Macedonia could not field the number of Companions that Alexander could, suggesting the Asian wars really did constitute a permanent drain on the Macedonian pool of skilled cavalrymen.[17] The remaining survivors divided between the dynasts as chance and personal ambition dictated. It is probable that in the Successor armies they were organized in similar units and remained, like their progenitors, made up mainly of high-born Macedonians. The extent to which non–Macedonians were recruited to provide replacements for these cavalry is unclear but it must have occurred. At Paraetacene 1,000 are mentioned on one side and 900 on the other and this is, at least, as many as the number Alexander led into Asia. Some replacements came over in his lifetime but since his death we do not know of any major injections of recruits from Macedonia and in Eumenes' case this would anyway have been practically very difficult. High-born Iranians must have fleshed out the Companions referred to in the confederate army under Eumenes, just as they did in the Seleucid Companions who still retained the name a century later. More than this, these units of Companions were also where the friends and councillors of the new rulers fought. And, besides functioning as a powerful cavalry arm, these regiments acted as a continuing school for the young aristocrats whose families had attached themselves to the various dynasts. Blue-blooded young men who, from whichever polity they hailed, started their education as pages but then continued their schooling as the officers of the future in the Companion cavalry, just as had been the case in the days of Philip and Alexander.

Second only to this cavalry elite were the heavy horsemen from Thessaly; indeed some sources suggest they might be regarded as the equal of the Companions, 'being Thessalians exceptional for their courage.'[18] Northern Greek aristocrats numbering 1,800 initially went to Asia, where they provided much of the muscle for Parmenion (the largest squadron from Pharsalus acted as his bodyguard) when he held down the left wing in the great battles of the Persian conquest. They were equipped just like the Companions, and like them were recruited regionally, based on their home cities. But, unlike them, they were returned to Greece after a few years, when the invasion army had reached Media and Alexander was confident he had overcome all really serious Achaemenid opposition. Their presence as the key cutting edge of Greek forces in the Lamian War shows they were still the best horsemen around, and that they were available in their thousands on the Greek mainland at a time when the Macedonian state in Europe was desperately scraping round for any sort of cavalry. Apart from that significant eruption they played little role in the *Diadochi* wars.[19]

The Macedonians generally fought in a wedge formation, which they had probably learned from the Thracians, who had themselves learned it from the Scythians. This was an effective offensive formation where the unit leader could keep good control of the troopers behind him as all of them had a good view of him; 'since all have their eyes fixed on the single squadron commander as is the case also in the flight of cranes.'[20] But all these cavalry might fight in longer lines a few ranks deep or even in squares depending on what the circumstances required, and it was usually at the head of these ancient cavaliers that the army leaders would place themselves when battle was to begin. A regular squadron of 250 horse in a wedge formation would have had a frontage of 45 yards or so, thus 1,000 Companions, that often are described, would have had a frontage of around 180 yards, However, this should be doubled to give a decent interval between squadrons (cavalry would need more room than infantry) so that they are not crunched up against each other. The resultant 360 yards when extrapolated for the 3,700 horse reported on Antigonus' right at Paraetacene would have resulted in a cavalry line not much under 1 mile in length.

The 600 allied Greek horse that are mentioned by Diodorus going east with Alexander (as *hegemon* of the league of Corinth) in 334 BC may have been heavy cavalry, equipped like their Thessalian cousins, or lighter troops with little armour and using javelins for combat. An indication that most were heavies is that at Gaugamela in 331 BC they are brigaded on the left under Parmenion with the Thessalian horse. After Darius was finally defeated in 330 BC they, like the Thessalians, were offered demobilization at Ecbatana but many opted to stay on in the ranks of the mercenary horse. How many allied Greek horse there were at this juncture is difficult to determine since we only know of one definite reinforcement of 150 mounts arriving at Gordium in 333 BC, but there must have been others. In any case, they are still recorded under arms during the years of the Successors but following their progress is very difficult. Certainly 500 allied horse are mentioned on Antigonus' right at the Battle of Paraetacene, but whether this refers to these same men is unclear. Here, as at Gaugamela, they are brigaded with the heavy cavalry, like the Companions and Antigonus' bodyguard, so it is probable they were heavy horse rather than skirmishers.

The troops that we know definitely were light cavalry in Alexander's invasion army were the scouts (*prodromoi*), numbering 900. These were troopers whose only protection was a helmet and their offensive weapon was a very long spear described as a *sarissa*. This was presumably longer than the 12-foot spear carried by the other heavy horsemen, or it would not be so particularly specified. But practicality would surely mean it was shorter than the phalangite's pike which as a two-handed weapon would not have been feasible for horsemen, who needed at least one hand to control their steed. Though, of course, later *cataphracti* (completely armoured cavalry) used a two-handed *kontos* (barge pole) and this is attested for Parthians, Sassanians and even Romans, these were very heavy horse expected to move forward in steady and irresistible manner, not to perform the kinds of agile manoeuvres expected of light horse. These *prodromoi* may have come from Macedonia or

Thrace but other units definitely came from the 'barbarian' marches, like the Paeonians and Odrysians whose rulers had been reduced to subject allies of Greater Macedonia. The role of all these troops was to act as scouts and skirmishers, a sword would have been carried but only as an arm of last resort. The long spear was intended to keep enemies off so they would not need to fight hand-to-hand or require the protection of body armour. What is interesting is that these troops are little mentioned after the Macedonians had got well into Asia. The invaders discovered and co-opted troop types that did these jobs better, most particularly the horse archers they came across on the central Asian steppe.

Mercenary light horse are not mentioned as going over to Asia but are heard of by the siege of Halicarnassus and are frequently noted as active in Alexander's wars. They are described at Gaugamela as providing a screen in front of part of the right and left wings; acting as the cavalry equivalent of infantry skirmishers. But a good number, up to 800, were killed off in an ambush by Scythians near the Polytimetus River in Sogdia, in 329 BC. Though 500 of this troop type are mentioned in Antigonus' battle line at Paraetacene, what relationship they had to the mercenary horse utilized by Alexander is unclear and we can really say little specific of the national origin or equipment of these men.

Though the *Diadochi* war machines were created by the fusion of European and Asiatic power, money and techniques, the Alexandrine core remained the same. But, of all the arms concerned, the cavalry arm saw most change. This should be no surprise as Asia had always been the home of celebrated horsemen. Alexander encountered not only formidable exemplars of the kind of cavalry with which he was familiar in the cavaliers of Persia, Media and Bactria, but also light horse archers typical of the peoples of the steppe. Before reaching inner Asia, he would have had little experience of this sort of warrior but, once encountered, he clearly liked what he saw and lost little time in incorporating many of them into his military caravan. Arrian mentions 'Scythian cavalry, and the mounted archers of the Daae' as a main component, 1,000 to 1,500 strong, of Alexander's task force as he heads off to confront Porus at the Hydaspes and, indeed, these were the first to strike a blow against the Indian monarch's army.[21] Under the *Diadochi* we look in vain for troops described as Scythian or Daae, though, if these actual men were not kept on in large regiments, some may have remained in the retinues of the satraps who gained control of the regions near their steppe homelands. The horse archers we do know of are recorded usually as Parthians and are often brigaded with Median light horse.

The horsemen who had initially ridden out of Europe were fairly few in number, perhaps 5,000 all told, though by Gaugamela they had increased to

7,000. But, with Persia fallen, Scythia visited and India part-traversed, the invaders recruited non-European horsemen, who remained formidable and sometimes decisive throughout the *Diadochi* wars. The Median, Persian, Bactrian and Sogdian aristocrats who had initially fought Alexander, now joined him and stayed on with his Successors in some numbers over the years to come. The best of them were well-armoured in scale corselets, helmets and even with armour covering their legs. Their horses were big and strong and we know, in the era of Xenophon, that some of them were protected by armoured bards of cloth faced by scale armour. It is unlikely that this was discarded when the Macedonian kings took over, as 100 years later the Seleucids were fielding *cataphracti* wearing full body and horse protection, making such a breach in continuity unlikely. The most useful of these troops would have stayed on and travelled west, with their conquering commander, before, on his death, joining the entourages of the satraps who took over their homelands. They were recruited and fought again in the great battles, particularly those of 317/316 BC, and after these combats some would have been demobilized or gone back home with their satrapal commanders, but enough would have stayed in the main army. Others would undoubtedly have fought for and against Seleucus, as he first established himself and then went on to fight wars in east Iran, India and Anatolia.

The heavy cavalry battle winners were the apple of the Successors' eyes, just as they had been for Alexander. They personally led these troops, riding with their greatest subjects, councillors and friends, even when the main strength of their army might lie in their heavy infantry phalangites. This was the place of honour, traditionally on the right of the battle line and though the serried ranks of horsemen might be more exotic, drawn from a greater range of peoples, their role, like the Companions of Alexander, was that of Homeric heroes. It was a dangerous post; Leonnatus, Craterus, Neoptolemus and possibly Lysimachus perished leading these troops into battle, but it was at the heart of things. However, if from Cannae in 216 BC to Rocroi in 1643 AD, a successful attack by the cavalry wings to finish off an army (effectively occupied in front by the infantry) is a military truism, what the story of the *Diadochi* also illustrates is some of the more problematic qualities of these blue-blooded cavaliers. History equally has many examples, from Raphia in 217 BC to Naseby in 1645 AD, of such cavalry defeating the men in front of them and then heading off in pursuit, never to be seen again and leaving their comrades to suffer for it.

If the heavy cavalry remained the queen of the battlefield, the usefulness of light horse was also well appreciated by Alexander's Successors. It was fully understood by these commanders that these troops could hold an enemy in play at one part of the line while the killer blow was struck elsewhere. Eumenes and Antigonus both employed this tactic in their great battles, using many of the sorts of light cavalry that had been hoovered up along the way by Alexander's army. Indeed, it is clear that in most combats for which we have information, one wing was intended to hold back and skirmish rather than get fully involved in deciding the battle, while the other wing was anticipated to win the day.

Elephants were the big new thing in Hellenistic warfare, the one particular feature that would have stood out as different from a Greek battlefield thirty years before. They first seem to have been encountered at Gaugamela, when Darius fielded fifteen. These had no impact and the first time they were recruited was in India when a friendly prince gave Alexander some. These were not used by Alexander in battle and the first belligerent experience of these beasts for the Macedonians was at the Battle of Hydaspes in 326 BC, when they found themselves very uncomfortably on the receiving end. In that encounter they caused numerous casualties and engendered great terror but the side they fought for still lost.

It is often thought that Alexander, himself, did not seem to have a great deal of time for the beasts, thinking them very unreliable. Yet, he still kept several hundred in one part of the army or another in the last years of his life; perhaps it was a matter of prestige, the connection of elephants with royalty that mattered. They are depicted as an integral part of his army on one side of his death cart (the other three sides show cavalry, infantry and warships) and reluctance to put them in the front line certainly did not extend to his successors.[22] What information we have suggests, whether it was Polyperchon, Cassander, Olympias, Eumenes, Antigonus or Demetrius, they were prepared to spend much to keep up their herds and, as often as not, used them as the spearhead in battle.

How they were equipped and armed is made clear by Diodorus when he describes the death cart. 'They carried Indian mahouts in front with Macedonians fully armed in their regular equipment behind them.'[23] With an Indian driver sitting on its neck and fully armed phalangites sitting on its back, they towered above all the other warriors in any battle array. Even so, it is likely that the animals on occasions went into attack with just a driver, as fighting from the back of an elephant must have been very difficult for those unused to it. And anyway, the essence of the elephant as a weapon was the beast itself. It is also unclear whether elephants, at this period, carried missile troops. One occurrence suggests not, as before the Battle of Gabene, Eumenes' elephants were ambushed by Antigonus and they could not reply to the missiles of the men who attacked them. Though, of course, it is always possible that, as they were unprepared for battle, they did not have their fighting crews on board. Certainly the Indians had mounted bowmen and javelineers on them and it is more than possible that their Macedonian pupils would have followed them in this too. Plutarch suggests elephant towers were used at Paraetacene 'and on the backs of the elephants the towers and purple trappings were seen', but the first hard evidence for their use is from Pyrrhus' campaigns in Italy.[24] They were certainly worn by the Seleucids' animals in 273 BC when Antiochus I defeated the Gauls of Asia Minor in the 'Elephant Victory'.

Their tactical organization is described by Asclepiodotus as being like the phalanx, with a division of sixteen animals being called an *elephantarchy*. But some idealized arrangements see them acting in great squares of animals. However, in all the battle descriptions we have, they seem to have fought in a single rank. The whole corps was commanded by an *elephantarch* who, probably, was not just an *ad hoc* posting for a battle but was retained for a period. Certainly, Eudamus seemed to have had some such role under Eumenes, while Antiochus the Great seems to have had the same officer called Philip fulfilling the post both at Raphia in 217 BC and at Magnesia, twenty-seven years later. The creation of such a rank seems eminently sensible given that if any part of Hellenistic warfare was a real specialism it was the use of elephants. How actual command during the battle might have been arranged is another matter, as the beasts seem usually to have been strung out all along the battle front. The elephants were accompanied into battle by a light infantry guard of fifty men interspersed between each animal.

Their usefulness in battle in the *Diadochi* era is somewhat inconclusive and only at Ipsus was their use decisive. But the elephants' ability to frighten horses by their smell and noise made them particularly attractive as a weapon. That and their initial impact on troops who had never seen them before made them well worth having. No doubt, several of the *Diadochi* who became kings remembered the day Alexander's army had refused to carry on in India and the straw that had broken the camel's back for them was the thought of facing an army of 4,000 elephants. To own a weapon that had brought terror to the hearts of even Alexander's conquering veterans must have appealed to the king's old officers, whatever the risks and costs of pinning their fortunes to these behemoths.

Some of these formidable beasts became famous and their names well known to the troops, in the same way huge cannons were given names like Big Bertha in a much later age. Pliny the Elder, in his *Natural History*, mentions one named Surus, possibly Hannibal's own elephant, who had fought valiantly in the Punic War and had lost one of his tusks.[25] Pliny also tells of two elephants in Antiochus' army (which Antiochus is not specified) named Ajax and Patroclus after the Trojan War heroes. It was certainly understood they might vary in fighting quality as it is specified that when Eumenes deployed sixty beasts about his left wing at Gabene, these were the very pick of the bunch. Equally, being herd animals, the fate of their leader could be as important to the elephants as was the fate of a beloved general to soldiers. Eumenes was one who suffered from this in his last battle, when he was holding on against an enemy, who much outnumbered him, until his lead elephant was downed and his whole line fell apart.

What is also very noticeable in our period is that elephants are mainly valued as a deterrent against enemy horsemen. These are the troops that they are seen as particularly useful against, most emphatically shown at Ipsus, when the failure of cavalry to go near a line of elephants decided the outcome of the battle. This is in marked contrast to subsequent periods when elephants were used. In the battles fought against Rome by Hellenistic armies or Carthaginians it is often the heavy infantry of the legions that the great animals are directed at and often with impressive effects. Perhaps the change of tactic can be explained by the fact that infantry of the *Diadochi* had become used to the animals over a period of years under Alexander so were never afraid of them in the way the Romans were when they first encountered them. However, the Romans eventually got used to handling them and, understanding their characteristics, used tactics that nullified them. For example, at Zama in 202 BC, Scipio organized lanes so the beasts were harmlessly corralled down them.

There is no question the army used and honed under Alexander and his Successors remained a military exemplar for generations and indeed millennia to come. Even Livy could not resist the lure of this force as the great acid test of quality for his ancestors from the beginning of the third century BC. The state and army that had come to dominate the central and south Italian peoples was still required in his imagination to be tested against the institutions, arms and personalities that had developed across the Adriatic and then conquered the whole world to the east.

The issue Livy addressed in his *History of Rome* was: could those Romans who were contemporaries of Alexander and his Successors have faced their war machine with any chance of success? First, he concentrates on personality and claims a parity of skill between Alexander and many of the Roman military leaders of that era. Marcus Valerius Corvus and Titus Manlius Torquatus, both memorable duellists who later became generals, are portrayed as the equal of the Macedonian leader when it came to bravery and skill in battle. While this does not hold up when he matches them to Alexander himself, it might be nearer the mark with at least some of the *Diadochi*. Livy also makes the good point that as kings, both Alexander and his Successors had the advantage of providing unified command, but the great drawback was that if they were killed or debilitated everything fell down. Thus, if one of these kings had invaded Italy, to exterminate them would have been at the forefront of the thoughts and actions of all the brave young men of Rome. Pyrrhus encountered this phenomenon in his first encounter with the Roman army, when he had to change armour with a friend because of the vicious attacks on his person that the royal regalia attracted.

This is interesting but does not really test Roman valour, talent, techniques and organization against a Macedonian model. Yet it would be possible, in a virtual way, to explore a situation where the conquering Macedonians turned from Babylon at the end of the 320s BC with plans to immediately invade the Italian peninsula. This was at a time when they still had available all the power of their original army, but were expanded and increased by the wealth and manpower of Asia. This is perhaps not a probable scenario, but nor should it be completely dismissed out of hand. After all Alexander of Epirus (Alexander the Great's uncle) had not long since died fighting on campaign in Italy. Also, if this supposition is allowed much of interest is raised. If, almost 100 years later, Hannibal Barca could get most of Rome's subject people to rebel, what greater success would these extraordinary Macedonian warlords have had if they had arrived in the plains of Apulia or the hills of Campania? Could Rome have triumphed when so many of the lands she had just conquered would have risen up to regain the freedoms so recently lost? Livy claims they could but it is very possible to argue the other case.

Equally, what he says about the comparative military puissance of the two sets of armed forces is debatable. Livy claims a Roman population of 250,000 was capable of fielding armies of 50,000 just based on the city itself, never mind colonies and allies. Furthermore, that often four and five armies were kept 'on active service in Etruria, Umbria (where the Gauls frequently joined their enemies) Samnium and Lucania.'[26] In contrast to these mighty numbers he suggests that that the invaders would have been largely dependent on the Macedonian component of their army. Only that part would be formidable, that the levies of Asia would be of no moment and indeed even that the Macedonian core might have been badly debased. As Livy says, Alexander 'would have been more like Darius ... by the time he reached Italy, leading an army which had already forgotten its Macedonian origins and was adopting degenerate Persian habits.'[27]

While this was not the whole truth, and indicates common prejudice against Asiatic soldiery, it is true that the main heavy infantry they could field would either be Macedonian or troops trained in a similar fashion. Against his Romans, Livy considered the Macedonians would only be able to field 30,000 heavy infantry and 4,000 cavalry, if the Thessalians were included. But the whole assumption that the Macedonian military machine could only dispose of 30,000 pikemen is debatable. Just twenty-two years after Alexander's death, well over double that number of drilled and trained phalangites came together in combat at Ipsus. If these numbers had been united under Macedonian leadership, with skilled auxiliaries and a range of eager local allies who hated Rome, Livy may not have had such cause for confidence.

As well as claiming a numerical advantage, Livy contends superiority in the value of fighting men; asserting an edge for the Roman soldier, with javelin and *scutum* against the round shield and pike of the Macedonian, because of their personal hardiness and the variety of weapon systems that allowed the legion a decisive flexibility. But he forgets the qualities that had seen Alexander's troops overcome every type of people and terrain from the Danube to the Indus and also that any Macedonian force would have included an array of its own specialists: bowmen, slingers and numerous peltasts; a force of all the arms that would allow for a considerable amount of tactical agility.

For Livy to have compared the GDP of these Roman and Macedonian virtual contenders would, of course, have been valuable, if not decisive, in understanding this potential conflict, but the financial and economic dimension are seldom dealt with in any period of ancient history. Most sources are pretty reticent about giving us a sniff of information on the matter of money. Only occasionally, when somebody heads for the hills with the loot, like Harpalus, do we get an inkling of how crucial filthy lucre could be. But his outcome showed that just plundering was dangerous and that it was necessary to have armed might to give the security to enjoy gains ill- or well-gotten. In the end, Harpalus' bullion led to his death and ended up funding the Athenian contribution to the Lamian War. Still, always money was key but we are seldom given details of how it was garnered. Finance is rarely mentioned by Diodorus; one of the few times is when Antigonus takes centre stage. Having taken control of the 10,000 talents from the treasury at Cyinda, he is then reported as receiving 11,000 talents from the annual revenue. Philip II, in contrast, only got 1,000 talents from the gold mines that were such a major component of his revenue from Greater Macedonia. We also hear of the great windfall of 8,000 talents that Ptolemy got when he disposed of Cleomenes and how crucial this was in stitching together a military establishment in double-quick time that allowed him to see off the threat from Perdiccas. But, if little is known of the actual finances, what is clear is that the world divided by Alexander's Successors was a rich one which allowed ambitious projects to be essayed that their forebears, a hundred years back, could not have dreamed of. Alexander himself crossed over the Hellespont with a war chest of only seventy talents. There is no polyphony of voices when it comes to describing *Diadochi* finances at this time, but the general picture is clear. These people had riches, released from Asian treasuries not known before; gold and silver ran through their fingers, luxuries filled their lives in a way just not known in the Classical period. Considerable inflation was probably one result and another was a world where conspicuous consumption became a curse and a worry that seems very modern.[28]

All this is fascinating speculation that tells us something of what an early imperial Roman knew of the war machine deployed by Alexander and inherited by his Successors. But Livy, even if some of his assumptions can be queried, would always have had the last laugh, as indeed he himself points out in this discourse. That is that his people in the test of real history came out on top. Less than a generation later against Pyrrhus, a second cousin of Alexander the Great, who was blessed with many of his warrior qualities and much of his glamour, they survived. Then less than a century after that the Romans began the overthrow of the armies of Philip V of Macedonia, then Antiochus the Great of the Seleucid kingdom and then trounced King Perseus to such an extent at Pydna in 168 BC that the greater Macedonia created by Philip actually ceased to exist.

All this unhistorical construction may have entertained the Roman historian but the reality was that it was a different foe who first challenged the armies of Macedonia immediately after Alexander' breath had finally left his body. It was an old enemy from their own backyard who took up cudgels against them. And, despite the fact that most of what comes in the story of the *Diadochi* concerns officers who were hardly past their young manhood when the story kicked off at Babylon, the first chapter of this epic would not centre on these comparatively young Turks. Next to take the strain of maintaining Macedonian hegemony was an old man who could reasonably have felt that he had already done his fair share of national work in a very long life.

Chapter Two

The Lamian War

Alexander's death in 323 BC threw the sticks in the air the world over, but it was back in Europe that the pot boiled over most dramatically and where we discover a war, germinated before the death of the conqueror, which is well reported by our sources. Old belligerents from across Greece looked down the tempting road of resistance and saw hope of the old days of power shining at the end of it.

What was in so many heads and hearts had taken some form, the year before Alexander's death, when, in July 324 BC, Leosthenes had been elected one of the ten Athenian generals. He had an interesting past, having fought as one of Darius' mercenaries before defeat forced him into retirement. He had gained considerable kudos by undertaking to arrange the transport of Greek soldiers back home. The alternative for these men was bleak exile in the new Macedonian foundations in Asia. When even more were left rootless with the disbandment of the satrapal armies, Leosthenes used his contacts well to muster a considerable force of soldiers for hire at Cape Taenarum in the southern Peloponnese.

When Leosthenes suggested that they take part in a war against Macedonia with Athens' backing he found a receptive audience. Athens, for her part, was eager to use these potentially crucial auxiliaries and promised 50 talents and sufficient weaponry to equip all who did not have their own armour, spears and swords. Leosthenes planned as his officers distributed the arms and money around the mercenary camp. He needed allies, so his first stop was across the Gulf of Corinth from the Peloponnese into Aetolia. Here, he picked up 7,000 soldiers from a people who were always open to offers from those who wanted to kill Macedonians. From Aetolia, his agents spread all over central Greece enrolling Locrians, Phocians and many others while he moved his growing army to the pass at Thermopylae. Yet, he hardly had settled in the historic defile when he discovered enemies in his rear looking to threaten his communications with Athens and his allies in the south. He was a brilliant and energetic general having had experience of the lightning style of warfare Alexander pioneered in Asia. Prepared to risk deserting his defensive post alongside the Malian Gulf, he aimed a decisive blow against the Boeotians who had mobilized, with help from those Macedonians present in the region, and were in camp near Plataea.

Marching southeast as fast as he could push his men, Leosthenes attacked at Plataea, in conjunction with the Athenian army which had come in force from the south comprising 5,000 citizen foot, 500 horse and 2,000 more mercenaries. Together they administered a crushing defeat to the heavily outnumbered Boeotians. Leosthenes, having accomplished his objective, hardly halted to deal with the dead and set up a trophy to victory before he hurried his way back to Thermopylae. In this adventure, fortune had favoured the brave as the Macedonians had still not arrived at the hot gates.

Antipater had had plenty on his mind as the world turned upside down in the last year. First, it looked like he was to be replaced and forced to carry his old bones to Babylon, as news arrived that Alexander had sent off Craterus to take over as his viceroy in Europe. Then, after Alexander's death, he kept a job that now included facing a Greek uprising. After leaving Sippas in charge of home defence, with orders to recruit more troops where he could, Antipater led out an army that only amounted to 13,000 Macedonian foot, presumably mostly phalangites, and 600 horse.[1]

He crossed the border into Thessaly, following the coast road, and here many thousands of the local cavalry joined his army. But their mood was sullen and unenthusiastic and, on the road south, their shaky morale deteriorated towards open mutiny. In Thessaly, support for the Macedonian cause was evaporating and changing to outright allegiance to the Greek coalition and, as Antipater approached the Greek defences at the pass of Thermopylae, it became common knowledge that the native cities of his Thessalians had declared for the enemy en bloc. The Thessalian cavalry, taking stock of both their interests and their inclinations, deserted and went over wholesale to join Leosthenes' side.

Leosthenes' strength and confidence was increasing daily and, with the unexpected arrival of these excellent heavy cavalrymen, his strategic position dramatically changed for the better. He no longer needed to confine himself to a defensive posture in the coastal defile of Thermopylae but could look to take the offensive and face Antipater in the open. His opponent still had faith in his previously-undefeated phalangites and accepted battle somewhere north of the pass. Though heavily outnumbered in both foot and horse, the old marshal had known a history of victory and achievement that meant he felt he had at least to try his luck in battle. Still, his situation must have given him pause, even as he showed a brave face to his men at the start of the encounter. His worst fears were realised and 'the Greeks who far outnumbered the Macedonians, were successful'.[2] This was a famous victory but we know absolutely nothing of the details. From what we know of the battles that were to follow it is not unreasonable to conjecture that it was the allied cavalry that carried the day. We know Leosthenes had at least 500 Athenian horse added to his 2,000 Thessalians and whatever cavalry the other allies had provided, while all that is reported for Antipater is 600 and this imbalance surely turned the combat, rather than an infantry struggle, where it would be difficult to believe that Greek hoplites with their shorter spears would have easily driven off their *sarissa*-wielding opponents.

Whatever, the reverse was far from total and Antipater managed an organized retreat north. The Greeks had failed to destroy their enemy and the lack of close pursuit allowed the Macedonians a space in which to regroup. But, if the extent of the defeat was limited, Leosthenes had full command of the open countryside. Unable to forage far from camp, the Greeks' superior cavalry arm made it difficult for Antipater to see a way to safely get back to Macedonia. He took his battered army to Lamia (the one city in the area that had stayed loyal) where at least he could hope for refuge behind the town walls. But the corollary of this was that it handed over the initiative completely to Leosthenes. This man was a first-rate general; he did not allow his men to be distracted by plunder but followed on the heels of the Macedonians and led his victorious men to immediately make an attack on Lamia itself. He led them out in battle formation and challenged the Macedonians to come out from behind their defences and face him in the open. When Antipater sensibly declined another combat against the odds, the Athenian ordered an all-out assault. This unusually determined attack continued for several days and only by an equally determined and well-organized defence did Antipater keep his enemies at bay. In the limited time available to him, Antipater had worked a small miracle in strengthening Lamia's defences and mounting artillery on the walls. In this he had been aided by the sailors and marines from the Macedonian fleet stationed in the Malian Gulf.

The coalition army soon sustained considerable casualties and the waves of attackers began to lose some of their early enthusiasm. Calling off the assault, Leosthenes made preparations to blockade the city and its formidable garrison. As the lines of defences rose before his eyes, Antipater heard, at last, news which offered some hope. Predictably, the coalition army, made up of so many disparate peoples, had begun to show its fragility and parts of Leosthenes' army began to drift away. The Aetolians had requested and received permission to return home temporarily for what is described as 'national business'.[3] Whatever the lack of reliability of some of his units, Leosthenes had achieved great things in the last few months. Unbroken success since he had taken the field had made him for the moment, at least, the most powerful man in the Balkan Peninsula. Though, by now, he was also in command of the Athenian army, his real strength lay in the mercenaries he had recruited. As long as he could pay them, he had the potential to be an independent power, a warlord in his own right.[4]

He reflected the growing development and importance of mercenary armies in the fourth century BC.[5] Since the zenith of Theban power in the 370s and 360s BC only Macedon had had real success with a citizen army. Most of the other powers in the Hellenic world had come more and more to rely on hired bands of soldiers who usually had no connection with the state that paid them. Men like Jason of Pherae could make themselves the greatest men in the Greek world on the back of large mercenary forces, the only drawback being that they needed to be paid and this could lead these dynasts into deep and difficult waters. Twenty years after Jason, Onomarchus of Phocis had to plunder the temple treasury at Delphi in order to pay his troops; that action brought a Sacred War on his head and gave Philip of Macedon a doorway through which to enter the world of Greek politics.

Unfortunately, Leosthenes was not to have the opportunity to fulfil his potential. Antipater's men made a sortie in an effort to frustrate the completion of the siege lines around the city of Lamia. The Macedonians rushed out and attacked the enemies who were digging out the ramparts and, though only intending a raid, they had some unexpected luck during the day's fighting. Leosthenes, observing his men being overrun, gathered together the immediately available troops and hastened to their support. During the resultant melee he was struck on the head by a missile fired from the city walls and within three days had died from his wounds.

> For Leosthenes perceived that the whole of Greece was humiliated and ... cowed, corrupted by men who were accepting bribes from Philip and Alexander against their native countries. He realised that our city stood in need of a commander and Greece herself of a city.[6]

So Hypereides, the great Athenian orator and enemy of Macedon, lauded the patriotism, intelligence and courage of the dead man in the funeral oration for the Athenians who had died outside Lamia. The speech is largely extant and, apart from its intrinsic interest, it serves to temper a tendency that sees in the death of Leosthenes the beginning of the end of the coalition cause. The whole feeling of the piece is upbeat and optimistic, a call to arms to repeat against the Macedonian 'barbarian' the triumphs achieved against the Persian invaders in the fifth century. Leosthenes' death may seem, in hindsight, to mark a watershed between triumph and decline towards eventual defeat but this is contrived. Internal weakness in the alliance had anyway manifested itself before his demise and in Antiphilus, another

Athenian, the coalition found a brave commander and sound tactician who would be ably seconded by Menon of Thessaly.

For Antipater, if comfort could be drawn from the disruption Leosthenes' death had caused, substantially his situation was unchanged. He was trapped and reluctantly had to reconcile himself to a winter in northern Greece. The one consolation was that, as the seasonal rains began, his men had proper roofs over their heads in contrast to the tents and makeshift huts of the Greek army's encampment outside the city walls. His greatest problem, after fighting off the initial coalition assault, was how to supply the army he had brought down from Pella. This was no mere garrison that he was responsible for feeding; if that had been the case Lamia's granaries would have been sufficient. Antipater managed this prodigious feat and the army survived without any great hardship the whole of the winter of 323/322 BC. One consolation in his having very few cavalrymen in his army was that only a small number of horses needed to be kept fed, and finding forage for these animals would plague the commanders of all armies down to very recent times. During the middle of the winter, news at last began to reach the besieged army that help was on the way. Leonnatus was on the march to try and prevent a victory for the Greek coalition that would threaten the very root of Macedonian imperial power. With his province including the Asiatic shores washed by the Hellespont, Leonnatus had the advantage of proximity in reaching Europe with his army. Marching through Thrace and Macedonia he recruited as he went. The army he brought over was not large and most of the force he took into Greece was mobilized en route. Sippas, Antipater's governor in Macedonia, would not have been able to spare him many of his already depleted garrison but somehow Leonnatus assembled an army of over 20,000 men. Antipater was very short of experienced soldiers when the war began and no large body of veterans had returned to Macedon from Asia so Leonnatus had to recruit the untrained and the young. These men were not part of the trained national levy and as raw recruits their inexperience was to play a part in the battle to come.

This glamorous, high-status officer had been years in the east with Alexander, rising to a command in the Companion cavalry. He had now come back to his homeland. The year 322 BC would be a fatal one for him but, as he rode out of Pella in the spring, he showed no signs of having any premonitions of trouble ahead. His makeshift army came down through Thessaly taking the most direct route to the theatre of war. No army blocked his way but most of the Thessalian towns shut their gates against him, hoping that their sons away fighting with the coalition cavalry would give short shrift to the intruder, who was marching over their ancestral lands and past their walls. But exact news of all this would probably never have got through to Lamia and only when Antipater saw his besiegers packing up, burning their encampment and sending their camp followers away to Melitia for safety, did he realise that possible relief was so close at hand. He tried vainly to draw his men up in battle order and break out to join the army that was approaching to relieve him. But, after the rigours of a winter in Lamia. his men were not ready to march at a moment's notice and when the coming battle occurred Antipater was not there to second Leonnatus as he met the coalition army in battle somewhere north of Lamia town.

The Greek army consisted of 22,000 foot and 3,500 horse while Leonnatus could boast 20,000 infantry and 1,500 cavalry. It was again the cavalry in which the Greeks had the significant edge, because of the presence of 2,000 first-rate Thessalians: cavalry destined to decide the day. They were led by Menon, a great aristocrat of Pharsalus in Thessaly (his daughter had married Aeacides, the Epirote king and was mother of Pyrrhus). With them were the 500 Athenian horse, recruited from the bluest bloods of that city, but this still left 1,000 cavalry who must have come from the Allied cities of Phocis, Locris and the rest. These others were on the left while Menon took up his position at the head of his Thessalians on the right wing of the allied army.

Antiphilus led the Greek infantry phalanx in the centre where problems were anticipated and his steadying presence would be needed. The heavy infantry there would have been traditional hoplites with *aspis* (shield) and 8-foot spear who had won glory for their cities on the battlefield for several hundred years. Some were the 8,000 mercenaries who Leosthenes had mustered in the Peloponnese, plus the 2,000 others that the Athenians had brought with their citizen troops up past Plataea where they had been instrumental in dispersing the Boeotians. These citizen Athenian forces were 5,000 in number, far more than anything other cities could provide, but still the other coalition cities must have brought in several thousand more heavy infantry. Who was still there and who had slipped away over the winter we don't know but, as Diodorus reminds us, 'all the Aetolians had previously departed to their own country and not a few of the other Greeks had at that time scattered to their native states'. So, though they must have fielded some light troops in front of the eight-deep ranks of the main phalanx, these would not have included the Aetolians who produced some of the best of this troop type.[7]

The opposing 20,000 in the Macedonian army are not described in any detail at all but most would have been *sarissa*-armed phalangites with some light troops, probably recruited from Macedonia's borderlands, to offer a protective screen in front of the heavy infantry. The Macedonian phalangites at the centre of the battle line were for the most part untried and presumably only briefly drilled in the complicated manoeuvrings of the phalanx, but their great reputation still went before them.

Despite the fear they inspired, Antiphilus could not afford to wait and decided he had to engage Leonnatus before Antipater could join the man from Asia. The Hellespontine satrap, on his part, had always been inclined to boldness and he took on the enemy as soon as they came in sight. No doubt, he thought victory unshared with Antipater would be all grist to the mill when it came to deciding on the governmental pecking order once the war was done. Menon attacked on the right and his brave and well-armoured cavalry had immediate success. Our source suggests that Leonnatus himself bore the brunt of the attack by the Thessalians which indicates he had taken place on the left wing, not the place of honour on the right. He may have realized that this was the place of greatest threat and there he would be most needed. Whatever the exact details of the deployment, Leonnatus only had 1,500 troopers, so his wings were bound to be stretched thin to avoid being overlapped. Still, they made a stern fight of it until numerical inferiority inevitably took its toll and they were pushed back. Driven onto marshy terrain the horses were unable to find firm footing and their order disintegrated. Separated into small groups, they had to defend themselves against the rampant Thessalians as best they could. They fought valiantly but it was in one of these vicious small-scale combats that Leonnatus received a fatal wound. This brave, but foolhardy, general, who had escaped major injury in years of campaigning in Persia and India, met his end on the very doorstep of his own country. Servants and bodyguards managed to rescue his body and escorted it back to the baggage train.

When the commanders of the Macedonian phalanx (we do not know whether the push of pike had begun, or if both sides had waited to see who won the cavalry combat) realized their flank had been exposed to the Thessalians and that Leonnatus was dead they conceded the battle and ordered the undefeated foot soldiers to retire towards their baggage camp:

> the Macedonian phalanx, for fear of the cavalry, at once withdrew from the plain to the difficult terrain above and gained safety for themselves by the strength of the position. When the Thessalian cavalry, which continued to attack, was unable to accomplish anything because of the rough ground the Greeks, who had set up a trophy and gained control of the dead, left the field of battle.[8]

Here, in hilly country, they would be less vulnerable. The blood of Menon's followers was up after turning the tables on their usually-dominant neighbours and they pursued the retreating Macedonians even though once out of the open ground where the battle took place they, in turn, found it difficult to keep formation. The Macedonians, though left leaderless, were resilient and fought back from the advantage of steeper ground, the

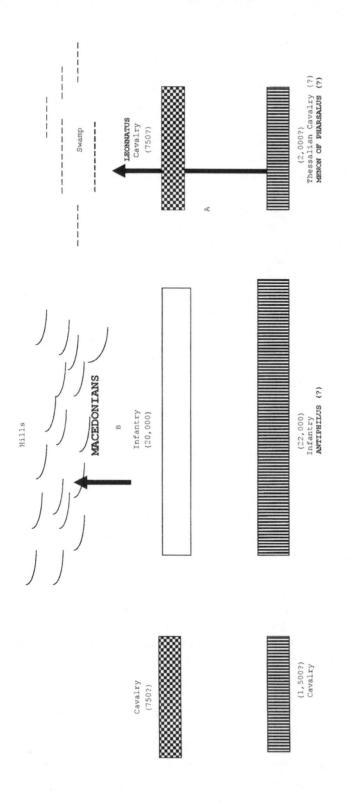

Hills

MACEDONIANS

B
Infantry
(20,000)

Cavalry
(750?)

Cavalry
(1,500?)

Swamp

LEONNATUS
Cavalry
(750?)

A

(2,000?)
Thessalian Cavalry (?)
MENON OF PHARSALUS (?)

(22,000)
Infantry
ANTIPHILUS (?)

GREEKS

A Thessalian Cavalry drive Leonnatus' cavalry back to swampy ground where he dies.
B Macedonian phalanx retreat to higher ground after defeat and death of Leonnatus.

Leonnatus' battle, 322 BC.

charging enemy squadrons found themselves disorganized and began to sustain such casualties that they were forced to break off the fight.

What had occurred on the other cavalry wing, where the Greeks had their non-Thessalian horse including the Athenians knights, we do not know, but the fighting altogether had gone sufficiently well for the Greeks to claim a great victory. The reality was less decisive; the army that Leonnatus had brought with him had not been hugely depleted. The core of the infantry was still intact, even if most of the cavalry had been destroyed or dispersed. Antipater arrived the following day, too late to help Leonnatus, but in time to take command of the leaderless warriors he found encamped amongst the hills north of Melitia. He could not stay there in the face of a rampant coalition army and instead followed the open road north, keeping up on the hills where Menon and his Thessalians could not get a good run at them.

Good news at sea, with the triumph of Cleitus over the Athenian fleet, gave some succour to Antipater and his men as they leapfrogged north and even more heartening was the realization that further help from his erstwhile colleagues in Asia was likely to be forthcoming.[9] Craterus and his veterans had left Cilicia and were on the road to Europe. Around 6,000 of Alexander's old veteran Macedonians, 4,000 more who we are told were recruited on the march, 1,000 Persian bowmen and slingers and, crucially, 1,500 front-line cavalry were on the way. He travelled up over the Taurus across the Anatolian plateau into regions he not seen for over ten years. This was a homecoming the troops had waited a long time for, even if it involved seeing off some Greeks to enjoy it. They had even mutinied against their beloved king Alexander to get their discharge and now these world conquerors intended to settle down and enjoy their portion of the loot of the Persian Empire, that would make them very rich Macedonian farmers indeed. Thrace was traversed, and presumably Pella was visited, on the way to Thessaly but now Craterus was not dawdling as he aimed to join up with Antipater. With his arrival, the old man found himself in command of the agglomeration of three forces, a truly formidable army. Antipater had the phalangites he had originally brought south from Macedonia, a long year ago, and with whom he had seen the siege of Lamia through. Added to these were the very substantial rump of the army Leonnatus had led to defeat and now the impressive array brought by Craterus. With this superfluity, he could contemplate taking the initiative with considerable confidence.

Mainland Greece, south of Thermopylae, had so far been defended from the hitherto-invincible armies of Alexander; driving them back deep into Thessaly, the Greek army had looked set to bundle the enemy unceremoniously over the border into Macedonia itself. 'Antiphilus, the Greek commander, having defeated the Macedonians in a glorious battle, played a waiting game, remaining in Thessaly and watching for the enemy to move, reports Diodorus'.[10] If this indicates that the Greeks had no intention of actually invading Macedonia, the difficulty of establishing an attainable strategic aim may have doomed the rebellion from the start. It is almost inconceivable to imagine any Greek coalition army having the determination or resources to completely crush the might of the Greater Macedonia that Philip had built, and yet failure to do so would mean it would only be matter of time before the northern imperialists returned in new puissance. None the less, Antiphilus and his officers were still borne on the crest of a wave of optimism as they led their men north towards the Peneius River, where they encamped close by the position occupied by Antipater and Craterus. When the coalition leaders realised the full strength of the force opposed to them is not clear. But it must have come as a considerable shock to them when they discovered the true numbers of the opposing army, as surely they would not have encamped so close if they had known the odds they faced. Antipater had concentrated 40,000 heavy infantry as well as 3,000 light infantry and 5,000 cavalry. The number of cavalry now present indicates that the combined presence of the old regent and Alexander's greatest general had possibly enabled some recruitment, even amongst the local Thessalian squirearchy, to supplement the Macedonian horse.[11]

The Greeks realized that, against these odds, they were in no condition to challenge the enemy to battle and withdrew their army to a defended position. Antipater, at last, had control of events which, after long months on the defensive, he had no intention of losing. Deploying his forces in the plain below the coalition army's position, he offered battle, intending to bring on the decisive encounter before the enemy could be reinforced by any returning allies. This challenge was repeated on several days running, while the Macedonian cavalry denied them supplies. Antiphilus was still hoping more troops would be coming into his army from those that had gone back to their homes 'to look after their private affairs'.[12] But fighting or starving soon became the only options that faced the coalition forces and Antiphilus decided to accept battle while at least his men's morale was high and before his own horses were debilitated from lack of forage. To have delayed further would have undermined his army's strength, whilst in battle tactical brilliance and bravery might yet compensate for numerical inferiority. The Greeks could only field 25,000 foot and 3,500 horse, but they still had great faith in the quality of their cavalry which had brought them two famous victories already. The climactic fight took place not far from Crannon in early August 322 BC. This town was once as important as Larissa (the richest, largest and most powerful city in Thessaly) but had been in decline since the middle of the fourth century.

Some manoeuvring had gone on before the two sides met in combat; Crannon is half a day's march south of the Peneius River where Diodorus' account firmly placed the two sides at the outset. No doubt the coalition army had been attempting to work their way back south, so they could have an unimpeded line of retreat if things went against them. When battle was joined, Antiphilus deployed his horsemen in front of his infantry phalanx rather than on the wing, hoping by this unorthodox formation to decide the battle before his weaker infantry became too involved. This is the only occasion this unusual deployment is mentioned in the Successor wars; in every other affray the horse were always positioned on the wings. Interestingly, however, at the Battle of Leuctra fifty years before, Epaminondas of Thebes set up his cavalry in the same manner. But, on that occasion, it seems he was using his horse to screen his weak allies on the right of his phalanx while he won the battle with his own Thebans on the left. Eumenes would later try a similar ploy to ensure that the battle was largely a cavalry affair, but he still kept his wings separate. Nothing is reported but probably Antipater lined his forces up in the traditional fashion with the foot in the centre and the cavalry divided on either flank. His strength lay in the Macedonian phalangites and he had no interest in keeping them out of the front line of battle. When he saw the enemy troopers coming in a mass along their whole front he ordered his cavalry out to confront the menace. What would have happened had he not is difficult to say as even Thessalian horse would surely not have flung themselves forward onto the *sarissae* of an unbroken phalanx. In the event, a huge melee developed with almost 9,000 men and their animals involved whilst the infantry on both sides stood and watched. Late summer is incredibly hot and dry in Thessaly and the dust raised by these myriad swirling hooves must have made it impossible to make out the progress of the fight for those watching, whether they were the rank and file or commanding generals.

Antiphilus' confidence in his cavalry was not misplaced. The Macedonians were driven back by the fury of the Greek attack and swiftly put to flight. But this reverse only served to clear the battlefield and allowed Antipater to push his phalanx forward against Antiphilus' infantry. In action at last, they closed in on the Greek hoplites who, outnumbered almost two to one, had no answer to the long *sarissae* of their opponents. The coalition phalanx was forced to fall back, but they were first-class troops, and keeping discipline they withdrew, in order, to the rougher terrain behind the plain where the battle had been fought. 'Thus they occupied the higher ground and easily repulsed the Macedonians thanks to their possession of the superior position.'[13] The many mercenaries in the ranks hated and feared their Macedonian foes who they had fought at Granicus, Issus and Gaugamela. They could not forget how their comrades were mercilessly massacred after defeat in the first of those fights, and they might well have anticipated such treatment for themselves.

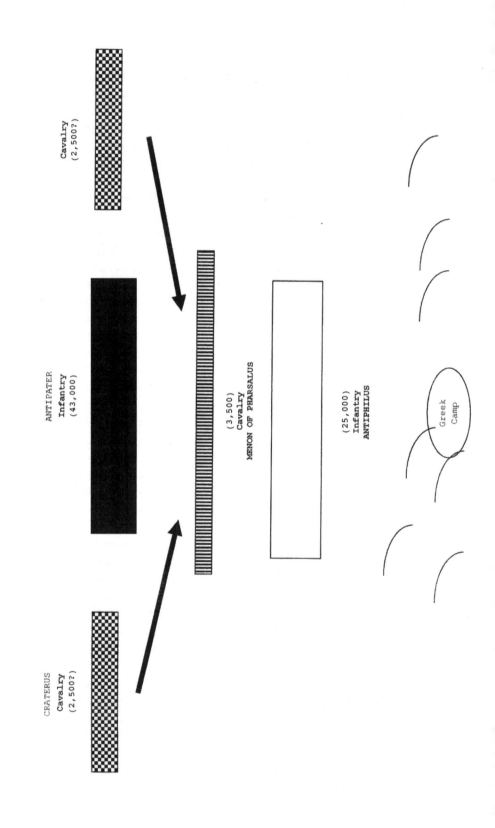

There are a number of outcrops near Crannon and it was to these that the Greek army retreated, where the terrain allowed them to hold their own against the Macedonians' continued assaults.[14] The coalition cavalry, seeing the defeat of their infantry, curtailed their pursuit of their fleeing enemies; these were impressively disciplined warriors who could be so kept in hand, and returned to support their comrades in the hills which effectively brought the encounter to an end. If the sources are to be believed, the casualties of the battle were minimal, with only 130 Macedonians slain and 500 from the Greek army. The very modesty of these figures argues for their plausibility, when so often the dead from ancient warfare are counted unbelievably high. Whatever the truth, this had been no crushing defeat for the coalition. The Macedonians held the field at the end of the day but apparently little more. Antiphilus' army was still in being and had fought splendidly against the odds. Antipater and Craterus had much to occupy their thoughts as the victory trophy was set up and the dead and wounded dealt with. Three battles had been fought, two had been lost and one won only on points, but none of this had finally brought a conclusion to the conflict.

Actually, this casualty-light skirmish would turn out to be epochal. From the year 322 BC nothing would be the same in Greece. Never again would any Greek people or even a Greek coalition of cities, unaided, be able to take on the power at Pella. Crannon had finally buried any chance of revival by any of the mighty independent states of the Classical era. Chaeronea in 338 had really written this death sentence but Crannon put the full stop in place. Muscle flexing in the future by Athens, Sparta, Thebes, Corinth, or Aetolian or Achaean leagues would need to be sponsored and seconded by a great power from outside for the combatants to stand any chance in a stand-up fight. But this would not have been clear to the combatants as the sun rose on the day after the combat. Antipater certainly had put the stop to a losing streak, but almost the whole of Greece still stood against him, with no friends raising their head above the parapet south of the Peneius River. The coalition army was still very much intact, and the Thessalian horse had shown again that head-to-head in the crucial cavalry melee they would still come out on top. But this picture was deceptive. In fact, all had changed. The corporate commitment of the Greek communities to the ruin of Macedon had been undermined by the failure of some of the detachments to return to Thessaly after the winter demobilization of 323/322 BC. The encounter at Crannon may have been little more than a skirmish but its effect on the will to fight both in the army and the cities was considerable. To blame this disintegration of morale on the comparatively-young generals in charge, as Plutarch does, is understandable but hardly fair. Both Antiphilus and Menon had shown real mettle against enemies who had just conquered most of the known world. It was not the failings of military leadership that had turned the war in Antipater's favour but the political failure of the Greek communities to maintain the enthusiasm and energy that had buoyed up Leosthenes' original success.[15] And, merely by surviving, Antipater had conquered; once the resources of the Macedonian Empire slowly began to seep back along the road Alexander trod over a decade before, it was only a matter of time before the Greeks would be overwhelmed.

Chapter Three

Eumenes' War

Perdiccas had won out at the army assembly at Babylon, ending as regent and guardian of Alexander's heir, and now it would be him and his erstwhile comrades who would come to blows. For, though now apparently confidently seated at the centre of the Macedonian Empire, cracks were showing elsewhere. As a companion bookend in the east to the Greek rebellion in the Balkans, the mercenary garrisons in Bactria and Sogdia had decided they had had enough of being ordered around by men from Macedonia. Pithon, the new satrap of Media, who had stood shoulder to shoulder with Perdiccas at Babylon, sorted this problem out. But this was only the first of many troubles that built up in the new regent's 'in tray'. Anatolia proved a can of worms which even his extraordinary lieutenant Eumenes could not handle alone. The regent came himself but, by drawing closer to the other power brokers in Europe, his actions only increased the temperature between men who had not long since been comrades under Alexander. Perdiccas campaigned against the king of Cappadocia and cities in Isauria but success in those places soon became marginal as he realized he would have to go to war with the other great Macedonian powers. It was the bodysnatching of Alexander's remains by the ruler from Alexandria, Ptolemy, that provided the final straw, but events anyway had been driving relentlessly towards the First Macedonian Civil War.

The exact sites of the battles of the western campaign of the first Macedonian Civil War are somewhat in dispute. Much suggests they took place near the Hellespont. Logic would urge that Eumenes, commanded to defend in the west, would deploy himself there; this crossing was a choke point, where an invading army might be held up or even destroyed. Diodorus specifically states Eumenes was sent by Perdiccas to defend the Hellespont, and that he had to send to some distance to his own satrapy of Cappadocia for horsemen, as the army the regent left him was deficient in that arm, which suggests he was near the Hellespont.[1] Plutarch, however, places a different emphasis. He describes Craterus and Antipater as planning an invasion of Cappadocia and Eumenes is specifically detailed as the commander with plenary powers over the armies in Armenia and Cappadocia. Perdiccas, in this analysis, seems to have expected Eumenes to defend deep, the regent sending letters to Neoptolemus and to Alcetas, off in Pisidia, to support the Cardian.

This position is given some credence when, at the battle with Craterus' army, it is mentioned that Eumenes persuaded his own men that they were facing just Neoptolemus and some Paphlagonian and Cappadocian horse.[2] This makes more sense if they were in that locality; if not it is difficult to see how it would be believable to Eumenes' followers that Neoptolemus, who had recently ran off with just a few supporters after defeat in battle, could recruit cavalry from so far away. But that he might have enlisted them locally would be eminently plausible. Plutarch also states that there were ten days between the two battles but this does not help at all, as how much distance was covered in this time period we have no way of knowing. A modern commentator certainly holds to the battle on the border of Cappadocia, and nothing intrinsic in the evidence bars the events occurring in either locality.[3] Cornelius Nepos offers no help as he merely says Eumenes was left to defend territory from the Taurus to the Hellespont.[4] But it is necessary to jump one way or the other, as to try and describe events hedging one's bets on the locality would be clumsy in the extreme. We have taken the view that the action unrolled near the waters of the Propontis where, so often over the centuries, the incumbent in Asia has stood fast to defy invaders from the west.

The manoeuvring that led to the two battles we are now describing certainly began where Europe met Asia at the Hellespont, a place that would figure much in the *Diadochi* story as both barrier and highway. The rest of this particular conflict played out in Egypt but on that front no major battles were fought and it was intrigue and treachery that decided the day, not military confrontation. Eumenes was left by Perdiccas as supreme commander in Anatolia on the western front of the coming world war. His responsibilities were huge, to counter what was bound to be the most potent thrust of the enemy coalition and guard a region that was far from easily defensible, but was rich and advanced, a part of the heartland of the Perdiccan realm whose loss could not be contemplated.

It is difficult to emphasise too much what major figures the people who Eumenes had to contend with were. Certainly he had, himself, been a senior bureaucrat who went back to Philip's reign but these, his two adversaries, were by far the greatest figures in the post-Alexandrine world. Compared with them even Perdiccas was almost a second division figure. Unlike what was to happen with the regent in the heart of Egypt, it is difficult to imagine either Craterus or Antipater struck down by a cabal of ambitious officers so early in the *Diadochi* epoch; their standing and repute would have made it unthinkable.

Certainly Perdiccas would not be the only one to suffer, Seleucus would fall under the knife of a murderous follower at the height of his success, but that was after forty years of chaos, bloodshed and fracture that changed the balance of men's loyalty in a world far gone in disintegration.

Antipater had grown old in service to Macedonia under Philip, even before the previous fourteen years when, with an absentee monarch, he had governed all of Macedonian Europe. He had taken on all-comers during that time, from Alexander's mother to the king of Sparta, and overcome them all. Despite this, and the fact that he had just gained a hard-fought victory in the Lamian War, it would be true to say that he was more of a politician than a military man, but this could not be said of his co-commander. Craterus was without doubt the greatest soldier of his day and had held that place after Alexander from halfway through that king's reign. After Parmenion was rubbed out in Ecbatana, there was no question that Craterus had expanded to fill his place. The extent of his services to his king were legend, whether from leading the main army forward at the Persian Gates as Alexander turned the enemy flank or holding the crossing at the Hydaspes River while Alexander took his strike force down river to cross and bring on battle with Porus. And since Alexander's death it had been his contribution that had decided against the Greeks in the Lamian War. And, at the time he was dragged away to this first Macedonian civil war, he looked on the brink of decisively dealing with the Aetolians (an achievement no one else came near in these years) despite their unorthodox strategy of defence, where they declined to fight in the open but took to the hills and fought a guerrilla campaign.

Apart from the calibre of the opposition, another drawback for the man from Cardia was that for subordinates he had a group of officers who were about as fractious as they could be. It would soon become clear that one of them was completely treacherous while the others, it seems, wanted Eumenes to fail in his efforts rather more than they ever desired victory for their own side. Neoptolemus was in central Anatolia, on the road from his satrapy of Armenia. This was the man who had twice fallen foul of Eumenes in the few years since the Babylon settlement. Neoptolemus had been made satrap of Armenia, but had found the task of imposing his rule very difficult indeed. A relative of Olympias, he had been little noticed in Alexander's wars except that he was at the forefront of the assault on the fortress of Gaza in 332 BC. He had also taken over the hypaspists after the Philotas affair, meaning he was Seleucus' direct superior for a time. Command of these foot guards was a prestigious office and an arduous one, as these veteran infantry frequently spearheaded Alexander's campaigns in Iran and India. He is not recorded as taking any part in the Babylon debates but as a royally-born, highly-experienced officer he was granted Armenia by Perdiccas, when the carve-up of the imperial satrapies took place.

This was no easy posting. Alexander had never been near Armenia in his great campaigns and it is unclear to what extent it was ever under Macedonian control. In 331 BC, Mithrines, a Persian officer who had surrendered the citadel of Sardis to Alexander, had been sent to take possession of the province, but whatever success he had did not last. By 323 BC Orontes, its original Persian satrap, had re-established himself, though whether as an Alexandrian protégé is not clear. There was no doubt this large province with considerable mineral resources had great potential, but governing it was always a dangerous business. How deep Persian control had ever gone is also open to question; the mountain tribesmen and baronial aristocrats of Armenia throughout the centuries had a deep reluctance to accept any foreign overlord.

The task that confronted Neoptolemus when he arrived had been further compounded by the fact that refugees from the king of Cappadocia, Ariarathes, just defeated and killed by Perdiccas, had fled to Armenia where they intended to fight on. Eumenes was despatched by Perdiccas to support Neoptolemus but, instead of this team approach making the difference in the real pacification of the area, all that happened was that a very deep personal antipathy arose between the two men. Eumenes offered his services to Neoptolemus on a second occasion after he had raised a large cavalry force in his own satrapy of Cappadocia. But again he was rebuffed by the Molossian and his officers, who resented deeply this intrusion by a man who, as a civilian foreigner, failed to tick the key boxes for these hoary Macedonian sweats on at least two counts.

The man who should have been Eumenes' other main support was Alcetas who, at that time, was ensconced in Pisidia. He was Perdiccas' brother with a history of considerable achievement under Alexander, in command of a *taxis* of the Macedonian phalanx. When ordered by Perdiccas to support Eumenes he refused, stating his men would not fight against Antipater and Craterus, who the Macedonians admired from way back. But, there is little doubt his real motivation was fuelled by resentment that his brother had not given the office of commander-in-chief in the west to him. With both these intended props showing they were inclined to flatly refuse the regent's orders, Eumenes was not clear what he could expect from any of the Perdiccan officers who controlled the Anatolian lands. He found himself left holding a poisoned chalice handed on by his leader, and only his extraordinary qualities allowed him to make a fist of it at all. He must have been close to despair, but it is extraordinary how loyal he stayed, despite the problems he encountered. Even when offered a very good deal by Craterus, he did not reconsider his loyalty to the Perdiccan cause. Eumenes' qualities were very impressive and loyalty was far from the least of them. In his whole career he displayed a remarkable adherence to the legitimist cause, whoever happened at the time to be in charge. An argument could be made that his own interest usually coincided with the cause he espoused, but equally a man more committed to personal survival surely would not have declared against Antigonus after he left Nora, at a time when the old marshal looked to be by far the most powerful star in the Macedonian cosmos.

Whatever his inner soul-searching, his situation demanded effective action, so he moved to the Hellespont where he could hope to close the crossing from Europe to Asia. Here were garrisons and strongpoints that with his own army in support might even stop the enemy getting across to challenge Perdiccan control of Asia. Strengthening the defences and garrisons occupied Eumenes' mind for the moment, in this, his first independent military campaign of any magnitude. He knew two of Macedonia's greatest soldiers were marching through the Thracian Chersonese to test his defences, certain components of which were bound to have a loyalty to their commander which was, at best, highly questionable.

While he waited for whatever, if any, reinforcements might arrive, Eumenes received news that made him realize he could not just sit and defend where he was. He heard news that his opponents' plans for invasion included a seaborne attack on the Aegean provinces far to the south of his position. In that region, Perdiccas' handling of the local elite had not helped the task of defence. The regent had been allying himself with Cleopatra, Alexander the Great's sister, and he handed overall control of the region to her, an act that alienated the officers who previously had enjoyed near-independent control of these provinces and now had to rule under her orders. In these circumstances, Eumenes would not have been so surprised that when Antigonus arrived with a small army in Caria, on ships provided by the Athenians, Asander, the local satrap, went over to him immediately and Menander of Lydia also seemed only too happy to co-operate with the one-eyed invader. Perdiccan control in the Aegean provinces looked set to be completely undermined in no time at all, and, with Alcetas well-placed in Pisidia but clearly doing nothing, Eumenes had to respond himself. Moving south by forced marches, he had not made contact with Antigonus when he heard that Antipater and Craterus with their main army had already crossed into Asia, apparently not opposed at all by the forces Eumenes had left deployed around the Hellespont. With his defensive line breached and the potential of being outflanked to north and south, Eumenes felt keenly exposed with only his own army under hand and none of his subordinates yet come up. In this predicament, he decided the only course was to withdraw into the interior of Phrygia.

Eumenes got away unscathed, but he now knew his position was such that the soldiers Neoptolemus was bringing with him were an absolutely vital ingredient if he was to have any chance of fighting the armies from Europe with any prospect of success. Eumenes' forces were well-mounted, mobile and knew the country and, even in the vastness of Western Anatolia, his Cappadocian troopers soon found what was supposed to be an important reinforcement for the Perdiccans. Somewhere east of the Hellespont the two forces encountered each other. When Eumenes ordered Neoptolemus to join him the worst followed. Clearly, Neoptolemus was disregarding orders to put himself under Eumenes' command, indeed his reaction showed that his plan was to join the invading army under Antipater and Craterus. This may have been because he believed the cause of opposing them was already lost but there was probably much personal enmity in it too. He hated Eumenes and the feeling was reciprocated. The Greek general at the head of his men found Neoptolemus with his army drawn up ready in battle array. It was clear this army was going to fight; Eumenes would need to clash with his own men before he even reached the main enemy. Now there were three armies ranged against him, Antipater and Craterus with one, Antigonus with another and now Neoptolemus as well.

In extradicting himself from this situation the Cardian would have to show persuasion, skill, resolution, imagination and courage and he never came up in short supply of any of them:

> He had managed to render the lives of his associates cheerful, inviting them all by turns to his own table, and seasoning the meal thus shared with conversation which had charm and friendliness. For he had a pleasant face, not like that of a war-torn veteran, but delicate and youthful, and all his body had as it were artistic proportions, with limbs of astonishing symmetry; and though he was not a powerful speaker still he was insinuating and persuasive, as one may gather from his letters.[5]

This social paragon's first move to resolve this difficult puzzle was enacted somewhere in Phrygia, where the terrain of that country was instrumental in the outcome of events. This was cavalry country of broad open valleys that invited the sweeping manoeuvres of skilled troopers and gave little natural protection for the vulnerable flanks and rear of ponderous infantry battalions. Eumenes was weak in the infantry he commanded: only a mixed force of mainly Asiatic foot, many of them light infantry with few Macedonians to give beef to his line. But Anatolian cavalry he had aplenty and in this undulating terrain he intended they should be the battle winner.

Neoptolemus' phalanx had a core of Macedonian veterans, a combination of those sent with him when he first received his satrapy and more, no doubt, sent as part of the support package of which Eumenes himself was an unwelcome part. Perhaps some were part of the 4,000 veterans that Craterus had left behind in Cilicia when he left for Europe and the Lamian War. Whoever they were, they very quickly dispersed Eumenes' soft infantry centre, an outcome that the Cardian surely must have expected. But he was still confident that his superiority in cavalry would tell. The cavalry left him by Perdiccas and his Cappadocian squires, born to the horse, spear and sword, had the Molossian's few cavalry on the run in double quick time. The desperate princeling, seeing his cavaliers scattered, almost made Eumenes' day by nearly getting himself killed in the combat. But his luck held long enough for him to escape from the melee with a few hundred horsemen, leaving his infantry leaderless after they had all but won him a victory.

The Cardian reformed his troopers and returned to confront the enemy phalanx who:

> intending to make their appearance have the most fearful impact upon the cavalry, they advanced in close order; and the troops behind them, those who were cavalry, began to fire javelins where the opportunity offered in order to throw back the cavalry charge by means of the continuity of their barrage. When Eumenes saw the close-locked formation of the Macedonian phalanx at its minimum extension and the men themselves heartened to venture every hazard, he sent Xennias once more, a man whose speech was Macedonian, bidding him declare that he would not fight them frontally but would follow them with his cavalry and units of light troops and bar them from provisions.[6]

This makes it clear the remains of Neoptolemus' cavalry had taken refuge behind the phalanx, which closed to locked-shield formation and were helping the infantry keep off Eumenes' triumphant troopers, who were surrounding them. It had all the appearance of a stalemate, with Neoptolemus' infantry impervious to the assault of enemy cavalry and, yet, not able to come to blows and defeat their more mobile adversaries. The decisive factor was that while pursuing Neoptolemus, Eumenes' men had captured his army's baggage train. Without supplies and unable to forage in the face of the enemy horsemen's control of the countryside, the infantry, though victorious in battle, were faced with both starvation and the permanent loss of whatever moveable wealth and dependents had remained in the camp. In these circumstances, the leaderless warriors had no alternative but to throw in their lot with Eumenes' army. They were an important addition but one whose loyalty was always questionable.

Only days after this action, while Eumenes was incorporating as best he could the remnants of Neoptolemus' troops into his own army, ambassadors arrived from Antipater and Craterus. The Greek was an old enemy of Antipater. It is certainly difficult to imagine a meeting of minds between the handsome socialite and the grumpy old man of Philip's court and they had been in that king's entourage long enough to dislike each other. And, more than this, Eumenes was close to Antipater's bête noir, Olympias, and even Cardian politics played a part with Antipater a partisan of an hereditary rival of Eumenes' family in that city.[7] But Craterus had always got on well with Eumenes in Alexander's time. Both hated the king's favourite, Hephaistion. Eumenes had most memorably fallen out with him when Hephaistion had tried to commandeer quarters set up for Eumenes, for a flute player who was part of Hephaistion's entourage. Furious, Eumenes had confronted Alexander who at first agreed with him but then changed his mind and berated Eumenes for his insolence.[8]

Now, it seemed this closeness might make negotiations possible. If these tentative discussions showed a disinclination to get down to battle between old comrades, this fellow feeling did not survive the arrival of Neoptolemus in Antipater's and Craterus' camp. He brought little from the wreck of his army but he assured his new friends that Eumenes' men would desert at the sight of Craterus, who the Macedonian veterans loved for articulating their deeply felt xenophobia that Alexander had so offended when he began to take on Persian ways as the heir of the Great King Darius. The two generals from Europe were easy to persuade and, with the talking over, Craterus led out his forces to confront Eumenes while Antipater took his part of the army and headed southeast towards the Taurus mountains and on to the Levant to try and bring succour to Ptolemy, who faced the brunt of the main Perdiccan army.

Top men from Alexander's time were squaring up to fight: Craterus, that epitome of Macedonian military virtue; Neoptolemus, a scion of the royal house of Epirus, a noble of the highest status, who had been part of Alexander's innermost circle in the later years; and Eumenes, as royal secretary, one of the key figures at the Macedonian court from even before the death of Philip. All had marched from Pella to Taxila and back with the greatest conqueror the ancient world had ever known and it is no surprise, now that blood was to be spilt between them, the shadow of their dead king hovered over events. Indeed, Eumenes, the night before the battle, was disturbed by dreams.[9] 'He dreamed, namely, that he saw two Alexanders ready to give each other battle, each at the head of a phalanx; then Athena came to help the one, and Demeter the other, and after a fierce struggle the one who had Athena for a helper was beaten, and Demeter, culling ears of grain, wove them into a wreath for the victor.'[10]

The Cardian comforted himself, somewhat, by interpreting the victory of the goddess of fertility as referring to his own corn-growing satrapy of Cappadocia, but his confidence really returned when deserters informed him that indeed the enemy password for the battle was Athena and Alexander. That this is an anachronistic confection, from the mind of Plutarch, a second century AD Roman provincial, does not detract from the reality that, in these first years of conflict, the common experience of the rivals under Alexander cannot but have affected their thinking.

True or not, Eumenes had given considerably more thought to this encounter than somebody who regarded the outcome as already decided by the machinations of fate. What he intended was that his Macedonian infantry would not hear that the general opposed to them was Craterus until he had been able to decide the fight with his horsemen. Craterus, now seconded by Neoptolemus, commanded a formidable array, of the quality that Alexander had taken over the same route fourteen years before. Of the 20,000 infantry a good proportion were Macedonian phalangites, veteran foot to be fielded at the centre of his battle line, men who had known very little defeat in their careers. They were a combination of those who had returned with Craterus, Leonnatus and Polyperchon from the eastern wars and the national levy. Some would have grown to manhood since Alexander had initially drained Macedonia of its manpower. They were an impressive combination of hardy veterans and vital youngsters, whose forest of pikes must have made a deadly show as they approached Eumenes' position. The rest of the infantry were the usual skirmishers, most probably recruited from Thracian and Illyrian tribes, who provided a screen in front of their heavier comrades. This was a very formidable force but the invaders' weakness was not in foot soldiers but in cavalry. Craterus had only slightly over 2,000 horse. After the Lamian War they would not have had many, if any, Thessalian or Greek horse. Such recent enemies would neither have had the inclination to join the invading army nor if they had, could they have been trusted. Interestingly, Diodorus states 'and more than two thousand horsemen as auxiliaries', not a designation often used for cavalry in this period.[11] This may be just a stylistic device to emphasise that the army was strongest in infantry. Whatever the truth, we know the senior generals took their posts with these horse soldiers on the wings. Craterus led 1,000 or so cavalry on the right wing, the place of honour, while Neoptolemus held the other side with what was left of the troopers present.

Eumenes equally had 20,000 infantry on hand but their quality was not comparable. There were a few thousand Macedonian pikemen, lately of Neoptolemus' defeated army, but the rest were mainly a muddle of mercenaries from the provinces of Asia Minor and light infantry from Mesopotamia and Iran, who had followed Perdiccas west from Babylon. In terms of both calibre and loyalty Eumenes was at a real disadvantage. He must have known he could not keep the identity of the enemy general permanently a secret from his Macedonians and when they did find out it was probable they would desert. This would be especially the case if some were part of the 4,000 veterans left by Craterus in Cilicia when he went to aid Antipater.[12] Eumenes was now trying to lead them in battle against Craterus himself. Eumenes was banking on his 5,000 horse against the enemy's 2,000 to win the day, well before the infantry got to grips. Yet, even his cavalry were not without their weak links. Some of them were Macedonians or others who had served in Alexander's army and allegedly the very sight of Craterus might cause them to change sides. To counter this effect, Eumenes, seeing that Craterus led on the right, 'arrayed against Craterus not a single Macedonian but two troops of foreign horse commanded by Pharnabazus the son of Artabazus and Phoenix of Tenedos'.[13]

These foreigners, non-Hellenic European and Asiatic horsemen, who would have had no link of affection to the great Macedonian marshal, formed the left of the Perdiccan array. But, it was on the right Eumenes intended to win the fight. Like Alexander, who had won his great battles with cavalry charges on the right wing, this was the pattern his old secretary intended to follow, with the best and largest body of the cavalry. To disguise the identity of the real enemy, Eumenes first gulled his followers into believing that it was not Craterus that was approaching but merely Neoptolemus with some Paphlagonian and Cappadocian cavalry he had recruited. But it was obvious this fiction could not be maintained when the armies closed and another policy was required to sustain the subterfuge. The terrain aided the Greek general as there was a hill between the two armies which masked Craterus and his army from sight. Instead of allowing his own infantry to get close before beginning the battle, he ordered the cavalry wings to attack while the main bodies of the armies were still far apart. This caused considerable consternation amongst Craterus' forces, as they did not know what to make of the enemy charging at them so unorthodoxly with the opposing phalanxes nowhere near each other.

> Now that Eumenes should learn beforehand of his approach and get himself ready for it in advance, one might consider a mark of sober generalship, though not of superlative ability; but that he should keep his enemies from getting any knowledge that would work him harm and besides this that he should hurl his soldiers upon Craterus before they knew with whom they were fighting and conceal from them the name of the opposing general seems to me to have been an exploit peculiar to this commander.[14]

Plutarch clearly feels this deception, achieved by a fellow Greek when he pulled the wool over these Macedonian's eyes, was much to be applauded. Perhaps, again, here we see a tendency for the writer to appreciate when his own compatriots outwitted people who were more powerful but regarded as less sophisticated. Only a little time later, when Antigonus had bested Eumenes in battle, the Cardian again outwitted his enemy by doubling back to the field of combat to give rites to his soldiers who had fallen there. Also, when tested by the insubordination of the Macedonian leaders of the Silver Shields, Eumenes used his brains to hoodwink them into thinking that

Alexander, in a dream, had inspired him to lead them by convening strategy meetings in a royal tent dedicated to the dead king.[15] Nor, if we are to believe Plutarch, was it just Eumenes who was the great manipulator. Crates, a renowned philosopher, is attested as cunningly inducing Antigonus' son, Demetrius, to give up the siege of Athens in 288 BC and head off on what was to become his final campaign in Asia.[16]

But still there were problems with this ploy for if Eumenes' horse was defeated the infantry would not be available to offer a refuge for them to rally on. On the right flank, dramatic events were soon under way. Here, Eumenes, protected by his personal guard of 300 veterans, was in command, leading his thousands of Cappadocian aristocrats and their retainers in what he intended to be the *coup de grâce*. Xenophon, who had encountered such cavalry in Persian service many years before, described them as having big horses, long lances and scale armour. Opposite stood Neoptolemus, a man whose personal dislike of Eumenes was matched only by the extent this antipathy was returned. Eumenes' history showed he knew how to hold a grudge and Neoptolemus' resentment against a man he considered an upstart bureaucrat all made this encounter a particularly vicious personal clash with few real parallels in these pages. To fight an enemy commander and strip him of his arms was a resonant achievement in most ancient societies and most certainly in the military worlds of Greece and Rome. This and the intimate loathing of the participants make a real gladiatorial combat of what is the unanimous evidence of our sources.

Eumenes and Neoptolemus charged at the head of their men:

They had long hated each other with a deadly hatred, but in two onsets neither had caught sight of the other; in the third, however, they recognised each other, and at once drew their swords and with loud cries rode to the attack. Their horses dashed together with the violence of colliding triremes, and dropping their reins they clutched one another with their hands, each trying to tear off the other's helmet and strip the breastplates from his shoulders. While they were struggling, their horses ran from under them and they fell to the ground where they closed with one another and wrestled for the mastery. Then Eumenes, as Neoptolemus sought to rise first, gave him an undercut in the ham, and himself got to his feet before his adversary did; but Neoptolemus, supporting himself on one knee, and wounded in the other defended himself vigorously from underneath. He could not, however, inflict fatal wounds, but was himself wounded in the neck, fell to the ground and lay there prostrate.[17]

The wrestling match ended with the two falling off their horses and onto the ground. In this Homeric struggle both men were wounded in several places, before Eumenes dealt his opponent a fatal cut, but not before Neoptolemus had, with almost his last breath, thrust the sword he still retained in his hand into Eumenes' groin, under the protection of his breastplate. With the death of Neoptolemus, his forces, who had previously been holding their own, as shown by the fact that at least three charges had occurred, lost much of their heart and soon were in retreat. Cavalry fights were more inclined to be affected by the loss of the commanding general than their infantry equivalents. These splendidly-armoured figures, with their bodyguards of friends and servitors, were required to give continual direction to their side of the combat; leading the squadrons in attack, reorganizing and rallying them when the impetus of the charge or enemy resistance had disordered their ranks.

On the other cavalry wing, Craterus (no doubt cursing his new friend, Neoptolemus, who had promised the enemy would not fight, which they now clearly intended to do) had led his outnumbered troopers forward to confront the enemy so his men might have built up some impetus when the squadrons clashed. 'Here Craterus did not disgrace Alexander, but slew many foes, and frequently routed the opposing arrays.'[18]

The two opposing wings of swirling squadrons seemed for some time an even match for each other but then, in the ensuing melee, an event of great moment occurred that would have a profound effect on the succession struggle. The greatest of Alexander's generals and veteran of most of his wars met his end. The sources are at some variance as to the exact details of Craterus' death. One account has his horse stumbling and throwing him off to be trampled to death and, if true, it might cause a mordant observer to see it as an apposite demise for this unlucky man. On Alexander's death, he had not found himself in the right place to go for the top job that his record and reputation undoubtedly fitted him for. But the more likely detail of his fall comes from Plutarch and has him valiantly beating down the enemy before being wounded by a Thracian warrior who came up unnoticed on his blind side. Such though was the respect that he was reputedly held in that an enemy officer called Gorgias[19] recognized him and actually shielded his defenceless body from further injury, though he was not able to save the dying general.[20]

With both Craterus and Neoptolemus dead, the horsemen on the flanks routed and fled towards the protection of their infantry. The foot soldiers had not even begun to fight by the time this occurred and Eumenes, having achieved so much, did not intend that they should. He brought back his cavalry from pursuit, an impressive performance in any age in the midst of battle, halted the foot and set up a trophy to his victory. The leaderless infantry of Craterus had halted where they stood, as going forward would

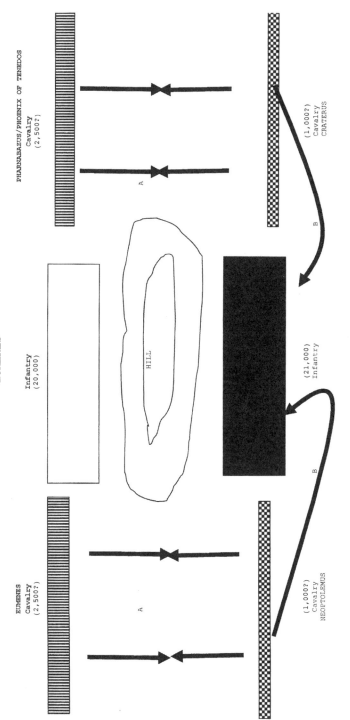

EUMENES

PHARNABAZUS/PHOENIX OF TENEDOS
Cavalry
(2,500?)

Infantry
(20,000)

HILL

EUMENES
Cavalry
(2,500?)

A

A

(1,000?)
Cavalry
CRATERUS

B

(21,000)
Infantry

B

(1,000?)
Cavalry
NEOPTOLEMUS

CRATERUS

A Clash of cavalry; Craterus dies and Neoptolemus killed by Eumenes.
B Both defeated cavalry wings flee for refuge to phalanx.

Battle of the Hellespont, 321 BC.

have invited attacks on the flanks and rear of the phalanx which no longer had an intact cavalry force to provide protection. The Cardian general, though wounded, was active enough to desire to reap all the benefits of victory. He wanted to recruit the extremely valuable soldiers that were now at his mercy and he sent agents over to offer them a truce. This was accepted as these formidable warriors had lost their commander-in-chief and did not know what to do. They knew they could not fight on, but equally, they were not prepared to change sides. Eumenes realized most would not actually join his army but at the very least he hoped to neutralize them for the campaign to come. While negotiations were under way, Eumenes allowed them to occupy some local villages to live off the supplies they could find there. However, these loyal warriors were determined not to abandon the cause of Antipater and after they had recuperated and got together provisions, they secretly set out on the road to find him. So, the wily Greek failed to achieve the neutralization of these constant soldiers for even one season.

This loyalty to the cause shown by these soldiers is interesting. The facility with which soldiers changed sides at a later time had not yet become the norm. These men had followed Philip and Alexander in a corporate enterprise and they saw following Craterus and Antipater as a continuation of this. But this war they were involved in and the ones that followed would soon dissolve the ties that so far were so strong. Components of any ruling elite, split against themselves, find it difficult to long retain attachment unless it pulls off the trick of continuous success. Loyalty for most people is a crude dynamic, something simple to hold to that defends their interest, gives them worth, value and profit. But when the centre of loyalty is fractured then just narrow immediate self-interest takes over. Most people want something bigger to belong to, something grand and self-affirming but when it collapses then they will revert to the tribe of just their own selves and their immediate comrades.

Whatever this quality of fidelity really consists of, little enough was found by the banks of the crocodile-infested Nile. After some bad luck, not helped by poor local knowledge, Perdiccas was assassinated in an officer coup led by Pithon. This only left the main army, and in essence the heart of the now peripatetic Macedonian state, virtually leaderless as the First Macedonian Civil War drew to a close.

As for Eumenes, his first two battles show that as a commanding general he already had it all: happy to use ruses to confound his enemies and even to keep his own followers in the dark; making sure the decisive events occurred in those sections of the battlefield where his troops were strong on the wings and ensuring that what happened in his weak centre in the end did not matter; using terrain features to aid his battle plans; and, finally, fighting as a hero at the front of his own men and personally besting one of the opposing commanders.

Chapter Four

Gabene and Paraetacene

The settlement of Triparadeisus was only a semicolon in the *Diadochi* Wars, hardly bringing a pause to the ongoing saga of venomous embattlement. Antipater soon returned to Pella, leaving Antigonus at the helm in Asia. He, in charge at last, began to show the qualities of decisiveness, speed, imagination and determination that would define his career. But, for all his success against Eumenes, against Alcetas and in reclaiming the Aegean provinces from hostile satraps, it was only to be a prelude.

Everything draws the attention towards the campaigns of 317/316 BC; we have comprehensive details of the manoeuvring and the epic clashes that characterize this time, which is rarely true of other years. The thinking of the combatants is understandable; the very battle plans themselves are available, as is seldom the case in any period before modern times. The reason is that we have a real spy on the ground. Hieronymus of Cardia, who provides the main source for Diodorus at this time, was in a unique position to understand and report on events and probably would even have had access to recorded orders of battle. He was present at the highest levels for not just one but for both sides. In a long life he first spent years in the entourage of Eumenes and, on his demise, became a long-term officer in the service of the great Antigonids, father and son; and he was still active at the court of Antigonus Gonatus. Indeed it is possible to read an agenda into his work that while critical of Antigonus and Demetrius, he buffed with relish the reputation of the grandson in a period when that king was trying to establish a south Balkan hegemony. This remarkable chronicler who we are so dependent on (channelled through Diodorus) is even claimed to have lived to 104 years of age.[1]

The one great drawback in understanding these events is that the fighting took place in Susiane, Persia and the heart of Iran, not places familiar to those who described the course of events. Many informants may have been to these places with Alexander, or after, but they did not know the terrain, as they would have the country around Pella, Vergina, Thermopylae or the

Gulf of Corinth. So they are much less able to pinpoint where things occurred than they would have been in the familiar terrain of Greece, or even Western Anatolia. And this ignorance from the start is compounded by the fact that for many generations little in the way of archaeology or even historical geographical exploration has been possible in an area wracked by war and foreign invasion. People do try and make guesses where the events were placed but it is all conjecture of the least convincing kind. How can a comment in the sources about where a ridge, a river or a salt plain were really enable somebody to pinpoint the great battlefields of this war? All that is possible is to suggest the general region where the specific conflicts were played out. Yet, the drama of the two greatest of the commanders to emerge in the decade after Alexander's death slugging it out with the most formidable armies fielded by any of the *Diadochi* none the less makes it compelling.

Antigonus, in late 319 BC, looked to many unstoppable, but that was only a local perspective. While he pushed all over before him in Pisidia, then Hellespontine Phrygia and Lydia, a brew of troubles was being concocted for him by a formidable trio. Polyperchon, as guardian of the kings, egged on by Olympias, mother of Alexander, had mobilized that temporarily dormant genius, Eumenes, to get back in the ring. Credibility, legitimacy and the money it opened up meant this brilliant man had been able to create a force round the veteran Silver Shields that he would wield with lambent intelligence in the couple of years to come. He had retreated into the heart of Asia, as Antigonus harried him again, but it was not just to get away but also in the hope of finding friends there. Seleucus, at Babylon, had not been responsive but as he approached the Iranian satrapies, the rulers there, already united against their problematic neighbour, Pithon, satrap of Media, had joined him in Susiane.

As campaigning opened in 317 BC, Eumenes had both his own army and the combined forces of the satraps that consisted of 18,700 foot and 4,600 horse. But the group that had come together so recently was not without its fissures. The personal dynamic was fraught with individual rivalries as, apart from Peucestas, there were a number of formidable leaders present. The satraps of Carmania, Arachosia, Aria and Drangiana had all contributed troops and Eudamus had come from India, where the Alexandrine settlement was crumbling, with a considerable army that included 120 elephants. Tension amongst these egos was inevitable, as all of them could boast years of experience in the army of Alexander and their very survival in positions of great importance, since his demise, labelled them as veterans of considerable stature and ability. They knew Antigonus had disposed of most of their colleagues around the Aegean and would be bringing a huge army with him. He had followed Eumenes across

Mesopotamia, but to reach them there were still natural obstacles in the way. But, soon enough news arrived that the intruders had thrown a pontoon bridge over the Tigris and their army was across the last great natural barrier between them and Susa. Eumenes and the satraps, despite rivalry over command, had come to a modus vivendi that, at least, allowed key decisions to be made. The first of these was premised on the fact that they were outnumbered and so they decided to decamp.

As they struck their tents and marched out south, the coalition leaders were on the look out for a place that they could hope to defend with confidence. They thought they had found it at the Pasitigris River, a waterway which Alexander himself had cruised down to the sea in 324 BC, shortly after the Susa weddings. This, they decided would provide a front line that any attacker would find difficult to pierce with an active defender ensconced on the other side. The great drawback was the extent of the shield which they sought to utilize; it was bound to try the abilities of any defender to watch over its whole length effectively.

Pickets were posted along the bank, from the source of the river to the sea, to ensure the enemy could not slip by unnoticed. To cover this vast front was no small matter. In fact, it required Peucestas to call on the resources of the province he had controlled since before Alexander's death. Officers were despatched back to his adjacent satrapy to raise 10,000 more Persian bowmen. And, there is little question this display of local might was not intended to be lost on both the leaders and the soldiers of the coalition. This was not the first time Peucestas had shown what a cornucopia of military resources he controlled. In 323 BC, he had provided Alexander with 20,000 soldiers who it had been intended to incorporate in the body of the Macedonian phalanx. It was planned that each file of the new combined units would consist of four Macedonian pikemen and twelve Iranian troops using lighter local equipment that would provide the new regiments with missile-hitting power. This experiment was not destined to last long; as soon as Alexander died it was shelved, never to be resuscitated.

Antigonus, meanwhile, had joined the Royal Road to Susa, after crossing the Tigris. Days of marching in the late June heat had meant very real attrition for Antigonus' men. Trekking when the sun was down helped a little but still the temperatures were almost more than the body could bear and, on top of this, the road to the Pasitigris was far from clear. Before reaching this watercourse, the invaders found themselves confronted by a considerable tributary called the Coprates.

Eumenes had been keeping Antigonus under surveillance all the way and scouts in forward positions kept him well informed on his movements. At the Coprates, Antigonus found himself in some difficulties, as his officers could not find sufficient boats to transport the army across the river. He immediately began ferrying what men he could across the river to build, as quickly as possible, a defended camp that could hold the position while the rest got across. When this was reported, Eumenes decided on a surprise attack. Covering the 9 miles from his encampment to the Coprates at great speed, he and a small force of 4,000 foot and 1,300 horse fell on the Antigonids. About 9,000 men had crossed when Eumenes launched his attack but 6,000 had dispersed to forage. Whether this was indiscipline, or even if sanctioned by the high command, it was very foolish when such an active commander as Eumenes was not far away. The remainder of the soldiers had begun to dig a defensive ditch and to construct a palisaded bridgehead, but the stockade was incomplete and the defenders had their backs to the river, with no room to manoeuvre when the enemy arrived. The Antigonids did not have time to put down their tools, pick up their arms and get into proper fighting formations. As all they could do was defend themselves as best they could against superior numbers, this was not likely to be successful. The faint hearted soon started to run for the boats and what order they had struggled into began to crumble. Soon, all organized resistance ceased and the only thought that Antigonus' men had was to get back over the river to the protection of the main army. The old man looked on helplessly as the debacle was completed when the very numbers of terrified fugitives capsized the boats and dumped his soldiers into the rushing waters, which carried most away to their death. The men who had gone off to forage now returned in dribs and drabs and, unable to put up any defence at all, were killed or captured. Eumenes was outnumbered and his command structure fractured, but he was an extraordinary talent and this coup had cost Antigonus as many as 8,000 casualties including 4,000 prisoners.

The Antigonid army was hot, frustrated and confused; a weaker foe was keeping them at arm's length, causing great loss, and there seemed no likelihood of the decisive action that Antigonus craved. To try and winkle the confederates out of their position by force seemed futile and another strategy needed to be tried. He decided that to revitalize the army's sagging spirits, progress and success were needed. The lands of the upper satrapies were relatively unprotected, with their rulers and their best troops away with Eumenes. This, potentially a rich source of plunder, was attractive because it would both encourage his followers and it would make the generals with Eumenes squeal and insist he leave his hidey-hole to return to protect their holdings. Antigonus, decided on this course of action, set off north to Ecbatana, formerly the Persian king's summer capital in the hills of Media, where his men could also escape the roasting climate of Susiane.

Antigonus, in putting his plan into practice, showed less intelligence than in preparing it. Displaying an impatience that on several occasions would lead him into trouble, he determined to march directly north over the mountains instead of the army taking the longer but much easier route via the royal road, up the Tigris valley, before branching right through the Zagros range at the Median Gates. This way led through the territory of the Cossaeans. They were a hardy, aggressive and 'uncivilized' tribe who apparently still lived in caves and subsisted on acorns, mushrooms and wild game. But, if they lacked the amenities of life, their knowledge of the mountains made them formidable opposition on their own land. The Persian kings had sensibly left them untamed and paid tribute if they wished to use the routes through their territory. However, Alexander had not been prepared to suffer their presumptuous independence and campaigned against them. The Cossaeans could not have chosen a worse moment to challenge him, as he was suffering from massive bereavement at the death of Hephaistion, his chiliarch and favourite. Alexander vented his grief; harrying them for forty days through their glens and forests, massacring or deporting those he found. Almost seven years had passed since this humiliation and many had forgotten this unpleasant taste of Macedonian might, so they again demanded tribute from Antigonus. He compounded his already dangerous decision to march this way by refusing to pay. Pithon, more familiar with local customs, advised against such arrogance but Antigonus would not be swayed. The Cossaeans decided to take their tribute by force of arms.

Realizing he would have to fight, the old general ordered his line in a competent manner. His missile men, peltasts, bowmen and slingers were divided into two parts; one to go ahead and occupy the main passes and the other to be distributed amongst the whole army and give it protection. In charge of the first detachment was Nearchus, Alexander's favourite admiral and a man who had disappeared from view since Babylon, where he had tried to foist Alexander's illegitimate son, Heracles, on the Macedonian assembly.[2] Antigonus marched with the phalanx in the middle of the army, while Pithon brought up the rear with selected light-armed troops. All these preparations could not ensure protection from the fierce Cossaeans, especially as Antigonus had a massive army with camp followers and baggage, particularly vulnerable, as it snaked its way along the seemingly never-ending passes. Nearchus faced strong opposition and lost many men while the main body found itself under pressure all along the route as the Cossaeans occupied the high ground and rained missiles down on the Antigonids with impunity. The horses and elephants suffered particularly severely and many did not survive.

As for the troops led by Antigonus, whenever they came to those difficult passes, they fell into dangers in which no aid could reach them. For the natives, who were familiar with the region and had occupied the heights in advance, kept rolling great rocks in quick succession upon the marching troops.[3]

After a harrowing eight days, they finally managed to reach the safety of Media. Though an ordeal of shorter duration, this episode is very reminiscent of the march of Xenophon's 10,000 and after their travails Antigonus' men must have greeted the end of the Cossaean hills with as much relief as those earlier Greeks did the Black Sea coast. Morale, though, had again been heavily shaken and Antigonus must have rued his refusal to pay tribute. For once, he should have listened to Pithon.

In Media, Antigonus' first concern was to revive the flagging spirits of his men who, in the last month and a half, had suffered much from both the hands of man and nature. They were rested and fresh supplies brought in, while he personally visited as many troops as he could to convince them that the setbacks were only temporary. Pithon, back in his old province, was sent to get reinforcements. This he did with some élan, bringing back 2,000 horsemen and an additional 1,000 mounts as well as numerous pack animals and 500 talents from the eastern treasury at Ecbatana. By giving the horses to those who had so recently lost their own and distributing the pack animals as presents, Antigonus did much to restore spirits. The Antigonids in Media were also much relieved when news arrived that the ploy to draw their enemy out from behind his entrenched position had worked as well as could have been expected. The arguments in the coalition command tent had been bitter and protracted, but eventually things had fallen out as Antigonus had hoped it might.

The Cardian and the officers who had come with him saw an opportunity with Antigonus far to the north to retrace their steps back to Babylonia and the Levant. This open road to the west would put them, with a mighty host, at the centres of power in Syria, Phoenicia, and Cilicia and not far from the great cities of the Aegean. But the satraps were not prepared to leave their provinces open to depredations by the invader. A reluctant Eumenes had to fall in with men whom he knew, at bottom, that he absolutely needed. So, the mix of Macedonians, Greeks, Iranians and Indians who comprised the coalition army moved away towards Persepolis, the capital of the Persian lands, where Peucestas had been the ruler for almost ten years. They took it easy, no foolish escapades against hardy locals for them; in fact, they went through country so bounteous it allowed them to flesh out both their numbers under arms and their quartermasters' stores.

Peucestas had, from the beginning, been intriguing to be appointed commander in chief of the allied army and took advantage of their presence in his own province. He laid on ostentatious entertainment:

With the company of those participating he filled four circles, one within the other, with the largest enclosing the others. The circuit of the outer ring was of ten stades (approximately 6,000 feet) and was filled with the mercenaries and the mass of the allies; the circuit of the second was of eight stades and in it were the Macedonian Silver Shields and those of the Companions who had fought under Alexander; the circuit of the next was of four stades and its area was filled with the reclining men – the commanders of lower rank, the friends and generals who were unassigned, and the cavalry; lastly in the inner circle with a perimeter of two stades each of the generals and hipparchs and also each of the Persians who was most highly honoured occupied his own couch. In the middle of these there were the altars for the gods and for Alexander and Philip. The couches were formed of heaps of leaves covered by hangings and rugs of every kind, since Persia furnished in plenty everything needed for luxury and enjoyment; and the circles were sufficiently separated from each other so that the banqueters should not be crowded and that all the provisions should be near at hand.[4]

Competition for command seemed to be really heating up and Eumenes, deep in the heart of Peucestas' satrapy, was becoming very concerned. He responded with both carrot and stick. First, he circulated a forged letter that peddled it that Olympias had gained complete control in Macedonia, had slain Cassander and sent Polyperchon into Anatolia. Indeed, it was claimed he had reached Cappadocia with an army that included elephants. With this making an impression (it looked to auger very well for the campaign now the Cardian was to be reinforced) he also threatened a slippery ally with dismissal and death.

This was Sibyrtius, satrap of Arachosia, a close friend of Peucestas and it is not difficult to see against whom Eumenes was aiming. In fact, this episode is a little unclear as Diodorus claims he was close to being tried by the assembly, at the behest of Eumenes, and only escaped death by flight. Yet, soon after, he is recorded as still *in situ* in his satrapy, though it maybe he fled back and found his old government loyal and stayed there until the outcome of the contest between Antigonus and Eumenes became clear. Finally, to bind his iffy friends even closer, the Cardian borrowed 400 talents from the allied satraps, turning them 'into most faithful guards of his person and partners in the contest'.[5]

The enemy was now near at hand, for Antigonus had broken camp in Media and set out for Persia. Eumenes must have been confident in the arrangements he had just made – that hindsight shows us were to prove very rickety indeed – as he moved his army towards his enemy clearly now prepared for a fight. Yet, he was still thinking about hearts and minds and, though not quite able to compete with Peucestas' munificence, he still threw a party for the army at which everybody indulged in the binge drinking that Macedonians were famous for. Eumenes, it seems, was first at the front of the wine queue, as he was so hung over and incapacitated that for several days the army was reduced to waiting for its commander to recover.[6] Indeed, even when they moved off, he was reduced to following his men in a litter with temporary command exercized by Antigenes and Peucestas. At least here was a safety valve, as these two hated each other so much that they would be unlikely to join forces to depose Eumenes.

The two sides, after many months of chasing each other, finally came face to face. Yet, even then the final denouement was not at hand. For both armies had drawn up on either side of a river in a ravine, making a battle impossible. For five days they swapped insults, skirmished and plundered the countryside; a hiatus in which an impatient Antigonus sent agents over to try and subvert the satraps. Strangely enough, their efforts seem almost open as Eumenes knew of their presence and even protected them from his followers who became enraged by their importuning at what Diodorus claims as an army assembly. This parallels the claim that Ptolemy spoke before Perdiccas' army prior to the invasion of Egypt but is perhaps slightly more plausible. In this case, Eumenes did not have the complete authority that Perdiccas had on the previous occasion, and, perhaps for the sake of unity, had to let the satraps hear what Antigonus had to say.

The coalition leaders would not hear of Antigonus' terms and by now his army had become desperately short of forage and was forced to move. Their destination was the plains of Gabene, a three-day march away, where there were ample supplies. However, dissatisfaction in the Antigonid ranks caused some desertions and, by this means, Eumenes got wind of their plans. Eumenes, showing the skills that made him probably the greatest general of all the *Diadochi*, proceeded to outwit Antigonus. He correctly guessed where Antigonus was heading and determined to get there before him and take up the best position. To do this, he needed a breathing space so he sent some soldiers over to Antigonus posing as deserters. They put it out that Eumenes was preparing a night attack, information that Antigonus readily believed. Eumenes, meanwhile, secretly sent his baggage on ahead and stealthily withdrew towards Gabene. After some time, Antigonus realized he had been duped and reacted swiftly. Leaving the bulk of the army under Pithon, he rode out at top speed with his cavalry. By dawn he had managed to overtake the enemy's rearguard and took up position on a favourable ridge. Giving the false impression that he had more troops than was the case, Antigonus forced Eumenes to turn and draw up his forces in battle formation. A manoeuvre that inevitably took up much time and allowed Pithon to arrive and now from high ground Antigonus could at last force a fight on his enemy.

Thus began the first of the two epic battles that are the centrepiece of this campaign and, it could be argued, the whole *Diadochi* era. Diodorus states Antigonus fielded 28,000 infantry (in reality this number is just those in the phalanx and does not include many thousands of light troops), 8,500 horse and 65 elephants. On the left wing, under the treacherous but competent Pithon, were drawn up the lightest of his horsemen and here the tactical intention could not be clearer, they 'were to avoid a frontal action but maintain a battle of wheeling tactics'.[7] These were the classic manoeuvres of steppe peoples that achieved so much for the Scythians, Sakae and Parthians, both before this and in generations to come. They were to use these tactics to occupy the strong right wing of Eumenes that Antigonus could see deployed below him from the heights. There were 1,000 Medes and Parthians described as lancers or horse archers. Then, according to Diodorus, came 2,200 Tarentines who were brigaded with them, 'men selected for their skill in ambushing'; an interesting new type of soldier who are given their first mention in this war; skirmishers who carried javelins and a small shield.[8] The association with the Italian city of Tarentum is real enough: coins from there show just such soldiers. In the cosmopolitan world that had seen Alexander's uncle fighting in southern Italy, it demonstrates the cross-fertilization of military techniques. The actual origin of these Tarentines is obscure; they are described as coming up from the sea but this is probably to distinguish them from the men who had joined Antigonus in Mesopotamia and Iran. A problem here is that this is a far larger group than you would expect from a new specialist troop type that had travelled up from the Mediterranean, even if not from Italy itself, and perhaps it is best to lose a nought from this estimate. Particularly as when Tarentines are again mentioned, whether when they ambush Eumenes' elephants or a few years later at the Battle of Gaza in 312 BC it is usually in numbers of a couple of hundred or so, never even close to the 2,200 recorded here. To reduce the number of Tarentines would also help solve the arithmetical dilemma that Diodorus poses when he states Antigonus had 8,500 cavalry but, in fact, all the separate units mentioned add up to 10,600.

After the Tarentines came 1,000 Phrygians and Lydians, gentry from West Anatolia with long association with Antigonus. Then 1,500 horse with Pithon, who we have no evidence about, but common sense suggests Pithon would have had with him good horse from his satrapy of Media. The last units on the left flank were 400 lancers under a Lysanias. Being on the left, these were probably light lancers rather than heavies who confusingly can also sometimes be designated by the same name. The rest of the left wing was made up of the 'two horse men' and 800 colonists from the upper satrapies. We know nothing of either of these regiments though presumably the former actually brought an extra horse to battle. Most cavalrymen had spare mounts; Alexander, famously, would only saddle up Bucephalus, his favourite warhorse, just before battle, using another one to get him to the field of combat. But, to get such a designation these men must have actually brought the spare mount into the line of battle, though it is not clear what great advantage this would give. If it meant they had a fresh steed immediately available, it also meant they needed to use one of their hands to hold the halter of the led horse which must have considerably impaired their fighting ability. What is interesting is that there are no figures given, so perhaps there were only a few of them and they had a specialist role. Last in the left wing were those 800 colonists already mentioned and all we can surmise is that, as colonists in the upper satrapies, they were most likely European or Anatolian horse who could have been settled by Alexander, or any others who had passed through the east in the years since his death. But, as the whole of the left is specified as being required to skirmish rather than charge straight home against the enemy, it is reasonable to suggest they again were light horse with either javelin or lance and with no armour except possibly a helmet. There was something around 7,000 all told on this wing if the high figure of Tarentines is accepted, but about 5,000 if the lower is used.

The 28,000 infantry mentioned are all attested in the phalanx. On the left 9,000 mercenaries; then 3,000 Lycians and Pamphylians (Anatolians who are perhaps specifically designated thus because they were old soldiers of Antigonus); more than 8,000 mixed troops in Macedonian equipment and then the nearly 8,000 real Macedonians who had come courtesy of Antipater at the start of the war. This indicates that 16,000 men in the phalanx carried *sarissa* and *pelte* as opposed to the classical panoply of *aspis* and shorter spear carried by the rest. What this leaves out is many thousands of light-armed troops that must have been fielded. Eumenes, for his part, had almost as many light troops as he had soldiers in his phalanx but he would have certainly had a higher ratio than Antigonus as many of his allies brought large numbers with them from satrapies that specialized in producing this kind of missile-armed warrior. Yet still Antigonus must have had many thousands; he would have needed at least 3,000 just to provide guards for his 65 elephants.

The horsemen on the right wing were intended by Antigonus as the battle winners, the clunking fist to compliment the defensive jabbing of Pithon. Nearest the infantry came 500 mercenaries, some may have been the Greek light mercenary horse who survived the massacre of their fellows in Sogdia while Alexander still lived. Next came 1,000 Thracians, who may have been light cavalry of the type Alexander brought with him from Europe or heavier armoured warriors typical of the aristocratic horse of that region. Then 500 who are described as from the allies, perhaps the cavalry from the allied Greek horse who stayed on while their units were demobilized at Ecbatana, after Darius had been defeated. How they were equipped is unknown but it is probable that most, if not all, were heavies, wearing body armour and welding the long cornel wood spear. The Companions, 1,000 strong, came next under Demetrius. He is on this occasion mentioned as specifically in charge of just these heroes as he was 'now about to fight in company with his father for the first time', while at the next battle he would be attested as in command of the whole right wing of the army.[9] And in the place of honour at the very edge on the right stood the old marshal himself, with his personal guard (*agema*) of 300. Placed in advance of them were 100 Tarentines and three troops of what are described as his slaves; we have no idea who they were but they would not have been servile retainers but brave and tried warriors. Their position as an advance guard in front of Antigonus' own *agema* suggests they, too, would be light horse deployed, no doubt, to clear the way of enemy skirmishers, enabling Antigonus to fling his heavy men down the throat of his opponent. This made 3,700 men in the whole wing, so in numbers they were considerably weaker than the left wing but in quality they included the very best. In front of this splendid assembly of mainly heavy horse, thirty elephants were drawn up, with most of the rest in front of the infantry phalanx and just an unspecified few guarding Pithon's front on the left. Antigonus led this awesome array down the mountain ridge they stood on towards the coalition army waiting for him.

Eumenes fielded 35,000 foot, 6,100 cavalry and 114 elephants. Much was analogous in his array to that of his counterpart and here, too, the allied left was intended to hold back and soak up the enemies' blows rather than deal the *coup de grâce*. In command was Eudamus, who had brought the crucial elephants, fresh from the Indus valley. As well, there were fifty mounted light horse lancers posted as an advance guard at the base of the hill that the rest of Eudamus' bodyguard was deployed on. After these men on the hill, to anchor the line came Stasander with 950 light horse from Aria and Drangiana, after him came Amphimachus, satrap of Mesopotamia, with 600 horsemen. This man may have been the half brother of Philip Arrhidaeus but what sort of cavalry he commanded we do not know.[10] Then came 600 Arachosian cavalry, no longer under Sibyrtius who had fled, but led by Cephalon, 500 Parapamisadae from the Hindu Kush and again most probably light horse like their comrades from the Indus. Approximately 500 Thracians from the upper country, troops planted in townships in the upper satrapies at some time since Alexander passed by, were on the right side of the left flank and thus adjacent to the infantry phalanx. Forty-five elephants stood in front of them with bowmen and slingers to protect the great beasts. Most of the horse on this left wing were light horse, unarmoured javelin men or lancers, best for scouting and skirmishing. The troops from

Mesopotamia may have been a heavier type and the same is true of the Thracians, though being arrayed with their lighter comrades might suggest they too were of this type. But, it is not impossible that some heavy armoured men, fit for close combat, were placed there to stiffen the whole left wing just as some would have been bodyguard troops, well armoured and fit for hand-to-hand fighting. Altogether they amounted to 3,400 horsemen.

In the centre came the phalanx, first 6,000 mercenaries and then 5,000 equipped like Macedonians 'although they were of all races'.[11] Next came more than 3,000 Silver Shields and then, more than 3,000 'from the hypaspists' taking the place of honour on the right.[12] So Eumenes fielded 11,000 *sarissa*-armed phalangites with the other 6,000 most probably classically-armed hoplites. Forty elephants stood arrayed in front of these spear and pikemen.

On the right of the phalanx were fielded most of the heavy cavalry Eumenes had at Paraetacene. First was Tlepolemus with 800 cavalry from Carmania, they came from the country east of Persia, itself, and probably produced warriors similarly armed to their cousins from that country. Then, 900 Companions, the heirs of Alexander's own, and then 300 cavalry under Peucestas and Antigenes (who though recorded as commander of the Silver Shields, with Teutamus, did not lead them in battle but took his place with the other commanders with the cavalry) where these two presumably shared charge as they had shared command of the whole army when Eumenes was indisposed. They led the quality of Persia; many were moneyed enough to equip themselves and probably their mounts with protective armour. They and their Median comrades had, since just before Gaugamela when Darius refitted them, taken up the longer, stronger lance used by the Macedonian horse. About this group, Diodorus says 'which contained three hundred horsemen arranged in a single unit.'[13] This is not explained, but it may refer to a specially strengthened *ile*, a bodyguard such as Alexander's royal squadron of the Companions that was just the same strength. If so, it was most probably Peucestas' bodyguard.

After this was Eumenes on the far right wing leading a complex array of horsemen. First were 300 cavalry, again the figure suggests it was his personal *agema* of heavy cavalry, many were surely his loyal Cappadocians who are not placed elsewhere but would still have been with him. They would have been looking to continue receiving the benefits of following a victorious patron. We know the Cappadocians who fought for Darius sometimes wore a full covering of scale armour and with Eumenes' elite it is likely they were as well protected. And they seem always to have wielded the long lance (*xyston*) with which the Persians and Medes had been re-equipped. As an advance guard in front of him were two lots of fifty mounted soldiers of what are called his 'slaves'. They are otherwise not

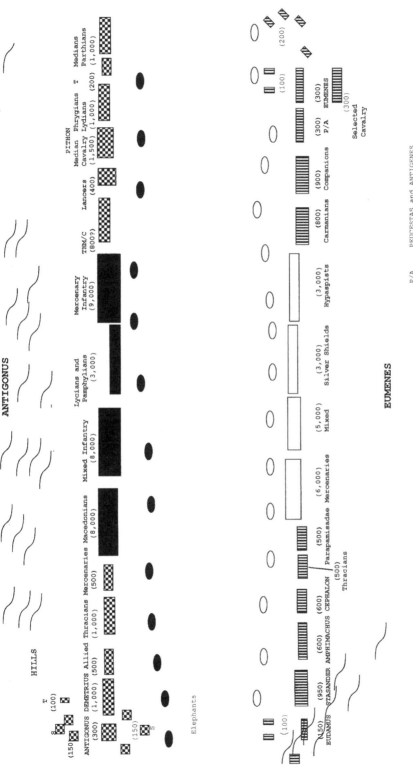

Battle of Paraetacene, 316 BC, initial deployments.

ANTIGONUS

HILLS

| ANTIGONUS (300) | DEMETRIUS (1,000) | Allied (500) | Thracians (1,000) | Mercenaries (500) | Macedonians (8,000) | Mixed Infantry (8,000) | Lycians and Pamphylians (3,000) | Mercenary Infantry (9,000) | THM/C (800?) | Lancers (400) |
| | | | | | | | | | | |

PITHON

| Median Cavalry (1,500) | Phrygians Lydians (1,000) | T (200) | Medians Parthians (1,000) |

T (100)

S (150)

(150)

Elephants

EUMENES

| N.50) EUDAMUS | (950) STASANDER | (600) AMPHIMACHUS | (600) CEPHALON | (500) Thracians | (500) Parapamisadae | (6,000) Mercenaries | (5,000) Mixed | (3,000) Silver Shields | (3,000) Hypaspists | (800) Carmanians | (900) Companions | (300) P/A | (300) EUMENES |

(100)

(100)

(300)

Selected Cavalry

(200)

P/A   PEUCESTAS and ANTIGENES
T   TARENTINES
THM/C   TWO HORSE MEN AND COLONISTS FROM THE UPPER COUNTRY
S   SLAVES

described, but as this is one of very few occasions any group of soldiers are so referred to in our period it suggests they were specially attached to their leader whether Eumenes or Antigonus. Furthermore, as slaves, in the sense usually used, were very seldom armed for battle (except *in extremis* when the very state was threatened with extinction as at the siege of Rhodes by Demetrius) it is likely they were some of his very best troops of light cavalry. Then, at an angle, guarding the wing were first 200 selected men in four groups and then another 300 described by Diodorus as 'selected from all the cavalry commands for swiftness and strength'; presumably these were the best equipped and bravest men from all the satrapal retinues picked for the purpose, kept in reserve behind Eumenes' wing.[14] In front of all these were forty elephants[15] with some of them positioned round and backwards to match the front of the flank guard.[16]

The two armies fought from afternoon to midnight. Pithon, on the Antigonid left, seems to have been unable to resist pressing where he had superiority in numbers and manoeuvrability. He pushed hard against the enemy elephants, worrying them with missiles; they were caught mesmerized, unmoving and taking considerable punishment. 'They kept inflicting wounds with repeated flights of arrows suffering no harm themselves because of their mobility but causing great damage to the beasts, which because of their weight could neither pursue nor retire.'[17] Pithon's horse archers were performing as intended and Eumenes, with only heavy cavalry and elephants, seemed to have no answer. But, by taking the offensive, Pithon was to bring on unforeseen consequences. Understanding what the problem was, the Cardian determined to respond by bringing round the most mobile of the light horse from Eudamus' wing to help counter Pithon's attack. When this reinforcement arrived, having moved behind the infantry phalanx, Eumenes made a concentrated push using light horse, elephants and light infantry to attack Pithon's men, who found the combination too strong and his remnants were pushed right back to the foothills behind the Antigonid battle line. If Antigonus had hoped his left wing would keep just to a holding role to occupy his enemies strongest wing he had been sorely disappointed.

While this was going on, in the centre the greater number of Antigonus' infantry was countered by the fighting qualities of the Silver Shields, who won success after a stiff contest. Some of these veterans are claimed as 70 years old which seems excessive even in an era when many of the Successors, themselves, campaigned into old age. Whatever the real age of these Methuselahs, they it was, with *sarissae* levelled and shields locked, who with younger men in the *taxis* to their right and left, ensured the enemy infantry were defeated and pushed back towards the higher ground from which they had descended not long before.

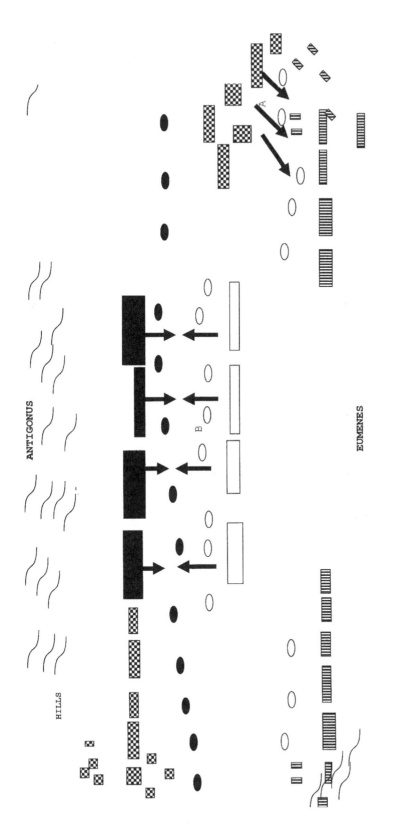

ANTIGONUS

HILLS

EUMENES

A   Pithon's cavalry attacks on the flanks of the opposing wing avoiding the elephants.
B   General engagement of infantry.

Battle of Paraetacene, 317 BC, phase 1.

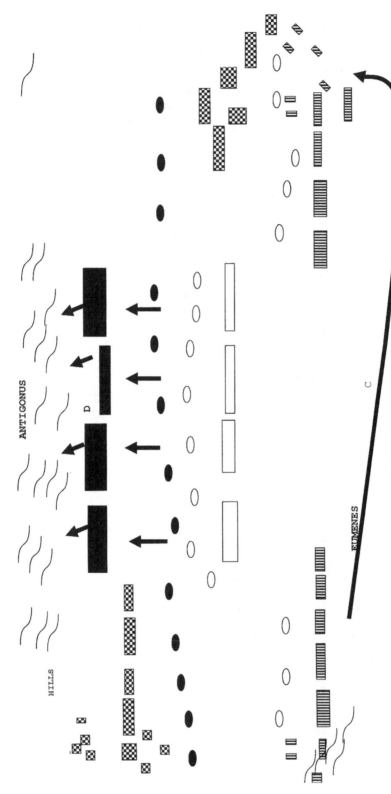

ANTIGONUS

HILLS

EUMENES

C

D

C Eumenes, seeing his right wing in trouble, summons help from some of the light cavalry of Eudamus.
D In the engagement of the phalanxes the Silver Shields win the day and force Antigonus' phalanx to retreat.

Battle of Paraetacene, 317 BC, phase 2.

But Antigonus now showed his quality, despite seeing his phalanx pushed back in defeat, if not in rout, and news reaching him that Pithon too had been overcome. He did not panic and felt no inclination to accept the outcome, withdraw back to the high country and attempt to rally what he could around his own undefeated forces. By his own swift action, he saved the army from destruction when he charged through the gap opened by the forward progress of Eumenes' phalanx, following in pursuit of the Antigonid phalanx opposed to them. Through this breach Antigonus found himself behind the enemy phalanx and on the flank of the cavalry commanded by Eudamus, who, having sent many of his troops across to Eumenes' wing, had remained immobile. This meant Antigonus was coming in from the flank; an attack from an unexpected quarter that proved a complete success. Many men were killed and the rest of Eudamus' left wing cavalry driven away. Now Antigonus sent 'out the swiftest of his mounted men and by means of them he assembled those of his soldiers who were fleeing and once more formed them into a line along the foothills.'[18] This is confusing, but what must have occurred is that the thousands of his cavalry in the rear of the enemy battle line and the resultant danger they posed brought the advance of his opponents to a halt. Eumenes, thinking victory almost won, stood in the light of a full moon to harangue his generals into one last effort. Both armies had, by now, moved a long way from the original field of battle and reformed and faced each other. At only 400 feet apart, Diodorus seems to suggest the newly ordered armies began again to prepare to fight.[19] But it was not to be, the hour having reached midnight and only the Cardian was prepared to fight on. His men would not countenance it with so much blood and effort already expended. So, reluctantly, the belligerent general withdrew and submitted to the insistence of his men that they get back to their baggage train which was now some miles in the rear of the main army.

Antigonus saw the enemy columns march away into the night with some relief; his army had missed being severely defeated by a hair's breadth and only his own leadership in the crisis had averted disaster. His casualties amounted to around 4,000 foot and several score cavalry, many more than the few hundred dead the enemy had sustained. The consolation of camping his men on the battlefield, and technically being able to claim victory, did little to relieve the frustration that had been building since the setback on the Coprates River. The significance of setting up a victory trophy (usually of captured enemy panoplies hung on a convenient tree or frame, built if no trees were available), and of camping on the battlefield was very important. It meant that the victor could enjoy the fruits of looting the dead and also were able to most effectively try to identify their own dead and give them proper rites. And, just as Antigonus accomplished this, Eumenes also was

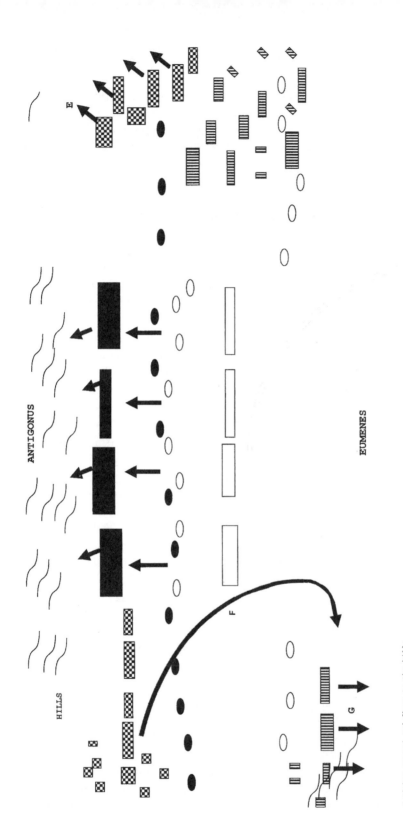

ANTIGONUS

HILLS

EUMENES

E Pithon routed and flees to the hills.
F Antigonus takes advantage of gap in enemy line and charges what remains of Eumenes' left wing.
G Eumenes' left wing put to flight.

Battle of Paraetacene, 317 BC, phase 3.

forced into the other great ritual act of accepting defeat by sending to the enemy for permission to collect his own dead. This setting up of a victory trophy might help a little in retrieving the soldiers' morale but the hollowness of the Antigonid claim to triumph was soon exposed when the orders were given to withdraw to Media, rather than pursue the enemy.

Yet still, what had occurred did highlight one great advantage Antigonus had over his opponent. He could command his men to stay put and camp on the battlefield whereas for Eumenes 'there were many who disputed his right to command'; he had to cajole and persuade and at this time, in a way that presaged later developments, it was the baggage train that was the centre of many of his followers' interests.[20] However, Eumenes had much to be satisfied with. His own soldiers had fought remarkably well and his confederates had stayed loyal, despite the lack of a clear-cut victory and the withdrawal from the battlefield. It had been all hard campaigning since his men left Babylonia and, with the end of the year approaching, he led the army to the lush and unplundered land of Gabene to enjoy the winter in comfort. It had been in competing for control of this region that the Battle of Paraetacene had come about, leaving no doubt who had been the real victor.

Antigonus had been severely blooded and he wanted to put some distance between himself and his active enemy to gain time to recuperate, particularly as winter was coming on. By prevaricating as heralds talked about disposal of the bodies from both sides, he earned time to send off his baggage and wounded.[21] He then forced-marched the rest of his men back to the city of Gamarga. Here, in Media, they could recuperate in a rich place with an administration well organized and loyal to his lieutenant, Pithon.

Eumenes had stayed where he was whilst the ritual of burial was accomplished and, at this time, Diodorus notes a particular event that indicates there was a strong Indian element in his army: 'Ceteus, the general of the soldiers who had come from India', had died in the battle and was cremated in the Indian fashion and both his wives, who were with the army, accompanied him into the flames.[22] After the dead were given due rites, Eumenes did not pursue Antigonus but moved to enjoy the abundant resources of Gabene. So, as the year ended, the two forces rested several hundred miles apart.

Antigonus had shown qualities of grit, ambition and some tactical brilliance over the previous year but his performance had been far from flawless. He had received a bloody nose from Eumenes, shown bad decision making over the Cossaeans and had even been hoodwinked by his talented opponent on one occasion. But, whatever had gone before, it never affected his self-confidence or his determination to act. What was typical of him in a complex and difficult situation was his preparedness to bend the rules: to make war in the winter when custom and weather dictated a hiatus, to achieve what he could not the year before and bring the enemy to decisive battle.

Winter was just begun as Antigonus collected his men and animals from their camps in the hills and valleys of Media. He intended a surprise and though winter warfare had been pioneered by Philip II, to great effect, it was still the exception rather than the rule. He banked on Eumenes expecting him to remain under cover in a region where winter conditions could be fierce. It was twenty-five days' march to Gabene by the regular road but there was another way. It had been learned, from local inhabitants, that Eumenes had distributed his units far and wide over a large area to make use of all available forage for the winter, and they would need several days to concentrate together again. By crossing the Dasht-e-Kavir Desert, the Antigonids could complete the journey to Gabene in just nine days. But it would be dangerous and uncomfortable across a grim waterless waste in the middle of the Iranian plateau, where hardly anything grew except a few shrubs that sustained the goats of the nomads who passed there on the way to better pasture. None the less, surprise was of the essence and many officers present knew that Alexander had traversed the fringes of this sterile region when he was chasing the fugitive Darius. But he had only taken a light-armed pursuit force across the edge of the desert while Antigonus intended to take the whole of his army through the heart of it.

This risky strategy had a particular advantage; the region was so inhospitable that it was not expected they would encounter any inhabitants who might alert the enemy. Great lengths were gone to in order to disguise their intention; word was spread that the preparations were for a move northwestwards to Armenia, a plausible enough plan after the defeats of the previous campaign. Ten days' rations were distributed, leaving no room for error on the route and, in December 317 BC, the army set out. The forced march typified the qualities of Antigonus that would take him to the very pinnacle of success; a dash across harsh terrain at a time of year when custom and conditions demanded a cessation of fighting: all this to steal a march on an enemy who had recently handed out a bloody reverse that would have kept lesser men quiet for some time.

This Alexander-like enterprise did not meet with Alexander-like success. Eumenes was renowned for the quality of his intelligence system and on this occasion also had more than an element of good fortune. After five days marching across the desert with no night fires to warm them (Antigonus had strictly ordered this precaution against discovery), the soldiers could no longer bear the freezing temperatures (it has also been suggested the elephants particularly needed to be kept warm) and flagrantly began to light campfires whenever they stopped, day or night.[23] Local people living near the edge of the desert saw the glow in the night sky. The speediest dromedaries were used to take the news to alert the Cardian general to the approaching threat. Peucestas was with Eumenes at his headquarters and allegedly panicked when he heard of the development, advising immediate flight. His commander was made of sterner stuff and responded with great invention. He ordered the units that were with them to light hundreds of their own campfires to give the impression to observers that the whole of the army was there. Again Eumenes' cunning paid off; some shepherds, who had previously served with Pithon, when he was satrap of Media, saw the campfires and informed their former master that the whole enemy army awaited them at the edge of the desert. Antigonus and his officers, convinced that their surprise had failed, reluctantly redirected their route away from Eumenes' headquarters. Bitterly disappointed, Antigonus took his men off to a position where they could camp in safety and comfort to recover from the rigours of the hard and ultimately futile desert journey.

Eumenes used the time his subterfuge had gained to send off to all the winter camps and ordered the units to converge on his own position. The vast bulk of his army had marched in and defended themselves in a palisaded camp by the time Antigonus was able to try to interfere. Antigonus knew he had been tricked but nothing could dampen his aggression and every reverse made him more eager to achieve something in compensation. The need to sustain his men's confidence was pressing and the opportunity presented itself when he learned the enemy elephants had not yet reached the main army but were still plodding along a road nearby. He determined to ambush them; a success here might at least rectify the previous imbalance he had suffered from in this arm. He sent 2,000 Median lancers, 200 Tarentines and all his light infantry in an effort to cut off this slow-moving detachment. At first, it seemed his luck would hold. Overtaken, the elephants and their guard suffered considerably against greatly superior numbers of attackers. It would have been quickly over but for the officer in command of the elephants who kept his head and drew up the animals in a defensive square, with the baggage in the centre and 400 horse guards bringing up the rear. The Antigonid cavalry drove off the Eumenid horse but were unable to overrun the elephants' formation because of the horses' fear of their noise and smell but, even so, they would have succumbed had not Eumenes reacted quickly. Guessing they were in danger when they did not appear, he sent a relief force of 1,500 of his best cavalry and 3,000 light infantry. They arrived just in time and, taking the Antigonids by surprise, drove them off and escorted the bewildered but unharmed beasts safely to the main camp. Antigonus' feelings of frustration can only be imagined, with all his best laid plans countered by an almost-miraculously well-informed rival.

But nothing could keep the effervescent old marshal down; he wanted to pin down and destroy these gadflies who had frustrated him at every turn since he entered the lands of Iran. 'Antigonus perceived he had been out-generalled by Eumenes and in deep resentment led his forces forward to try the issue in open battle.'[24] He was determined on battle and with his army rested he moved to bring it on. Days were short in this winter season and the weather was unpredictable but still he intended there to be a decision, he could not allow this war to drag on. Eumenes was also disposed to accept the test, he worried the Antigonids would get stronger with the passage of time and he always had the anxiety that his fractious army might split apart if not bolstered by a victory. The two armies found each other with ease and for a time manoeuvred, keeping several miles apart. But, this was just a preliminary, a warming up, for armies that in these cold and dismal circumstances were about to go at each other's throats. The battleground has not been identified but it was known to have been a vast plain, largely uncultivated because of the salt content of the earth, and with a river something over a mile behind Eumenes' position.

The night before the battle, Antigonus waited in some trepidation, at his camp on the higher ground above the plain. His men had surveyed the field of combat to ensure there were no unexpected effects of terrain or traps laid by the enemy. Now the 5,000-odd campfires he could see sparkling in the cold night air on the horizon really did represent the whole of his opponent's army and from the experience of Paraetacene he had some understanding of their strengths and weaknesses. The Silver Shields, pikes bristling, were vicious fighters and would be formidable opponents even for the Macedonian veterans that Antigonus could field in even greater numbers. Whether they could stand against a push of pike with these violent old veterans was a very moot point indeed.

Antigonus was not particularly noted for his piety but on the evening before the battle he would have given offerings to any Hellenic deities that might have been observing the dramatic events in prospect, so far from his homeland. In open combat against the greatest general he would ever meet, he needed all the help he could get, particularly as the open country and mutual familiarity seemed to rule out any ruse that might have increased the odds in his favour. In his command tent the council of generals entered a tactical debate. Present were men who had made great reputations under Alexander. Pithon led the officers in discussion; he had shown himself to be a cautious but intelligent tactician in the past months and he, like the Cretan Nearchus, could talk from their experience in these very hills years before. But the one-eyed old general had the final say and the battle plan he favoured was much like the one he had tried to put into effect at Paraetacene.

The battle tactics of the Successors are often derided as a decline from the flexible use of all arms that had characterized Alexander's genius. Although the assault on the right with a strong cavalry wing (the classic approach of the Successors) was clearly derived from the tactics of Alexander and Philip, it seems to have been an atrophied version. The subtle surgery of Gaugamela and Issus, where the infantry pinned down the enemy and the Companion cavalry carved a way to the centre of the opposition battle line, had degenerated from a deadly stab at the heart into a peripheral melee on the wings, with the outcome of the battle being decided by merely the brutal push of pike of the two phalanxes. But, in fact, this analysis fails to understand the differences in the problems faced by the men who came after ,Alexander. He had confronted an enemy who, though numerically strong, could seldom field an infantry force capable of facing down charging cavalry in the open. Darius, and his generals, had squandered the majority of their good Greek infantry at Granicus and in the ensuing campaigns in Asia Minor. Without this hard defensive core, the Persian battle line was very vulnerable, once Alexander's Companions had eluded the opposing cavalry. But in the inter-Macedonian affairs after his death, both sides could field a phalanx of levelled pikes at the centre of the line that could not be ruptured by an attack of horsemen, however disciplined or brave they were. Horses just would not throw themselves suicidally onto the line of spear points that faced a squadron coming in from the right centre. To disrupt and penetrate these fearsome formations, the cavalry had to get right round the flank or into the rear of the infantry. To do this required not just that the cavalry that defended the flank be fended off, they also had to be crushed and driven off to allow the time and space to attack the phalangites on their unguarded side. These cavalry fights on the flanks were longer and harder fought affairs which were often not settled before the foot soldiers had got at each other's throats. And, the combat decided by a ferocious bloodletting in the centre of the battle line.

But, if new realities forced some changes in the pattern of battle, inevitably similarities remained and Antigonus, like his erstwhile king, used a deputy who could command on that side of the battle line, where he himself could not be. Pithon had taken on the mantle of Parmenion to Antigonus' Alexander; he it was who held the left wing tight while his commander took the offensive on the right. The comparison does not stop there, he (like Alexander's general) urged caution when Antigonus inclined to a too adventurous strategy.[25] And, like his role model, Pithon would suffer at his leader's hands when it seemed his power was at its height; though Antigonus had more cause than Alexander for the radical disposal of his right hand man.

For this the decisive encounter, the details of the formations are sketchier than in the previous one. But, as the tactics decided on by Antigonus very much mirrored those at Paraetacene, we can reasonably assume both cavalry wings were composed roughly as before. Pithon was apparently given fewer men this time, about 4,500 horsemen to again hold up the left flank of Antigonus' array and by skirmishing occupy the enemy horse opposite him. Whether this smaller number of men was due to attrition from the previous battle and desert march or if the previous higher figure was exaggeration is unclear. His forces would have comprised Median gentry from his own satrapy, splendid in their colourful trousers and caps. The wealthier men wore gilded body armour that extended to frontal protection for the horses they rode. They had been, with their Persian cousins, the backbone of the Achaemenid imperial army and in a new world the fighting spirit Alexander had recognized had not deserted them.[26] The horses they rode were some of the best in the world. Pithon would also have commanded mounted archers from Parthia whose descendants, under the leadership of a Scythian ruling clan, would inherit the eastern Empire of Darius and Alexander in just over a century's time. We are not told where the 1,000 Phrygians and Lydians, the Tarentines, the lancers of Lysanias, the two horse men or the up-country colonists were, but they were presumably under his command too.

These units were designed to absorb the blows of their opponents and not give way. As at Paraetacene, they were not expected to make the decisive breakthrough but to occupy the right wing of Eumenes' army while Antigonus and his son led their own right hand flank to victory. Demetrius, we are told, now commanded the whole of the right wing, not just the Companions, but no explanation is given of why the change was made. It is possible that Antigonus was gradually increasing the responsibilities of his heir as a part of his education in power, and as Antigonus, himself, remained in the same part of the battlefield he could supervise or take direct command if necessary. At this station of honour on the right flank were about 4,000 horsemen, whose equipment, morale and discipline were second to none; the very heirs of those men who had chased Memnon, Darius and Porus off the battlefields of Asia. There were hundreds of picked Greek mercenaries and 1,000-odd ferocious Thracians, wild and uncivilized but well armoured and brave; we know of them from the previous battle and they almost certainly were arrayed on this wing. And then there came the Companions themselves, almost 1,000 strong; the very best of Antigonus' Macedonian horse, with a sprinkling of Greek and Levantine aristocrats, armed and mounted to perfection. The commander-in-chief, a huge man in breastplate and crested helmet, would have seemed almost a mythical giant, on the biggest Nicaean horse that could be found, as he dressed the line and took up his place with his glamorous son at the head of the right flank cavalry. The customary appeal to the army dwelt on past success; he reminded them of their victories over the last few seasons. How Alcetas, Arrhidaeus, Cleitus had all fallen before them and that having chased Eumenes from Cappadocia to central Iran they could now finish off this pest too.

The dressing and encouraging of huge battle lines of around 40,000 men a side must have taken much of the short winter morning, before any blows were exchanged. Eumenes, seeing how his opponent had deployed his army, decided to arrange his men in exactly the opposite way. He took command on the left wing directly opposing Antigonus. Against his enemy's 4,000 or so, he fielded his best cavalry. He positioned himself on the left of these squadrons with his personal guard and perhaps again, as at Paraetacene, supported by the 300 selected best of the satraps' horsemen. After them came the massed retinues of the eastern satraps, splendidly armed and mounted heavy cavalry intended to close and fight hand-to-hand. The end of the left wing nearest the infantry centre was held by Peucestas and his Persian cavaliers, whose ancestors had conquered the world under Cyrus and Darius I. Indeed, at this point Diodorus emphasizes the Iranian dimension by mentioning the presence of one Mithridates, whose lineage went back to the seven illustrious warriors who killed Darius I's rival and helped that great man to his throne. In front of the horsemen were sixty elephants, spread in a curve that extended around the far left of the cavalry line. They are described as the strongest of these beasts in the whole army and the intention was that they would stop Antigonus from using his superior numbers to outflank Eumenes.

On this side of the field, Antigonus had only thirty or so of these beasts to face the enemy's 60 but they (like their counterparts all along the line) stood forward to begin the battle when the trumpets sounded the advance on both sides. The dust these animals and their infantry guards kicked up as they jousted with each other was incredible. The loose saline soil rose like a thick mist to obscure the position of both friends and foe for several minutes at a time. Even before the real battle had begun between the cavalry and infantry, Antigonus decided on a stratagem to utilize this peculiarly poor visibility. He had been informed that on Pithon's flank the enemy had not extended the elephant line to prevent outflanking, so he sent to his subordinate to try a raid wide out to his left. Diodorus' wording actually suggests that the troops in this enterprise came from Antigonus' own wing, but the fact that they are specified as Medians suggests they were Pithon's men. Whatever, a detachment was organized and orders given for the squadron leaders to gallop around the elephants and the enemy formations whose armour could be glimpsed shining through the choking air. The dash

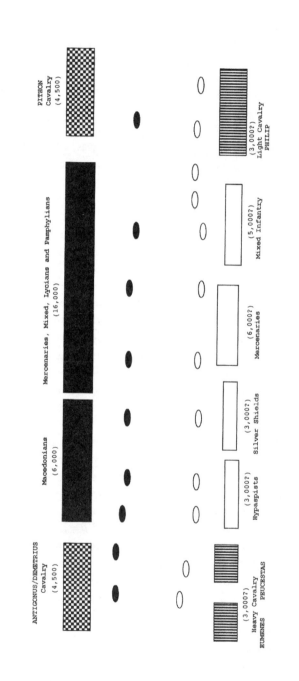

Battle of Gabene, 316BC, initial deployments.

through the dust, around the enemy flank, took the Medians and Tarentines out behind their opponents' battle line and ahead of them they saw the pack animals and loaded carts of the enemy baggage camp. The booty of years of campaigning, protected only by unarmed non-combatants, drew them on like a magnet and soon the whole camp was in uproar with the overrun defenders captured or killed. No line of reserves was there to help out, and the whole of their adversaries' material wealth came into the hands of Antigonus' men.

This manoeuvre is claimed as intended, Diodorus states that 'such a cloud of dust was raised by the cavalry that from a little distance one could not easily see what was happening. When Antigonus perceived this, he dispatched the Median cavalry and an adequate force of Tarentines against the baggage of the enemy.'[27] But to be sure of this is to try and resolve an insoluble mystery. To unravel the plans and events in ancient battles is a notoriously pitfall-ridden form of analysis. The probability is that an outflanking manoeuvre was ordered but once this was accomplished the capture of Eumenes' baggage camp was an act of inspired local initiative.

What is certain is that Antigonus had little leisure to think on the implications of this local success (even if he was aware of it) in the maelstrom of events elsewhere. The squadrons under his command each formed in offensive wedges and tried to manoeuvre through or around the elephants in preparation for an attack. On this occasion, sufficient gaps showed in the ranks of enemy beasts and light infantry in front so that Antigonus was able to lead his own wing forward against Peucestas, immediately opposite. That he aimed here, rather than directly for Eumenes, suggests he intended to force a gap between the enemy's left wing cavalry and their infantry centre just as he had so successfully at Paraetacene. The satrap of Persia fled, taking with him not only his own followers but also 1,500 troopers that were posted next to him in the line. These must have been mostly from the eastern satraps' retinues and suggests subversion or disenchantment with Eumenes amongst a large group of his allies. The dust of the retreating masses of enemy cavalry was a gladdening sight to the Antigonids clamouring for pursuit but they were not allowed the opportunity to succumb to this temptation. Eumenes could move his cavalry regiments quickly too, when required, and he responded to events by leading his own squadrons to attack Antigonus.

The Cardian showed extraordinary spirit against an antagonist who had outnumbered him even before over half his horsemen had fled; 'preferring to die while still upholding with noble resolution the trust that had been given him by the kings'.[28] Many of the men left were his own Anatolians and personal companions, who had been with him since the triumphs on the Hellespont and the setbacks at Nora. And, on his side, he had his sixty

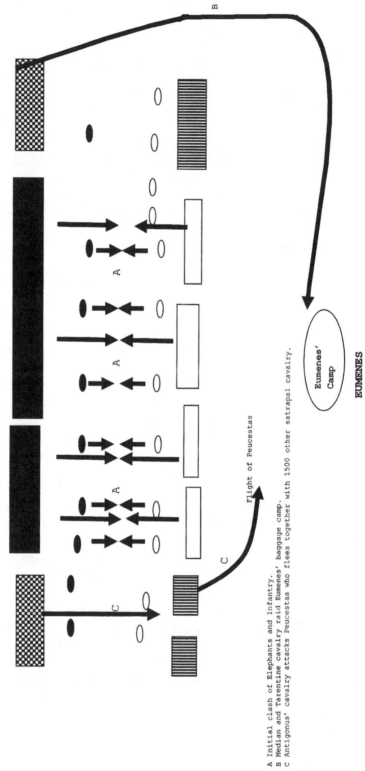

ANTIGONUS

EUMENES

Eumenes'
Camp

Flight of Peucestas

A Initial clash of Elephants and Infantry.
B Median and Tarentine cavalry raid Eumenes' baggage camp.
C Antigonus' cavalry attacks Peucestas who flees together with 1500 other satrapal cavalry.

Battle of Gabene, 316 BC, phase 1.

strongest elephants that might contain the enemy horsemen by their presence and stop them from exploiting the gap left by Peucestas. It was a bloody phase of the battle with charge and countercharge and generals fighting hand-to-hand alongside their men. It is, indeed, clear Eumenes hoped to bring down Antigonus personally as he had Neoptolemus on a previous occasion. Apparently, 'he forced his way towards Antigonus himself', but this time no such epic duel occurred and in this encounter the elephants were the key; while Eumenes' animal line held, Antigonus could not bring all his extra horsemen to bear.[29] 'It was at this time, while the elephants also were struggling against each other, reports Diodorus, 'that Eumenes' leading elephant fell after having been engaged with the strongest of those arrayed against it'.[30] With their leader down, these unreliably belligerent beasts gave up the struggle and it became apparent to Eumenes that his position on the left was untenable.

Leaving that part of the battlefield to the victorious enemy, with what men he could rally he withdrew to join Philip and the cavalry on the right flank. If in the fight on the left numbers had won out, the very opposite had happened in the centre. The Antigonids fielded 22,000 men in their phalanx, 6,000 less than at Paraetacene, indicating not just the inroads of the previous battle but the debilitating effects of the desert march. Assuming an even spread of casualties, 6 or 7,000 Macedonian phalangites must have remained to take up the position of honour on the right of the line. Next to them, the same number of other nationalities drilled and armed exactly as the Macedonians were. Then, between 7 and 8,000 Greek mercenaries and the balance made up of Anatolians from Lycia and Pamphylia, long-time loyal subjects of the Antigonids, all armed as hoplites or peltasts. Against them, waiting in the dust behind a line of 30 elephants, were 17,000 foot, deployed in a somewhat unorthodox manner. To ensure the Macedonians in Antigonus' phalanx were opposed by his best men, Eumenes had reversed the normal order of battle (just as he had with the cavalry opposing Antigonus). The 3,000 hypaspists, instead of the usual position of honour on the right, took post on the left of the phalanx. Next to them stood the Silver Shields, also to the number of 3,000, and then 11,000 'mercenaries and those of the other soldiers who were armed in the Macedonian fashion'.[31] We know from the previous encounter that 5,000 of these had been armed as pikemen but it may be that all the rest had now been so equipped and drilled. If this is the case, it might give some explanation of the ease with which they triumphed over an enemy who still fielded many troops carrying shorter spears. But, equally, it may be a mistake of the sources, as one must question whether even the extraordinary ability of Eumenes could reform and retrain these men in new arms and tactics in the short space of time between the two battles.

This encounter was preceded by some psychological warfare orchestrated by the general commanding the Silver Shields. Opposite them were Macedonian compatriots but men of a younger generation and, playing on a hoped-for respect for their elders, Antigenes had his agents go and yell at their opponents that they ought to be ashamed to fight against the veterans who had fought under Philip and Alexander in the great days of Macedonian power. Antigonus' men, who were mainly the younger levies brought over to Asia by Antipater in 320 BC, were affected by this and there were elements who were reluctant to raise their pikes against such national heroes. The veterans themselves had no such qualms about whose blood they spilt but were prepared to play the psychology game, shouting: 'It is against your fathers that ye sin, ye miscreants'.[32]

Then, on Eumenes' orders, these preliminaries were ended with instructions for the whole phalanx to prepare to attack. After the elephants had cleared the way, the awful lines of pikes faced each other. What is never explained in any of our sources is how a clear run was given to the phalanx infantry with many tens of elephants and thousands of their infantry guards fighting between the lines of pikes as they approached each other. Accounts of battles fought by Romans against enemy elephants suggest that they allowed lanes for the beast to be corralled down, but this is never mentioned in the sources for our period, and anyway unwieldy phalangites might have found this more difficult than the more flexible legions (though at Gaugamela they are described as forming lanes for Darius' chariots to harmlessly career down). Perhaps the phalangites were trained to push through the animals and men in front of them but unfortunately this process is not explained. This may be another reason to question our sources that try and paint the Macedonian formation as a clumsy battering ram, only effective when undisturbed by terrain or events.[33]

However they got to each other, they certainly did and the front ranks fell in heaps on both sides but, while the Antigonid foot were distressed by their losses, the Silver Shields and their comrades ploughed on unheeding. Like a steamroller they pushed over the enemy phalanx, though they were themselves far outnumbered. The hypaspists, no doubt, were alongside them in the fray but even with this support the Antigonids had several thousand more pikes at that part of the front. But this push of pike was a matter of discipline and morale, not numbers. In this rush of bristling enemy spears 5,000 of Antigonus' infantry fell, and after such loss of life retaining cohesion and discipline was out of the question. The bodies lay in piles, but the cutting edge of the veterans was hardly blunted as they chased the fleeing enemy off the battlefield over a litter of discarded *sarissae*.

Eumenes had expected to win his victory with the infantry and again they had done their job. But if events in the centre had seen his troops victorious, elsewhere it was a different matter. Philip, the commander on the allied right, had considerably fewer men than Pithon was fielding.[34] They were mainly light-armed cavalry who had been on the left under Eudamus at Paraetacene. They would presumably have again been the Arians and Drangians under Stasander, Paropamisadae under Androbazus and perhaps the colonial Thracians and Mesopotamians as well; mainly mounted javelineers, mountain Indians from the Hindu Kush and light horse from the eastern satrapies in the main. Their bravery was never in question but their equipment and tough, light horses, whilst effective for skirmishing, would never allow them to hold the line against Macedonian Companions or Nicaean-mounted Medes. The best of the satrapal horse had been stationed on the left to support Eumenes and Peucestas. Philip's regiments had, at least, occupied the enemy wing opposite, the horse and elephants in front had held the right wing tight as we hear nothing of Pithon's main force making headway against them as had happened in the early stages at Paraetacene.

To regain the initiative against Antigonus' rampant right wing cavalry, Eumenes needed the aid of Peucestas and his Iranian cavaliers who had fled at first contact with the enemy. He rode across to plead with his lieutenant but the satrap of Persia remained unmoved. 'Since Peucestas, however, would not listen to him but on the contrary retired still farther to a certain river.'[35] This must have been a dramatic encounter with few parallels in the pages of history but what is clear is that treachery had bitten deep into the ranks of Eumenes' generals and this was only the first of many bitter blows he would take from his own side during the next few hours. All was now confusion, over a battle line that stretched well over 2 miles in width. Opposed to Pithon were Philip and Eumenes, who, despairing of Peucestas and the others, had returned to his intact right wing with what remained of the routed left wing cavalry. In the centre, the ruin of Antigonus' phalanx was complete with the Silver Shields and hypaspists chasing them far from the battlefield. But Antigonus had the priceless asset of the allied baggage train. Antigonus' personal retinue kept him protected from the dislocated enemy units that careered over the plain whilst he tried to make sense of the chaos – the ultimate test of his generalship. The confusion in the reports of these battles must never be underestimated but, in this instance, we are fortunate that the original source for the events was a very competent eyewitness. Hieronymus of Cardia was able to record the course of the combat from the mouths of the contestants on the very heel of events. Their comments would have been partisan but fresh and, as far as is ever possible, the manoeuvres described at Gabene must be an accurate reflection of what actually happened.

Out of all the disorder one action, at least, is attested not just by its description but also by the events that resulted from it. While Antigonus sent orders to Pithon to attack the enemy infantry and he himself faced Eumenes' remaining cavalry, his officers made doubly sure that the enemy baggage train was made safe against counterattack. The Antigonid left, under Pithon, turned about and came in behind the enemy infantry, who were still in pursuit of the crumbled remains of the Antigonid phalanx. Yet, as they drew up in ordered squadrons in the rear of the Silver Shields and their comrades, they did not find easy pickings. These old sweats knew the tactics to counter this danger and 'formed themselves into a square and withdrew safely to the river'.[36] This is a remarkable testament to the qualities of phalangites already engaged in combat; to pull themselves up from pursuit and reorganize to show a hedge of bristling spears all round to the oncoming cavalry. With the salt soil in everyman's throat and night already on them, the generals on either side had no real idea of the overall situation. To reform and reconsider was the reality forced on them all and this breathing space became the end of the battle. In the dark, acrimonious debate characterized the council of Antigonus' enemy; Eumenes wanted to carry on the fight the next day, to exploit the virtual elimination of the Antigonid infantry as an organized force. His satrapal allies showed less fight and wished to retreat deeper into Iran. Revealing little belligerence in the battle, many perhaps shared whatever motive caused Peucestas to flee from Antigonus' cavalry.[37]

The atmosphere in the coalition bivouac as the soldiers settled down for what could only be a short night's sleep was very fraught indeed. Every man saw a traitor in another part of his own camp as well as feeling the ever-present threat of the Antigonid army over the horizon. The infantry knew that Peucestas and his Iranians had badly let them down by decamping without a fight and they were not backward in expressing their disgust. But, while cavalry and elephant-handlers looked to feeding and bedding down their beasts, the senior Macedonian infantry began to confer on a future that had their own very direct interest at its heart. The Silver Shields are specified but it must have been others as well who began to debate how to get back the baggage train that contained both the treasure and the families of these phalangites who had just fought so hard and successfully for their generals' cause. This was a roots-up movement (subsequent events showed that Antigenes and Teutamus would not have instigated any approach to Antigonus who was their vicious enemy) and with breathtaking felicity this Macedonian infantry 'co-operative' came to a decision. When their envoys found that Antigonus would only disgorge their worldly goods for Eumenes himself, they determined on the swap and marched to their commander's headquarters.

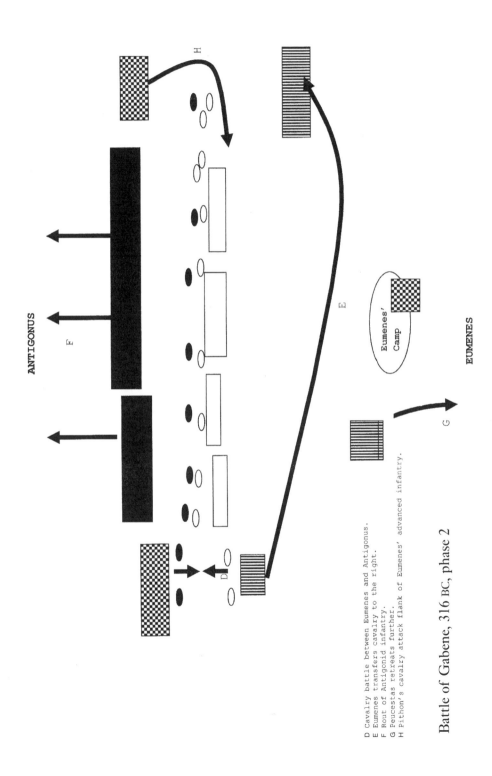

ANTIGONUS

EUMENES

Eumenes'
Camp

D Cavalry battle between Eumenes and Antigonus.
E Eumenes transfers cavalry to the right.
F Rout of Antigonid infantry.
G Peucestas retreats further.
H Pithon's cavalry attack flank of Eumenes' advanced infantry.

Battle of Gabene, 316 BC, phase 2

The Greek general was disarmed and restrained, despite some who felt ashamed of handing over their old chief, and word sent to Antigonus that he had been taken. He and Antigonus may have been personally quite close and had certainly known each other over many years. But he was too dangerous not to be eliminated and was executed. Antigonus could be generous to defeated foes but not in this case; the Cardian had cost him too much effort, given him too many frights and outwitted him once too often. Antigonus had sneaked success at Gabene but it was still decisive, for now he and his faction were the great power at the heart of the post-Alexandrine world.

Chapter Five

Battle of Gaza

Antigonus had been the centre of the military world of the *Diadochi* since he took up the command against the Perdiccan remnants after the Triparadeisus settlement and would remain so until almost the end of the century. But the next battle we can consider in detail, after the duel with Eumenes, saw him take no direct part despite the fact that his faction provided one of the sides involved. This time it was his son, the young Demetrius, who was in command when the might of the Ptolemies tested the empire the old man had constructed in the years from 319 to 312 BC. Antigonus, himself, was at the time of the encounter exploring various possible options of crushing Cassander and Lysimachus who looked back at him from the coasts of Europe. These opponents had been, since the defeat of Eumenes, his highest priority but it was other enemies who precipitated the events that would dramatically impinge on the military fortunes of his offspring.

It was the first time young Demetrius had left the protective shadow of his father. Antigonus had previously mainly used his nephews as lieutenants in independent commands but, at last, in his early 20s, his son and heir was to be trusted with major responsibility. From the time the elder Antigonid crossed the Taurus in late winter 313 BC to when the Byzantines scuppered his attempt to get at Lysimachus and Cassander in Europe, Demetrius had been in command in the Levant. This was a core region for the family's wealth and power; it was studded with cities rich from trade and manufacture and, apart from anything else, was the source of many of the naval squadrons that ensured the Antigonids' real control of the east Mediterranean seaways.

A council of veteran advisers were left with him to guide his steps in the crucial task of defending the Antigonid frontiers where they abutted those of their Ptolemaic rival. One of these men was Nearchus, the friend and admiral of Alexander, who had been with Antigonus for years and is mentioned in a command position during the march through Cossaean territory that so nearly ended in fiasco. Pithon (another Pithon, not the satrap of Media) was another, who had recently been made satrap of

Babylon replacing Seleucus, even though he had first fought for Eumenes, after coming up from his post in India. There was Andronicus the Olynthian, who is unknown under Alexander but had commanded the siege camp at Tyre when Antigonus struck with his main army against Joppa and Gaza; and Philip, another who had held a command in the upper satrapies and had served under Eumenes before joining the Antigonids.[1] The last member of the council we know of only from the battle casualties; this was a Boeotus who we learn 'for a long time had lived with his [Demetrius'] father Antigonus and had shared in all his state secrets'.[2] Most of these had been stalwarts under Alexander and together represented a considerable aggregate of experience and talent to advise the 22-year-old who now, for the first time, held independent command.

Demetrius had been left by his father with a considerable field army which he surely expected would face up to anything that Ptolemy might throw in his direction. These defensive arrangements were not immediately tested but then, in early 312 BC, the Egyptian satrap attacked north Syria and Cilicia. Several cities were sacked before Demetrius took action and saw the intruders off with some aplomb. The young Antigonid, in his first real test, showed well and after these efforts he and his men returned to Coele-Syria, which he had left in the care of Pithon, to enjoy some of the amenities of home. Since Alexander passed that way a number of Hellenic cities had been planted, where demobbed soldiers or enterprising civilians could provide the taverns, brothels, theatrical and musical entertainments and market produce to please the palates of men who came mainly from Europe or Asia Minor. Demetrius, no doubt, enjoyed his share of distractions; he certainly gained a reputation for enjoying his portion of debauchery in later life, but he had responsibilities too. Most particularly he needed to replace the cavalry mounts that had been lost in the hard march to Cilicia where 'on account of the excessive hardship not one of his sutlers or of his grooms kept up the pace'.[3] Fortunately, for him, in Media and Anatolia the Antigonids controlled lands where some of the best cavalry horses in the world were reared. But, the recuperation that the coming of winter normally brought was to be cut very short for the young commander and his relaxing soldiers. Ptolemy had organized a major army to continue his assault while Antigonus was still occupied in the west. Despite the winter season, he attacked directly, forcing Demetrius to prepare to defend the frontier of his father's empire.

We have noted previously that fighting in winter was still unusual, yet, while this remains true, at least three of the major battles in this history took place in that season. Paraetacene and Gabene, as well as Gaza, all occurred deep in winter and though all were fought in latitudes that meant the weather would not be completely debilitating it is still an interesting statistic. These Successor generals were not hidebound traditionalists. Just as that early Macedonian military revolutionary, Philip, would continue to fight when the time of year ought to see the soldiers back home on their farms, so would they. Even in the not-excessively severe climates of the Levant and Iran it was still difficult to operate in the winter months and in any case the crucial factor in this was social not meteorological. What Philip could occasionally do, with his core of mercenaries and a peasant levy which might make arrangements to stay on campaign when they would normally be on the farms, the *Diadochi* could do as a normal practice. The soldiers of 317 and 312 BC had no immediate farms to return to, in the way their predecessors had, and were available for their masters to call to arms all year round. Their homes were their baggage trains and encampments and these could function twelve months of the year.

The Battle of Gaza took place where now the mixed poison of neo-colonialism and monotheism has crushed the lives of people who 2,300 years ago would have given a more reasonable tithe to their gods and carried on with life more rationally than their descendants do today. Satellite imagery in the twenty-first century shows mainly a mass of dwellings very unlike the much less inhabited region fought over in 312 BC. The fighting occurred somewhere to the south of the old city of Gaza which had itself suffered much from Alexander's passing army a couple of decades before. The invading generals who now arrived there from the south had something of a military ragbag at their backs. The exact details of Ptolemaic Egypt's military establishment are not easy to accurately analyze. As a beginning, a garrison of 4,000 infantry and 30 triremes had been left there by Alexander, when he departed to confront Darius, and presumably they were mainly still in place when Ptolemy took over in 323 BC. These are described by Arrian as being based at Pelusium and Memphis and consisting of mercenaries. They were not front-line Macedonian phalangites and this suggests a reason why Ptolemy declined to face Perdiccas in open battle when the regent invaded Egypt in the first civil war. He also was, anyway, considerably outnumbered by the invader.

In this campaign, Ptolemy and Seleucus travelled from Alexandria but the army concentrated at Pelusium, further to the east. If the forces Ptolemy inherited on his arrival in Egypt had not been large, he had done all in his power to increase it in the meantime. An effort that allowed him to field an invasion force of 18,000 infantry and 4,000 horse. Some were Macedonians, which indicates a core of phalangites. But, their numbers must have been small, perhaps no more than a few thousand, comprising largely the men who had come over to Ptolemy's side after the defeat of Perdiccas. The bulk of the regiments Ptolemy led forward were made up of Hellenic mercenaries. These men, many of whom would have begun their career under Alexander, had thrived on the business of war ever since. Their calling in those days was considered honourable and a more pragmatic morality saves them from the pejoratives that sit naturally on their historical heirs, who have made the name mercenary an accusation rather than a description. They mainly came from the east Mediterranean littoral where Ptolemy's fleet allowed him easy access. Ptolemy had plenty of money to spend on them; he had taken 8,000 talents from Cleomenes who had been in command of Egyptian finances for some years before Ptolemy's arrival and who he eliminated straight away, despite Perdiccas having designated the Greek financier as his deputy in the Babylonian settlement. Apart from these veterans for hire, Seleucus would have brought several thousand troops from the army he had been shipping round the Aegean and east Mediterranean for the last two years. But, if this collection of foreigners provided the bulk of both the horse and foot there were also, apparently, many Egyptians present. This comes as something of a surprise as it was not until the Battle of Raphia in 217 BC, at a time when Antiochus the Great threatened the very existence of the Ptolemaic state, that indigenous solders were incorporated extensively into the fabric of the royal army. At that time, Egyptians were drilled into proper heavy infantry and, in fact, these local troops provided most of the main phalanx. And at Raphia it was their efforts in the crucial push of pike that mainly decided the battle, despite Antiochus driving off the Ptolemaic cavalry wing that he personally encountered during the battle.

That Hellenic xenophobia over arming the subject population was overcome as soon as 312 BC is extremely unlikely. Ptolemy and his people had only been in power for a decade and fear of a well-equipped native army as a tool of national rebellion would surely have been at the forefront of their minds. The Persian control of the country had been constantly disrupted by such independence movements. Defeat by Macedonian rivals could have dreadful consequences but not to the same degree as a national rebellion. It is certain that the people Diodorus describes as 'a great number were Egyptians, of whom some carried the missiles and the other baggage but some were armed and serviceable for battle' refers to servants or skirmishers, not front-line foot soldiers or cavalry.[4]

The army travelled the coast road with the bitter desert on their right and the blue sea on the left. The campaign plan was to take Gaza, the gateway to Palestine and from there on towards Coele-Syria and Phoenicia. This was a route that Tuthmose III and Ramses II had taken in the distant past to gain what Ptolemy had so far not, a lasting empire of the Levant. It was only a few days' march, but in that time Demetrius' soldiers had been massing in the rough barren country south of the old city. His army had been wintering in their billets near the southern frontier when word of the Ptolemaic invasion arrived and concentration on their headquarters at Gaza had been easy. The decision of the Antigonids to hold their ground, however, had not been automatically agreed and conflict marked the war council in the hours before the battle. Those officers left to guide the steps of Demetrius apparently opposed offering battle on the ground of the enemy's greater numbers and the military reputations of Ptolemy and Seleucus against the untried Demetrius. Though some hesitation before the fight is believable, the reasons given do not make complete sense. Certainly there was a disparity in the size of the opposing phalanxes, but as for the second argument, the very presence of a veteran group of advisors was intended to make up for the difference in experience between the commanders-in-chief.

This attitude of Demetrius' advisors to Ptolemy is interesting, if it is to be believed, because if his overall career shows him as a cautious, sometimes-irresolute imperialist, what this indicates is that at this period he was seen by contemporaries as a very great military figure.[5] He had fought with Alexander through all the glory years, he had been a bodyguard of the king and had fought a great set-piece duel with an Indian chieftain. He had possibly brought in Bessus, the Persian pretender, captive to receive Alexander's tender mercies and since Alexander's death he had conquered Cyrene, defeated Perdiccas, the great king's successor, personally commanding at the Camel Fort, and never yet been bested in battle. He was a great figure and now he was seconded by Seleucus, who could also boast a pedigree going back even before he commanded the king's guards (hypaspists) when they bore the brunt of the fighting in the battle against King Porus in 326 BC.

Whatever their individual ruminations, once the decision to stand was made a battle became inevitable and it seems neither side tried to manoeuvre much to gain advantage before they came to blows. But if the Antigonid had not been hard to find, Ptolemy did not rush to engage but camped to rest his men before the encounter. Demetrius was buoyed up by encouragement of the soldiery:

> When he had called together an assembly under arms and, anxious and agitated, had taken his position on a raised platform, the crowd shouted with a single voice, bidding him be of good courage ... For, because he had just been placed in command, neither soldiers or civilians had for him any ill will such as usually develops against generals of long standing.[6]

He decided to attack; in his life he seemed to know no other way of fighting. A cavalry assault on the left and the ponderous weight of his elephants (against an enemy who possessed none) he hoped would bring an easy victory. In infantry he was at a disadvantage; his phalanx comprised only 11,000 men, of whom 2,000 were Macedonians and another 1,000 were Anatolians (Lycians and Pamphylians). The latter are differentiated from the rest, as they had been at the battles in Iran, perhaps because they had long been regular soldiers of the Antigonid army. They, after all, came from countries that were close by the satrapy in Anatolia that Antigonus had governed since as far back as the 330s BC. The remaining 8,000 were mercenaries. This infantry force is definitely depleted from the 13,000 left Demetrius when he first took up his vice regal role; 2,000 mercenaries had been lost, but as wastage from over a year's campaigning perhaps this is not excessive. Most of these heavy infantry would surely now have been *sarissa*-wielding pikemen, there had certainly been a long enough period to re-equip and train those who were not so accoutred previously. To compensate for the disparity in the centre, where the enemy fielded 18,000 infantry, his own 11,000 foot soldiers were preceded into battle by 13 elephants and their light infantry guards.

No important role was envisaged for the right wing. Andronicus commanded 1,500 horse here and they were held back at an angle from the main battle line. The use of this oblique formation was more radical in intention than usual. The Antigonid high command did not just plan that their right wing would hold back in its attack, it was intended that this, the weaker flank, would not be strongly tested during the combat and, if possible, remain out of contact altogether. It, at the beginning, seemed an intelligent ploy but less so as the day developed with Ptolemy weakening his own forces on that part of the battlefield to the extent that Andronicus was eventually left with a three to two advantage in men on his front. The ploy of holding back a wing was one Demetrius was familiar with, from when he fought under his father in the great battles against Eumenes at Gabene and Paraetacene. On both occasions it was the left wing which had instructions from Antigonus to skirmish or hold back until the battle was almost won by the infantry phalanx or the heavy cavalry on the right.

Ptolemy foresaw the danger from the Antigonid elephant corps. He had none of these beasts himself; he had brought none from Babylon and was never in a position to recruit them from Asia. Not until the reign of his son did the Ptolemaic military establishment exploit the resources of their own continent to fill the gap. From Ptolemy II Philadelphus' time regular hunting expeditions marched south deep into Ethiopia to capture the forest elephant, indigenous to parts of ancient North and East Africa. This species, now probably extinct (though a similar African forest elephant does survive) were far smaller than the African elephant that inhabits the tropical country to the south and indeed considerably smaller and weaker than their Indian cousins introduced into Hellenic warfare by Alexander. In the Battle of Raphia, almost 100 years later, the smaller species did not hold up well against the bigger ones when they met head to head. That said, in a different time and place, the great Hannibal had enough faith in the African beasts to make great efforts to ensure some were available for his battles with the Romans.

The Ptolemaic high command was familiar enough with the elephants' powers since their days in India and knew their weaknesses as well; one of which was that the soles of the animals' feet were very tender. A deterrent was prepared that mirrored the technique used by Damis at the siege of

Megalopolis six years before. They constructed a form of caltrop, from planks with nails embedded in them, that pointing upwards would severely wound any animals that trod on them. The traps were portable and connected by chains and were used to protect the army's right flank. They may have been planted in front of the infantry phalanx as well, though their presence there was likely to have impeded the tightly packed pikemen when they tried to push forward to attack their less numerous opponents. It may well have been the view that the serried ranks of the infantry *sarissae* would be enough to keep the belligerent but temperamental beasts at bay.

If intelligence on the composition of Demetrius' army was sound, it appears from the preliminaries that the same was not true in respect of their disposition. Ptolemy and Seleucus had concentrated their strength on the left flank, only to find out from their scouts, that Demetrius had deployed his best horse on his left (opposite the Ptolemaic right) where the young Antigonid hoped to open the battle. This called for some swift adjustment and most of the troopers from the Egyptian left wing were brought over to the right to counter Demetrius' planned assault. Three quarters of all Ptolemy's cavalry, 3,000 horsemen, were eventually deployed in serried ranks on the right flank. So, only 1,000 were left to face Andronicus. All this must have taken a little time, and, as the winter day would anyway have been short, it suggests the battle could not have commenced until the day was well underway.

The composition of the Antigonid left wing, led by Demetrius, is known in some detail. The young general, himself, was stationed at the outer edge of the formation with 200 guard cavalry and kept company by Pithon (who seems to have acted as a co-commander in the battle) and most of his other friends and councillors. Also 300 more troopers were placed as advance and flank guards for the units around Demetrius and, reading Diodorus, it is difficult not to feel that these dispositions were made with protecting Demetrius' life very much in mind. The advisors left by Antigonus were determined they should not end up with the task of reporting to Antigonus the death of his favourite son. These 500 troopers were all specified as being armed with lances, but whether this would be the longer *sarissa* which was usually carried by light horse, or the shorter cornel wood spear of the heavier horse we are not sure. It is not, however, unreasonable to suggest they were heavy cavalry as these were usually the troops that were led by the commander who made the decisive assault. Whatever the case, out in front of all these were stationed 100 Tarentines, a warrior type that had only surfaced in the past few years. Having proved their worth in Antigonus' campaigns against Eumenes they had remained on the payroll and, though meagre in number, they were considered effective in disrupting enemy formations before the heavy squadrons were brought into play.[7] Then, next on the left were 800 Companion cavalry, all Macedonians, and on their flank 'fifteen hundred horsemen of all kinds'.[8] This was 600 horsemen fewer than

Demetrius had inherited when Antigonus left him, indicating he had perhaps not completed the cavalry refit after the brutal march to Cilicia. In front of them were thirty elephants which, with the thirteen spread thinly along the front of the infantry phalanx, made up the forty-three originally left to Demetrius by his father.

The Battle of Gaza was fought and won on Ptolemy's right but the first round was far from a success for his men. We hear of a conflict at the extremes of his right wing, between the advanced guards, beginning the battle. Demetrius' men proved too strong for the troopers of Ptolemy's vanguard who were badly beaten up. To remedy this development, Ptolemy knew he must support his forward units but with the elephants between the lines he could not directly attack the enemy horse. To bring numbers to bear, he ordered a large proportion of the cavalry to move to the right around Demetrius' flank. Both Ptolemy and Seleucus led these squadrons, who were drawn up in depth, to give extra impetus to their charge. The impact of this outflanking move initially fell on the 1,500 mixed horse on the left of Demetrius' line. The struggle is described briefly but dramatically:

> In the first charge, indeed, the fighting was with spears, most of which were shattered, and many of the antagonists were wounded; then, rallying again, the men rushed into battle at sword's point, and, as they were locked in close combat, many were slain on each side. The very commanders, endangering themselves in front of all, encouraged those under their command to withstand the danger stoutly.[9]

After the cavalry fight had been in progress for some time, the thirty elephants of Demetrius' wing were ordered forward to make the decisive breakthrough and drive a wedge through Ptolemy's battle line and expose the flank of his infantry. The animals and their drivers had no warning of the deadly spikes waiting in their path; and, more than this, when they blundered into the trap and were brought to a halt, they found Ptolemy had concentrated all his light infantry, who began to fire at the elephant drivers with their javelins and arrows. The beasts could not be driven through the barrier of spikes and with their drivers being shot down they panicked:

> And, while the mahouts were forcing the beasts forward and were using their goads, some of the elephants were pierced by the cleverly devised spikes and, tormented by their wounds and by the concentrated efforts of the attackers began to cause disorder. For on smooth and yielding ground these beasts display in direct onset a might that is irresistible, but on terrain that is rough and difficult their strength is completely useless because of the tenderness of their feet.[10]

Diodorus tells us bluntly that the discomfitted elephants were all captured and that it was the sight of this defeat that caused Demetrius' cavalry to give up the fight and run away. Though knowing his source at this point is most likely the usually accurate Hieronymus of Cardia, here common sense suggests Diodorus has not read him correctly. Elephants when gone berserk with pain from wounds in their feet and anger at the death of their mahouts are not readily susceptible to being brought under control. Though restrained and captured later, it is unlikely that many or any were taken at this juncture. Far more likely the animals ran amok back into the ranks of Demetrius' cavalry. With their horses driven wild by the sight, sound and smell of the elephants so near them, the whole of Demetrius' left wing dissolved. Leaving the young general to be caught up in the chaos and having to flee through the sunset plain to a place called Azotus, 30-odd miles from the battlefield.

But, whilst decisive events occurred on this wing, nothing is known of the rest of the battle. No mention of a contest between the foot soldiers is made, nor are infantry casualties detailed; only that after the battle 8,000 Anigonids (mainly infantry) surrendered to Ptolemy. Whether they stood and fought, fled or surrendered wholesale, they were no obstacle to the troopers who pursued Demetrius intent on filling their knapsacks with plunder from the baggage train left at Gaza. Their cupidity was facilitated by some of Demetrius' own men who took off to Gaza to retrieve their baggage and, when they got there, inadvertently kept the city gates open by the press of pack animals they had gathered to help carry their goods away. In the confusion, few got away with their belongings and Ptolemy's men were easily able to gain control of the city. The other wing under Andronicus also most probably saw no action with the 1,500 horsemen decamping when they saw the rout of the rest of the Antigonid army. In terms of battle casualties the Antigonids lost about 500 'the majority of whom were cavalry and men of distinction'[11] as well as Pithon and Boeotus who also lost their lives in the fray.[12]

It is worth noting that this is the second time that we know of when a commanding officer specifically changed their original formation to beef up one of his wings, when they found out where their enemy had collected their best forces and clearly intended to make their main attack. At Gabene, Eumenes, finding that Antigonus intended to weight his right for the decisive attack, accordingly moved his best cavalry to his own left to oppose them. But, more than this, when he realized that Antigonus had placed his best phalangites on the right of his centre, Eumenes then placed his crack troops, the hypaspists and Silver shields opposite them on the left of his centre. Now, at Gaza, when Ptolemy's scouts reported to him that Demetrius was concentrating his best horse and elephants on his left (Ptolemy's right) he then changed his formation bringing over many of his horse from his left wing to have sufficient cavalry to compete with the enemy's main thrust.

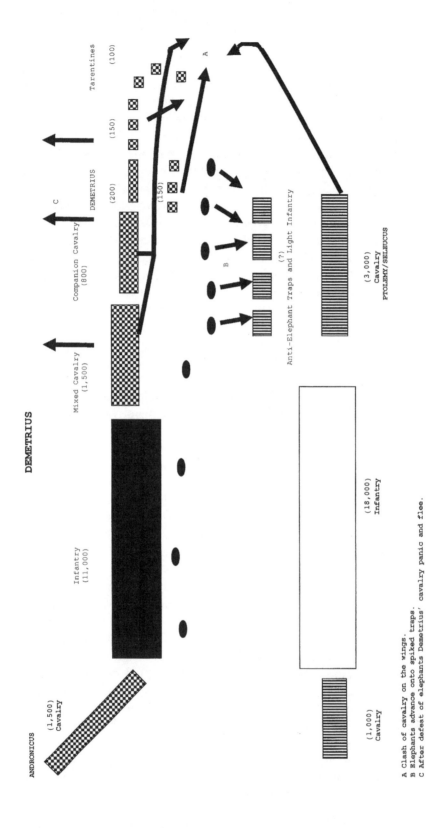

DEMETRIUS

ANDRONICUS

(1,500)
Cavalry

Infantry
(11,000)

Mixed Cavalry
(1,500)

Companion Cavalry
(800)

DEMETRIUS

C

Tarentines

(100)

(150)

(200)

(150)

A

B

Anti-Elephant Traps and Light Infantry
(?)

(3,000)
Cavalry
PTOLEMY/SELEUCUS

(18,000)
Infantry

(1,000)
Cavalry

PTOLEMY

A Clash of cavalry on the wings.
B Elephants advance onto spiked traps.
C After defeat of elephants Demetrius' cavalry panic and flee.

Battle of Gaza, 312 BC.

Aspects of this are difficult to interpret. Eumenes' ploy makes sense in that he would have initially, as in the earlier Battle of Paraetacene, deployed his strongest wing on the right and also his strongest infantry units on the right of the phalanx, the usual place of honour (because it was usually the most dangerous side with the unshielded side exposed). But, when he was certain Antigonus was emphasizing his other wing he responded. However, at Gaza it seems Ptolemy had, against tradition, decided to make his main thrust from his left and only when he realized Demetrius was making his attack on the other flank did he adjust. It is possible he assumed that Demetrius would conform to tradition and lead from the right wing and so Ptolemy had intended to oppose him with his best men on his left.

The question that is begged was why on these particular occasions the parties readjusted but on others they did not. Presumably one factor was that they were able to do so. Before Gabene the armies approached each other from 8 miles away giving time for redeployment to occur and at Gaza, again, some time was available before the fighting began. But at Paraetacene, shortly before Gabene, it was a more confused affair brought on by Antigonus' advance guard catching up with Eumenes which would not have allowed time for such a total redeployment. Clearly the tradition of the most prestigious units fighting on the right of the line was hallowed over centuries but it was far from an unbreakable rule. It had been breached by Epaminondas at Leuctra in 371 BC when he had brought the Sacred Band and his Boeotians to his left side, to ensure they would face the Spartans themselves, the strongest of his enemies. Even Philip, at Chaeronea in 338 BC, had posted the Companion cavalry under Alexander on his left to strike the fatal blow against the same Sacred Band, this time in the traditional place of honour on the right of the allied Greek line. Surprisingly Alexander had always conformed to the convention; in his four major battles he led the Companions on the right wing and the foot guards or hypaspists stood on the right hand side of the central phalanx. His Successors were more flexible but still, in most cases, conformed to what undoubtedly was expected by most of the troops. This is understandable and to change it willy-nilly might affect morale amongst extremely competitive warriors who valued reputation and worth almost as much as victory and loot. It is likely that if they did arrange their units in non-traditional fashion there would have been good reason for it.

That these officers of Alexander and their offspring were not always hidebound by tradition is equally shown here in that Demetrius was quite prepared to lead from the left, putting his best troops there as opposed to the traditional place of honour on the right. There seems no particular reason for this; the battle took place on an open plain, so terrain played no part in his decision making. Perhaps the reason was to do the unexpected, to try to outwit Ptolemy, and it almost worked with the enemy having to do some pretty sharp footwork to redeploy in time.

Another feature of this encounter is that the losing commander fled the field without apparently trying to get back to other parts of his army to try and retrieve the day. This was pretty unusual; most of the defeated generals we encounter either die where they stand, like Leonnatus or Craterus, or withdraw with their beaten forces like Antipater or Antigonus. The only other example in the battles of the *Diadochi* is Neoptolemus in his first encounter with Eumenes. But Demetrius at Gaza is the clearest example of one of them 'doing a Darius'. And, the parallel goes further, Demetrius, we know, was very far from being a coward; in combat before and after he led from the front, fighting hand-to-hand on the model of Alexander and the same is true of the Persian great king. He was no weakling who fled at danger; he was, in fact, a famous duellist who had killed a Cadusian chief in single combat and as a usurper in the Persian court he had to possess reckless nerve. With him, one feels, it was the responsibility he embodied as Great King that encouraged himself and those around him to make his safety the top priority. And, with Demetrius, there will be some of this; he, too, was surrounded by men determined he should not come to harm. His youth and his inexperience in command may also have played a part.

Gaza, at first sight, looks like one of the most decisive victories of the *Diadochi* era. Demetrius was completely defeated with hardly even a remnant at his back as he trudged north with bitter ashes of defeat in his mouth and the whole Levantine coast open to the advancing Egyptian army. Sidon was soon taken but they were stopped temporarily in font of Tyre, where Andronicus had made his way back to from Gaza and put some steel in their defences. But, even this very defensible place was taken soon enough.[13]

In the long run, the most important outcome of this battling on the borders of Egypt and Palestine was to be felt hundreds of miles away. Seleucus re-appropriated his old satrapy of Babylonia before going on to build a state in Mesopotamia and Iran that effectively changed the balance of power in the *Diadochi* world. From Gaza to the great denouement at Ipsus in 301 BC there are no great terrestrial battles fought for which the sources gives us any great detail. As well as a short peace there was plenty of recorded conflict; many sieges (most notably Rhodes), a great sea battle at Salamis in Cyprus, skirmishing in Greece and Anatolia. There was also the largely unknown and unrecorded Babylonian war between Seleucus and Antigonus which ensured the success of the Seleucid comeback. There may even have been a great battle with Seleucus against Chandragupta Maurya in India but again we have no details which can add to our stock of knowledge about this particular aspect of the military life of the successors.

Chapter Six

Battle of Ipsus

The last great battle that can be looked at in depth took place in 301 BC in the heart of Anatolia. The campaign, however, had begun the year before when Cassander and Lysimachus joined forces in earnest and sent envoys to recruit Seleucus and Ptolemy to the cause of a showdown with their dangerous Antigonid rivals. Lysimachus had begun the contest by invading Hellespontine Phrygia while Prepelaus, with an army seconded from Cassander, forced his way into Aeolia and Ionia. Together these armies secured most of the Aegean coast from Abydos down to Ephesus. Then, they moved inland; Prepelaus took the crucial west Anatolian administrative hub of Sardis through treachery while Lysimachus accomplished the same, in a like manner, at the old Antigonid treasure house of Synnada.

Preparing to absorb their new-won conquests and settle down for winter, the confederates were in for the shock of their lives. Antigonus, since receiving news of the attack, had dropped everything to bring his main army, in the last of those extraordinary forced marches so typical of his career, from Syria to Cilicia and on to Cappadocia before debouching into central Anatolia. When the coalition leaders realized that Antigonus was, at best, only a couple of days' march distant they called a full council to decide on their response to the threat. They agreed to avoid battle until Seleucus had arrived from the upper satrapies.

The strategy decided upon was to counteract Antigonus' numerical superiority by digging strong entrenchments, refusing battle and attempting to gradually withdraw north. Palisades and ditches were quickly dug as they awaited the enemy's arrival. Antigonus appeared, drew up his army and offered battle but, when this was refused, deployed his men to deny the coalition access to forage or supplies. Lysimachus was all too well aware of the exposed situation of his army's encampment and, when night fell, he marched them off over 40 miles to a place near Dorylaeum, where he would be able to better defend himself. Here, he built a solid triple-palisaded entrenchment on some convenient hills which were watered by a nearby river and had access to supplies from the city itself. Antigonus, frustrated, soon set off after them and when he found their second camp he ordered his men to completely invest the place so that they should not escape him again.

Lysimachus saw, with concern, preparations for what looked like a regular siege. Antigonus' men were not only throwing up earthworks but his engineers were constructing siege engines and setting up ballistae and catapults. The besieged sent out light troops to disrupt this work, but 'in every case Antigonus had the better of it' and his men protected by their trenches had the edge in these exchanges of missile fire.[1] The long march from Syria had not diminished the energies of the Antigonid veterans and, with the enemy skirmishers driven off, each day they were able to bring their siege lines a little closer to the ramparts of the camp. Soon Lysimachus' men were being hit at close range by the arrows and spears of the besieging light infantry as well as bolts and stones from the artillery. This battling amidst the trenches is very reminiscent of Roman warfare. The Roman legions were famous for their spadework, whether it was against national enemies, as at Numantia in 134/133 BC and Alesia in 52 BC, or in civil strife, as when Caesar fought Pompey at Dyrrachium in 48 BC and Anthony and Octavius battled Brutus and Cassius at Philippi in 42 BC. Hellenic armies were less noted for this tedious but effective tactic, and it is reported that Pyrrhus was the first general to systematically encamp his armies, while on the march, in regular defences. This campaign, however, shows that the sophisticated use of earthworks as a battlefield stratagem was well known and understood by these extraordinary military men who had learned their trade under Philip and Alexander.

Lysimachus was able to just about hold his own for a few weeks but his position ultimately depended on supplies lasting until Antigonus was forced by the weather to give up the contest. The old king's siege lines were drawn so tight that the besieged could hardly obtain any supplies from outside. Food became short and the besieging army showed no signs of quitting their post. Famine and enemy harassment looked likely to turn what had begun as such a successful campaign into a disaster. Lysimachus and his allied captains decided the only chance of survival lay in extricating themselves once more and moving further north. They knew that this would be a far riskier proposition than on the previous occasion and made preparations accordingly. There was still one part of the camp where Antigonus had not yet been able to completely encircle them but, even so, they would still need special conditions to cover their retreat. The coalition ramparts were well guarded until the moment of escape, partly to deceive the enemy into believing that they had determined to defend until the end and partly to ensure no deserters were able to alert Antigonus to Lysimachus' intentions.

A stormy night provided perfect cover for the deception, when driving rain forced Antigonus' pickets into shelter and made visibility extremely poor.

The bedraggled warriors somehow slipped out without alerting the guarding army and managed to put a few miles between themselves and their foe by the time dawn exposed the empty camp and the ruse. Antigonus organized pursuit, immediately sending his cavalry on ahead. This must have reminded the old warrior of his days of glory when he had chased the wily Eumenes across the plateau of Iran before he brought him to decisive battle. The gap between Lysimachus' rearguard and Antigonus' van was gradually diminishing and in the flat steppe country they were crossing there were no obvious defensive positions available to hold off pursuit. Lysimachus was a worried man when Antigonus' army drew level and marched parallel, only waiting for the most suitable site to bring on the battle. But the time of the year was against Antigonus and, as Lysimachus had banked on, the elements came to his rescue. The night storm that had covered his escape had been the harbinger of winter rains and these suddenly arrived in full force. The tracks of both armies were turned in a muddy quagmire. Pack animals were mired, horses began to founder and men found each step an effort of will. Antigonus realized he could not move his men with any felicity at all and that to try and instigate a battle would end in disaster. His troops were also suffering from exposure to the elements and this could only get worse unless he quickly managed to get them under cover.

This cut and thrust between the veterans in the heartland of Anatolia had worn down both parties, so everyone was relieved to pull apart and look for respite in winter quarters. For the coalition forces there was a long journey before them to reach the coast of Bithynia where they would be safe to settle. Antigonus took a shorter road back to Celaenae Apamea from where he had governed his old satrapy in the days when Alexander still lived. Here, an administration that had been familiar with his ways for three decades could provide provender for the animals and food and replacement equipment for the men and help construct a strategy for the following fighting season.

The old general was now in receipt of the news that Seleucus, his adversary from the Babylonian war between 310–308 BC, was coming to join the fight against him. This eventuality was not expected but it did nothing to discourage Antigonus; his intention was still to face and defeat all his congregating foes. These gathering enemies, meanwhile, enjoyed the amenities of Heraclea on the Black Sea and its surroundings where the widowed ruler, Amastris, was recently remarried to Lysimachus, who could act as host to his allies almost as if it had been his own capital. But, if the well-born hobnobbed in the palaces of the city and the ordinary soldiers took their relaxation with camp followers or local women attracted by the glamour of free-spending foreign warriors, it was not a time of totally unalloyed pleasure. News arrived at confederate headquarters that a considerable setback had occurred.

It had come about after Demetrius had taken a hand in his father's cause and returned to Anatolia. His landfall was Ephesus from where he had set out on his first great enterprise of Greece in 307 BC. He now took it and, after placing his men in the acropolis, headed towards Hellespontine Phrygia. If he could regain control there, it would threaten the enemy's lines of communication and deny them reinforcements from Thrace and Macedonia. He retook Parium easily, though Demetrius needed to defeat an enemy detachment posted near Lampsacus to secure that city. And, while overrunning the Illyrian Autariatae, who made up most of the enemy force, he took their baggage, which would have some consequence for the future. His next step choked off the last route between the confederates in Asia and Europe. Despite the approach of bad weather, Demetrius' force marched to the Bosporus. Once he reached the straits on the Chalcedonian side of the water he built strong defences for a garrison of 3,000 foot soldiers with orders to hold the crossing point and with them were 30 warships to patrol the adjacent waters of the Black Sea. With the campaigning season now definitely ended the rest of his forces were billeted on the Hellespont and amongst the cities along the Sea of Marmara.

Of course, when Demetrius left Greece, Cassander found himself freed from dire threat. His first response was to recoup what he could easily on his own doorstep and he 'took possession of the cities of Thessaly'.[2] But equally, he still saw the bigger picture and knew that the key events would unfold in Asia. He, as usual, did not venture there himself but ordered his brother Pleistarchus to take all the men he could spare to aid the cause. This son of Antipater had inherited his father's and brother's ambition but little of their talent. Cassander had several heirs and clearly Pleistarchus stood little chance of gaining the throne of Macedon. Asia Minor beckoned as a chance to carve out a realm for himself. A large portion of what remained of the Macedonian army were committed; 12,000 infantry and 500 horse. It was a long march, the easy way by sea was not possible in the face of Antigonid command of that element, but at least it was familiar territory and they could expect a welcome along the road in Lysimachus' kingdom. A greater problem was where to cross over to Asia as, at least for a short period, they would have to trust themselves to the water. The Hellespont was too well-held by Demetrius and it seems probable the intention was to cross further north near Byzantium, a longer journey but one that would allow them to disembark not far from Heraclea. The whole operation shows a remarkable degree of co-ordinated planning between the two armies and presumably Lysimachus was able to communicate with Pleistarchus with the help of ships of the Heracleian navy. But, on nearing the Black Sea coast of Thrace it became plain the Bosporus was also closed off by Demetrius' men. Agents from the Propontic cities informed Pleistarchus of the large garrison left to guard the strait and that Demetrius' fleet was patrolling the coast.

Diodorus' account of the subsequent events is somewhat difficult to follow in exact detail, but the outline is clear enough. Pleistarchus, blocked at both the main crossing points, now endeavoured to ferry his men by sea along the Black Sea coast. His point of departure was Odessus (Odessa), which is somewhat strange as this city is over 100 miles north of Byzantium up the coast towards Scythia. Why he needed to move so far away is not clear as there is no suggestion that Demetrius was preparing to attack him. Perhaps the most likely explanation is that this was the nearest port where shipping was available to transport his army. Pleistarchus needed a considerable fleet but had not brought one with him and Odessus also had the added advantage that news of preparations made there would take a long while reaching their enemies' notice. The boats collected at Odessus could not carry all the troops Pleistarchus had with him in one go, so he had no option but to try the long crossing in detachments. The first group got through, though we do not know how many or what units these comprised. The next party's journey was far less fortuitous. They hugged the coast south, as the previous group had done, but this time when they passed close by the Euxine mouth of the Bosporus the guard ships were on the alert and Demetrius' superior navy captured almost all the boats and soldiers on board. Pleistarchus, undaunted, obtained more ships and embarked the last units of his army. The commander, himself, was with 500 of his men on a 'six' but most of the rest of the flotilla were not large warships and certainly incapable of facing the patrolling enemy in open battle. Because of this they kept well off the coast to avoid them; a risky procedure now that winter had almost arrived. The armada was especially vulnerable far out at sea when a tempest struck. They were devastated; 'most of the vessels and men on them were lost' and Pleistarchus' flagship went down with only thirty-three men surviving.[3] Cassander's brother was one of them but as so often in his life, both before and after this catastrophe, he had been unlucky. Napoleon Bonaparte famously said the most important quality for a general was being lucky and one feels he would not have employed this bird of ill-omen in military command, however closely related to him he was.

Lysimachus had hoped for much greater reinforcements than the few that survived the crossing and the story they told showed that he could now expect no more help from Cassander. Morale in the coalition camp was not helped by these events and it perhaps explains the desertion of some hundreds of Lycians and Pamphylians to the Antigonids. More significant was a group of 2,000 'barbarian' auxiliaries who were originally from far off

Illyria and had been planted on the borders of Macedonia and Thrace for almost a decade. These were the Autariatae, who had lost their baggage to Demetrius on the Hellespont. Clearly the prospect of regaining it by joining what looked like the winning side was stronger than any sense of loyalty to Cassander who had found them a new home.[4]

Lysimachus, Seleucus and, presumably, a recuperating Pleistarchus prepared and planned for the coming campaigning season (Prepelaus also must have been involved but he is never again mentioned in the sources). They were all veterans and were familiar with their enemy from many years of rivalry. Their experiences over the last years had been very different and they had made their names in separate corners of the Macedonian world, but just their survival indicates most of them had qualities of determination and sufficient talent in command that ensured they would be formidable opponents for anybody. That they had now combined meant they were, at last, in a position to face Antigonus on virtually-equal terms even if there would be no more reinforcements coming. If they were going to act decisively then now was the time (what they hoped Ptolemy might do we don't know but there is no reason to think they expected him to arrive on the battlefield). It was as ethnically diverse an army as any Macedonian had ever commanded that packed up their bivouacs and marched out in the spring of 301 BC. Horses were sleek and well-fed and the men well-equipped and rested as they began on the road that would lead first to Dorylaeum, where 1,500 years later the first Crusaders would win through in their initial battle with the Turks. The coalition commanders were determined to bring on a fight as soon as possible, time was not on their side. Both Lysimachus and Seleucus could not have helped but be worried what was happening back home when they were hundreds of miles away from Thrace and Babylonia.

For Antigonus, the enemies who had eluded him in the previous year may have been reinforced but so, too, had he. Demetrius was with him and many thousands of his troops. When the two Antigonid monarchs paraded their army, it was almost as large as the force they had led against Egypt and most were seasoned veterans. Macedonian phalangites and the best mercenaries money could hire were at its heart. They also had excellent light infantry from Anatolia and unit after unit of aristocratic horsemen drawn from half the Hellenistic world. So they waited with confidence as spies, travellers and merchants were pumped to get word of where the enemy was and what they were planning. The Antigonids seemed to have been marching north when it became clear that the invaders were not far off and the combatants' paths eventually crossed 50-odd miles northeast of Synnada. It is possible that Lysimachus was aiming to cut Antigonus' communication to the east in a campaign of manoeuvre or in a ploy to ensure the old man would come out and fight. A threat to his communications with the Levant was bound to make the Antigonids react, especially as they would by now have known of Ptolemy's abortive invasion of Coele-Syria in the previous year. A return by the Egyptian satrap and threat to Antigonia must have seemed extremely probable.

Plutarch tells us a couple of tales which seem to imply a change in Antigonus' demeanour. Perhaps he had a premonition before the battle that made him more thoughtful than his normal bumptious self. Showing less than his usual contempt for the approaching enemy, he presented Demetrius to the army as his heir, a not unreasonable precaution for an 80-year-old on the eve of battle. Furthermore, he also apparently consulted his son before deciding on his battle plans and Plutarch contends that this was very much against character for a man who usually took no one into his confidence. Plutarch also repeats an old saw that on a previous occasion Demetrius had asked his father when they were striking camp and the old man allegedly replied: 'Why, are you afraid that you will be the only man who does not hear the trumpet?'[5] Plutarch also describes a dream Demetrius had before the battle. The dream, which inevitably featured Alexander, had the king ask Demetrius for the battle watchword.

> Demetrius said it was 'Zeus and victory', whereupon Alexander replied 'in that case I shall go and join your adversaries they will certainly receive me' for he was offended to find that Antigonus had not chosen 'Alexander and victory' for his watchword.[6]

These are stock fables reminiscent, for example, of a similar dream Eumenes is supposed to have had before his battle with Craterus. But perhaps it indicates a lack of confidence in the Antigonid camp before the battle, though we have no supporting evidence for this conjecture. In fact, Plutarch is, unfortunately, our only surviving coherent account for Ipsus and is mainly concerned with the part played by his 'hero', Demetrius. Diodorus remains in only the smallest of fragments for the battle; a great loss as the whole account, based on Hieronymus, would have undoubtedly answered many questions that now can only be guessed at.

Antigonus needed an open site where his cavalry could be brought into play and, in turn, the allied kings could only effectively utilize their elephants on level ground, so it is no surprise the encounter took place on a vast open plain. The exact spot has never been established but it would be wonderful to think that some day a metal detector enthusiast will crack this puzzle (as has happened quite recently with the site of the Battle of the Teutoburgerwald) and will be able to claim with a fair degree of certainty an epicentre for this Battle of the Four Kings.[7]

Something is known of the general disposition of the armies, particularly on the Antigonid side, but the details are far from clear. Of the 70,000 infantry they fielded, probably over 40,000 were armoured phalangites. Pikemen conventionally deployed sixteen deep. In the centre of the battle line they were solid and almost impossible to face down, but unwieldy and vulnerable on their flank and rear. The rest were peltasts or light infantry, bowmen or slingers generally not intended for hand-to-hand combat; they were still crucial in both acting as a protective screen for the elephants and shielding the vulnerable flanks of the phalanx, filling the gap between the heart of the battle line and the cavalry on the wings. Here in the middle of the battle line, protected by his bodyguard, Antigonus the One-eyed stationed himself, the greatest warrior of the age, whose life stretched back to a past that was almost legend to the young men in his army. The horse at the Antigonids' disposal amounted to 10,000. Some were deployed holding the left wing but the more numerous and the best quality were positioned on the right wing under the young king Demetrius himself. These were the king's friends (*hetairoi*), aristocrats in gilded armour and lavish finery, all eager to impress under the gaze of their glamorous monarch who represented the prospect of future advancement in a way his 80-year-old father could not. In front of this massive array of horse and foot were seventy-five elephants which, each with its fifty light infantry guard, would be expected to begin the fight. The two Antigonid kings hoped they would not find it impossible to compete against the much greater number of animals that they knew the enemy could deploy.

The tactical plan of the Antigonid kings was not innovative. The decisive blow was to be struck by the right wing just as Alexander, who had led them to glory years before, had done in his great battles against the Persians. Here, it was anticipated the high morale and superior training of Demetrius' cavaliers would make short work of the largely-Iranian horse facing them. These Antigonids were the traditional, and in some cases literal, descendants of Alexander's Companion cavalry, who had always bowled over such opposition at the charge. The weaker left wing was only intended to hold its ground while the centre pushed inexorably forward until Demetrius and his victorious horse returned to take the enemy phalanx in the rear and complete the triumph. As a plan, it was not over-elaborate and Antigonus had good reason to expect it to work. Intricate tactical schemes and deceptive ruses were the necessary armoury of a general commanding an intrinsically weaker force but Antigonus was not in that position. His was an army that had, for the most part, been together for years, not a disparate alliance of strangers who had joined each other only a few months before.

How the other side were drawn up is even less well attested. The coalition fielded 64,000 infantry, of which 20,000 must have been light infantry.

Seleucus had brought that many over the mountains from the east and it is unlikely that more than a few of his men were phalangites. In addition, some of his allies' infantry were also likely to be light troops. Thus, even if they deployed the remainder (between 30,000 and 40,000) in the central phalanx, the allied kings were at a serious numerical disadvantage in heavy infantry.

As to cavalry they, in fact, outnumbered the Antigonids, as altogether they fielded 15,000, of which 12,000 were Seleucus' Iranian cavaliers. They were probably divided evenly on either flank of the phalanx. For the actual commands of the allied army we have only one meagre detail. Antiochus, the young untried son and heir of Seleucus, was in charge of the left wing. His presence is noted because he happened to be directly opposed to Demetrius. That none of the senior commanders led on the left suggests this was, as was traditional, the weaker wing, with the coalition right being where the best cavalry and the commanding generals were positioned. Here would have been the Companion cavalry recruited in Macedon itself, and the heavily-armoured Thracian aristocrats, who Lysimachus had recruited to his own bodyguard. There is no actual record of where Seleucus, Lysimachus, Prepelaus and Pleistarchus were deployed and what is an even greater mystery than the stations of the allied commanders is the positioning of over 400 elephants and over 100 scythed chariots that had accompanied Seleucus in his epic march from the upper satrapies. The chariots are not mentioned at all in the battle but the elephants were to have a decisive influence on the outcome. A proportion of these were placed along the front of the battle line to face the seventy-five Antigonid beasts, but whether all were thus used or hundreds kept in reserve is in many ways the key to understanding the outcome of the whole battle.

Few of those present can have ever seen so many human beings gathered in one place, as the two armies dressed their ranks and moved slowly towards each other. There was the equivalent of the citizen populations of forty fair-sized towns gathered together on this dusty plain in Anatolia, almost 200,000 men. By the time Demetrius gave the order for his horsemen to advance, the dust kicked up by the myriad of animals' hooves and human feet must have made visibility all but impossible. In this murk, Antigonus' son had marked out where the elephants opposite him were placed and he carefully manoeuvred his units around them before leading a charge directly at the enemy horse under Antiochus.

The matter of the elephant/horse relationship can be confusing in these Successor battles. Clearly the big beasts were much prized for their ability to negate the effect of enemy cavalry, as horses were usually terrified by the sight, noise and smell of elephants. But it is clear that on this occasion some cavalry units manoeuvred nearby and through lines of their own elephants. Though not recorded anywhere it must be the case that some horses were trained to cope with being near elephants or otherwise such manoeuvres would have been virtually impossible. Whether any horses could become totally immune to the noisy, smelly beasts is not known. However, we do have at least one good example of the two species working together in some sort of tandem. When Antigonus attacked Eumenes' elephants before the Battle of Gabene we are informed by Diodorus that they formed a square with 200 horse as the rear side of the formation. This shows that they could be conditioned to work together to some extent.

In any case, squadron after squadron of Demetrius' cavalry charged into the fight, eager to bring to bear their numbers and superior quality. They rode in the wedge formation that had been so effective for the cavalry of Alexander when they shattered the battle front of Darius' Persian armies. Each unit had its commander leading at the point, able to manoeuvre easily on their officer's lead and effective as a spear in cutting into the formations in front of them. The assault was pressed with such elan that Antiochus' men began to lose cohesion and think only of their own survival. Soon they were in flight, carrying the son of Seleucus along as he vainly tried to rally the routed formations. However, Demetrius failed to keep his troopers in hand as they swept away in pursuit, an occurrence that was far from unusual in cavalry actions from ancient through to modern times.[8]

In the crucial clash of the phalanxes in the centre, the contest had begun with duels between the elephants. The great beasts fought tusk to tusk, with their riders lunging at each other with pikes and their light infantry escorts attempting to hamstring the enemy animals while protecting their own charges. 'In the battle', says Diodorus, 'the elephants of Antigonus and Lysimachus fought as if nature had matched them equally in courage and strength'.[9] All merely a preliminary to the main clash of the two great lines of phalangites. The push of pike began and both sides held firm, despite the carnage wreaked amongst the front ranks on both sides. Veterans now settled down to the process of jabbing and shoving by which they hoped to break up the opposition's formations.

We are told nothing of what had occurred on Antigonus' weaker left wing but it seemed that the outnumbered cavalry and elephants there were holding on as planned. Now was the moment for Demetrius' victorious troopers to return and charge the vulnerable flank and rear of the allied phalanx. Though they had gone further in pursuit than intended, the young king had eventually managed to regain control of his men who were then far in the rear of the allied army. He realigned his squadrons and turned them about to return to the main battle, but very soon found that his way was blocked. The enemy had drawn up 300 elephants in a great line across his path and his horsemen could not get through this cordon of beasts. The soldiers' mounts would not approach the elephants, such was their fear of

Artist's impression of a Macedonian heavy cavalryman, based on the Alexander Sarcophagus. He wears a linen cuirass amd Boeotian helmet and is armed with a sword and long lance. *(copyright J Yósri)*

Bust of a Macedonian soldier of the late fourth century BC, now in Naples Archaeological Museum. (*Authors' photograph*)

Artist's impression of a typical phalangite, mainstay of most Diadochi armies (*copyright J Yosri*)

Artist's impression of a light infantryman or peltast, a common troop type in all Diadochi armies. (*copyright J Yosri*)

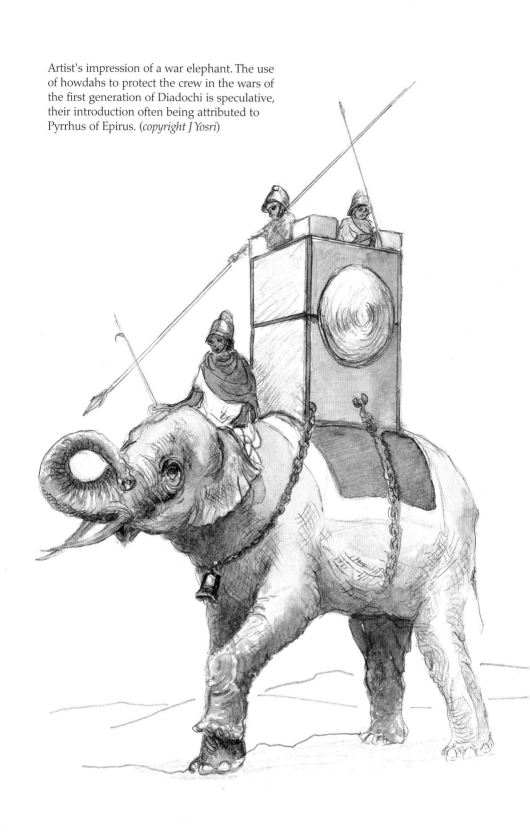

Artist's impression of a war elephant. The use of howdahs to protect the crew in the wars of the first generation of Diadochi is speculative, their introduction often being attributed to Pyrrhus of Epirus. (*copyright J Yosri*)

Artist's impression of an Iranian light cavalryman based on figures on the Alexander Sarcophagus. He is unarmoured, relying on speed and mobility to conduct hit-and-run attacks. (*copyright J Yosri*)

A detail from the Issus Mosaic, now in the Naples Archaeological Museum. It shows an Iranian cavalryman of the type that may have followed Peucestas or Pithon in the great battles of Gabene and Paraetacene. (*Authors' photograph*)

Artsist's impression of a Hellenistic *lithobolos* or stone thrower.
(*after Jeff Burn, copyright J Yosri*)

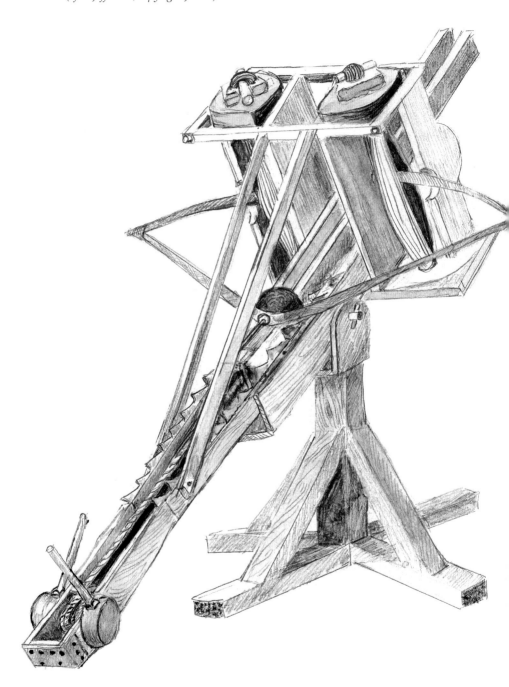

An example of 4th/3rd century BC Hellenistic walls at the foot of Phylae in Attica, near Athens. Such fortifications of large, precisely-fitted stone blocks presented a formidable obstacle to besiegers. (*Authors' photograph*)

Salamis port where Menelaus' fleet attempted to break out to join his brother Ptolemy but failed, allowing Demetrius to defeat Ptolemy in the epochal naval battle of 306 BC. (*Authors' photograph*)

The reconstructed Greek trireme Olympias.
(*courtesy of www.hellenicnavy.gr*)

the smell and noise and an increasingly-anxious Demetrius could not find a way round this living barrier.

The whole episode of the elephant manoeuvre at Ipsus has been the cause of much discussion and explanation, none of which is entirely satisfactory. The first question is where this number of beasts came from; it is unlikely they could been drawn from those already involved in the battle. To move elephants on this scale was difficult in any event and virtually impossible if they had to be withdrawn from the battle line before the manoeuvre began. The only other alternative is that they were kept in reserve behind the main formations but this is a tactic never heard of before in Hellenistic warfare, though a little later Pyrrhus kept elephants in reserve at Asculum in 279 BC and at Magnesia, in 190 BC, Antiochus the Great kept some of his beasts back in reserve. But if 300 animals had been held back, only 100 or so would have been available to clash with Antigonus' 75, thus giving up for the coalition army an opportunity to far outnumber their opponents at this key point.

However, the assumption that this number of elephants were kept back would support the proposition put forward by Tarn that the whole business on the allied left was a deliberate ploy in which Antiochus feigned retreat to ensure Demetrius was drawn away and his return blocked by elephants, kept in hand for that very purpose.[10] Attractive though this theory is, it is hard to believe that the allied kings would have countenanced such a gamble. A withdrawal of Antiochus' wing would have risked demoralizing the whole army, particularly with the polyglot nature of the allied forces. Lysimachus' men and the Macedonians in the phalanx would have certainly suspected treachery and the morale of the whole army crippled when the footmen saw Persian and Median cavaliers, so recently hereditary enemies, running from the field, having barely contested the fight on their wing.

If it was not a premeditated strategy then this manoeuvre with the elephants was a piece of inspired improvisation that turned the battle. It bore the hallmark of a leader very familiar with the use of massed elephants and Seleucus is the only senior commander who fits the case. He had seen, at first hand, their use in large numbers in India and may have fought a major battle with Chandragupta Maurya who would have fielded many hundreds, if not thousands, of these beasts. Perhaps Seleucus' role was to remain in charge of his elephants which were kept in hand until developments allowed their decisive use. But, even allowing for all this, there is still the further question of why the mobile horsemen of Demetrius' squadrons could not avoid the cumbersome beasts which confronted them and find a way round their line. One suggestion has been that behind the allied army was a wide valley out of which they had originally debouched to face their enemy in the plain.[11] Demetrius would then have pursued

Antiochus up the valley and on his return found this wide passage completely blocked by the elephants. They were spread thickly enough to prevent infiltration over sufficient distance to completely close the mouth of the valley and the sides were too steep for Demetrius' horsemen to ride up and over.

But, perhaps this detail of terrain is not even required. If each elephant was accompanied by its guard of fifty light infantry, or even if not, each individual beast would have had a frontage of at least tens of yards and probably much more. No sophisticated arithmetic is called for to see that 300 such pachyderms would create a huge barrier of several miles, especially for horses who might be distressed at the sound and smell of these beasts even from a good way off. A number of explanations are possible, if improbable, but what does not ring true is the chess-like precision of the movements of men and animals that is so untypical of warfare at any time and especially in the ancient world. The most tenable solution is that the meagre sources have rationalized a much more confused conflict between the young Antigonid's cavalrymen and the allied forces including large numbers of Seleucus' elephants that by chance or adept manoeuvring managed to keep Demetrius from the battle between the phalanxes until it was too late.

Initially, things had gone well for the octogenarian Antigonus, his pikemen outnumbered the opposition and even without his son's assistance it appeared likely that his veteran infantry would win the day. Problems arose when the enemy moved round them to attack the Antigonid right, exposed when Demetrius had chased headlong after Antiochus' horsemen. Light infantry would surely have guarded this vulnerable flank but they must have been driven off. Antigonus' phalangites then began to be harassed by horse archers and javelineers brought all the way round from the enemies' right wing. These fired missiles into the packed ranks of Antigonus' phalanx and threatened to charge against their exposed side. Unnerving even for these hardy fighters, to the front they faced the enemy pikes whilst their right, unshielded flank faced wounds from arrows and javelins against which they could not respond. Morale was inevitably affected and Antigonus looked desperately for the return of his son, who could even then have saved the battle. With no sign of his arrival some of Antigonus' warriors began to go over to the enemy. Desertion became infectious and whole units disintegrated. Once begun, loss of cohesion was fatal to bodies of ancient infantry and extraordinarily difficult to reverse in a huge melee of tens of thousands of battling soldiers. Antigonus attempted to rally those he could reach but his efforts were undermined by the increasing number of enemy horse and foot who were firing volley after volley into his ranks. Many of these skirmishers were closing in on Antigonus himself, his guards were falling around him and in the confusion the old man was eventually hit by several javelins. At 80, when most would have retired from the fight years before, he made a last stand but finally succumbed to wounds inflicted by the spears of what were almost certainly Seleucus' troops. When news of his death became known, what fight was left in the phalanx ebbed away and a total rout ensued.

Demetrius eventually returned but, by then, it was too late. Myriads of his father's veteran foot were dead, dispersed, prisoners or gone over to the other side. What happened to the cavalry on the Antigonid left we don't know but presumably they too had retired or transferred allegiance to the winning side. So, all the young king could do was collect the few thousand cavalry that he still had under his command and withdraw. With him was another notable refugee, Pyrrhus, the 18-year-old king of Epirus, who had fought valiantly under Demetrius in his first battle, and would show himself to be a very competent Antigonid officer, until he returned from exile to lead an expansionist Epirus in a direction that would not infrequently clash with the interests of the man he was following in defeat.

So as the century ended the man who had filled it most significantly in the last twenty years departed. What is odd, but perhaps appropriate, is that as this giant leaves the stage so the best and only continuous source crumbles into fragments. With the demise of Antigonus, the man who had tried and had the resources to restore the Macedonian Empire to a whole again, its fragmentation was entrenched. There no longer was a powerful, rich central power that might have contested with the houses of Ptolemy, Seleucus and the others to prevent the institutionalizing of the division of what Alexander had created.

Chapter Seven

Siege Warfare

The wars of the *Diadochi* are like so much military activity in ancient or modern times; capturing cities and strongpoints was the constant aim of many an enterprise. Sieges and escalades were what armies involved themselves in through almost the whole of the annals of organized conflict. Indeed, as often as not, if open battle came about, it was as the result of an army arriving to try and lift the siege put in place by their opponents.

Whether they are the boasts of Egyptian pharaohs inscribed on temple walls or Assyrian palace reliefs, the first examples of recorded campaigns most frequently consist of lists of sieges begun and towns taken. And this picture continues through Greek and Roman times down through the medieval period, when sieges were almost the whole of warfare with a battle only encountered every few years or so. Even the advent of modern war (when it is considered a Napoleonic revolution led the way in ensuring that bringing the enemy army to battle and destroying it was the new orthodoxy) did not see the end of great sieges. There were plenty of them during the Revolutionary and Napoleonic wars, Massena in Genoa, keeping the Austrians occupied while Napoleon prepared to cross the Alps and triumph at Marengo, and Davout holding on to the very end in Hamburg as his monarch was losing his whole empire. And, in the later years of the nineteenth century, the sieges of Sevastopol in the Crimea, of Petersburg in Virginia, of Lucknow in India and of Peking (modern day Beijing) in China are the events that punctuate the years just as much as the climactic battles that were fought. Indeed, by the beginning of the twentieth century, from the Russo-Japanese war fought round Port Arthur to the Balkan Wars and the First World War itself, the whole of military conflict had seemed to become one great siege – a complete matter of trenches and badly-bungled escalades.

The Macedonian kings of the fourth century BC, Alexander and Philip, his father, had been great besiegers of cities. The older king lost his right eye at the siege of Methone in northern Greece in 354 BC and, if he failed in front of the walls of Perinthus and Byzantium, this did not prevent his eventually achieving hegemony over the great cities of Classical Greece. And the younger conqueror punctuated his conquests in the Balkans and Asia with epic sieges at Thebes, at Halicarnassus, at Tyre; and if the great cities of Babylon, Persepolis, Susa and Ecbatana did not require reducing he found plenty of rock forts in Sogdia and India to test his mettle. Equally, the very same was true of his marshals when they fell to fighting for forty years over the world he left on his death at Babylon in 323 BC.

These Macedonians brought some celerity to the matter of assailing enemy strongholds. The sieges of Potidaea, Plataea and Syracuse during the Peloponnesian War, if not quite of the duration of the siege of Troy, were affairs of years not months. Though other strategies might be tried, starvation was, in the end, the main tool of subjection. Battles were fought around the walls to aid relief or to ensure complete isolation but often little enough was done to actually attack the garrison inhabitants and walls of the places themselves. To some extent ramps and ladders might be used but they were far from always effective and much work was put in to build earthworks both to enclose the besieged and to protect against attack from relieving forces. Battering rams were used, as were picks, to try to weaken the walls; they dug mines to bring them down or raised ramps to get up to them. But the masonry more often than not was the winner. Walls themselves were so important that they might be a pivotal reason for major warfare. The Athenian Long Walls, defending the lifeline to Piraeus and the sea, were so central to the city's survival as a great power that the destruction of them was the key condition of their Spartan enemies when it came to dictating peace.

By 360 BC or so, the Greeks showed that they had been thinking deeply about siege warfare just as they thought about everything else. At that time Aeneas wrote his *Tacticus* on how to fight a siege. Rams, towers and mines were threats that he was aware of and had suggestions to counter but what most concerns him is the threat from within. Dissident citizens, class spite and the presence of foreigners are his concerns and the history of the *Diadochi* suggests he was prescient in the extreme. If his advice to get rid of the untrustworthy residents and only allowing the most loyal of citizens to hold key posts had been adhered to, many of the campaigns described would have turned out very differently.

But new expertise and weapons had been changing the balance of power. Siege towers and sheltered rams and tortoises (to protect sappers filling in defensive ditches) were not as such new weapons (they had been in use in Asia for centuries), but their increasing size and sophistication was making them far more effective. The siege engineer and miner was becoming a dependable and highly-paid specialist in any army. Philip had Polyidus of

Thessaly who built a *helepolis* (siege tower) for his ultimately fruitless siege of Byzantium in 340 BC but we have no details of it. Alexander, never one to pass up the opportunity to be bigger and better than his father, reportedly had huge *helepoleis* built by Poseidonius of Macedonia and Diades of Pella for his sieges of Tyre and Halicarnassus. Demetrius, the son of Antigonus, is associated with many talented engineers, Epimachus of Athens and possibly Hegetor of Byzantium. And the weapons they could deploy had become increasingly devastating following developments in the middle decades of the fourth century. In particular, torsion-powered catapults and ballistae had become the regular artillery of ancient armies and would remain so down through the Roman period. The precursor had been the belly bow developed by the resourceful artificers of Syracuse. At the siege of Motya in 397 BC, Dionysius of Syracuse used them and possible catapults (belly bows placed on a stand with the cord winched back) as well as large towers to overtop the walls and drop men on top of the houses of the town.

In Macedon, others in turn had developed their ideas to make use of the propellant potential of twisted hair. Which, when kept under tension in great cords, was marvellously effective in giving far greater motive power to the catapult arm than anything possible with the wood, sinew and bone mixtures previously used. It also had the advantage of having no real limit to the size to which weapons could be constructed. Philip gratefully made use of the results of these experiments to add to the range of weapons available to his new model army. They could fire bolts at enemy soldiers as well as stones at their walls and ensured that, at least for himself and his son, an advantage lay with the besieger rather than the besieged. These weapons had really ratcheted things up. The use of missile men in the Greek world had already gradually increased as armies were no longer dependent on just hoplite phalanxes but these machines extended hitting power in an exponential way. With them missiles could be fired at defenders on the walls, making it possible to give cover to well-organized and effective assaults. They could keep the enemy heads down while the attacker attempted escalades or brought up towers, rams and the other paraphernalia of assault.

These developments seemed to have given siege warfare in this period a dramatic and epic quality and this form of warfare appeared to have appealed in a particular way to the first generation of Alexander's Successors. The size and complexity of the war engines that were made should not surprise us when it would only be a short time before scientists in Alexandria would be discovering steam power (although social factors would inhibit it being deployed as a power source, thus pushing back the Industrial Revolution 2,000 years). This fancy for engineering even had Plutarch, almost 300 years later, lovingly describe the machines brought out at Rhodes:

This was a siege tower with a square base, each side of which measured seventy two feet at the bottom. It was ninety nine feet high with the upper part tapering off to narrower dimensions. Inside it was divided into many separate storeys and compartments, the side which faced the enemy being pierced with apertures on each story through which missiles could be discharged

And very seldom showed much interest in the minutiae of military matters.[1] Despite this, and though many of the campaigns of this era are a catalogue of sieges, there are only two that are described in any great detail and where the sources allows us to understand what was really going on. Only at Megalopolis in 317 BC and at Rhodes in 304/303 BC are we given the kind of detail we could wish for in so many others of them.

The first of these affairs took place soon after Polyperchon had established himself as guardian of the two kings, following the death of Antipater, and promulgated the first decree of Greek freedom. He had descended from Pella, but arrived too late to forestall his enemies from securing the port of Athens. Although he had a considerable army of 25,000 men, 65 elephants and the support of the vast majority of the Athenian citizenry, he found Piraeus almost impregnable. It was surrounded on three sides by the sea and Cassander's fleet controlled the waters. Alexander, Polyperchon's son, remained with a force adequate to blockade Piraeus, while his father marched west on the Megara road and pondered developments. Rather than have his men idle, waiting upon events in Attica, he decided to try and complete his control over the Peloponnese. Encouraging news had already arrived from there that many of the cities had responded to his Decree of Freedom, expelled Antipater's oligarchic friends and were seeking alliance with the kings' guardian. These coups had in many cases been bloody, with massacre and exile of the old rulers. They were reaping their reward for the years of repression and savage treatment of the local democratic factions. Polyperchon had every reason to expect a warm welcome in the south as he and his army crossed the Isthmus of Corinth to take advantage of his new-found allies' successes.

But the city of Megalopolis was different. It was the one major place in the Peloponnese whose people had refused to depose their oligarchs and remained true to their allegiance to the family of Antipater. Their obduracy against the groundswell of regional support for Polyperchon seems initially inexplicable but it probably arose from a regard for Cassander, as the son of the man who had saved them from the vengeance of Agis' Sparta just over a decade before. Then, the Spartan king had besieged the town and would have wiped it from the face of Arcadia if Antipater had not arrived to save the day and put the genie of brutal Lacedomonian hegemony over the

Peloponnese back in its bottle. Another probable factor was the presence of an outsider, a man called Damis who we know was in the city. He was a veteran of Alexander the Great's army and had been active as a Greek messenger between the camps of Perdiccas and Meleager in those chaotic days at Babylon. Such a man knew a wider world outside Arcadia and had some idea that Polyperchon, though apparently dominant, had still far from won the day against Cassander. Damis was almost certainly Cassander's agent at this time and was subsequently raised to considerable heights when Antipater's son came into his own.

Polyperchon could not allow this important place to hold out against the royal edict of Greek freedom with impunity; if they would not get rid of their oligarchs themselves, he would do it for them. Accordingly the royal army moved inland in high spirits, having marched from Macedonia to the Isthmus of Corinth without any enemy opposing them in the field, and began to plunder the countryside around Megalopolis. The citizens were not unprepared, having had advance warnings of their enemies' intentions. They had called in the population from the surrounding farms and villages and set them to work, building a wide moat and a palisade around the walls. Catapults were constructed in large numbers to counter the ordnance that Polyperchon would be bound to bring in the train of his invading army. The defences of Megalopolis were impressive but Polyperchon had confidence borne of long experience in siege warfare in the armies of both Philip and Alexander, generals who had seldom failed in front of enemy walls. He divided his force into two, the Macedonians he encamped on one side of the city and his Greek allies on the other. Trenches were built between the two camps which soon surrounded the city. Whether he split up the troops on national lines because of animosity between them or merely for convenience is unclear but with the Lamian War only recently behind them it would not be surprising if some bad blood remained. The guardian of the kings had no intention of being delayed for too long in front of Megalopolis, if he could avoid it, and immediately ordered the building of siege towers, tall enough to overlook the walls, and the digging of mines under the defences.

Mining proved to be particularly effective and, when the pit props were burned and the tunnels collapsed, three towers and the intervening curtain wall came tumbling down. The besiegers poured into the rubble-strewn breaches and for a moment it seemed as if the city was bound to fall. The citizens, reacting swiftly, concentrated their best men to defend the breaches and Polyperchon's soldiers began to struggle to make progress over the broken masonry and debris. It is surprising how frequently in sieges of this era the obstructions created by the bringing down of city defences proved almost as much of an obstacle as the original wall itself. In any event, the struggle lasted the whole day and well into the night, with the bolt-throwing machines brought to bear by the defenders from their remaining flanking walls proving particularly effective in harassing the royal troops. It seems likely that Megalopolis had defences of the most up-to-date kind, the walls and towers having galleries where torsion-powered catapults were deployed. Severe losses were sustained by not only the soldiers in the breach but also those in the siege towers. While the Megalopolitan warriors had been defending the breach, the non-combatants had been busy throwing up a makeshift second line of defence, cutting off the area that had been exposed by the fallen section of wall. With darkness closing and further fighting difficult, Polyperchon reluctantly ordered his men to withdraw to rest, so they could return to the attack the next day.

The army's spirits had been affected by the rebuff and Polyperchon felt impelled to harangue the troops in a singular manner:

> Polyperchon inspired his own soldiers in face of the danger. He put on an Arcadian cap, fastened with a pin, double tunic and took a stick, and said to them; 'Fellow soldiers, these are the kind of people we are going to fight.' Then he threw off all these things and put on his full armour and said; 'And these are the kind of people who are going to fight them, people who up till now have won many great contests.' The soldiers hearing this decided to hesitate no longer but immediately go into battle.[2]

The old orator now showed he was very much a soldier of the new school, able to embrace the developments he had seen in the years with Alexander. He decided the second assault was to be spearheaded by the war elephants. How many were used in the attack is not known, but sixty-five had been available when the army marched south to Piraeus. Whatever the number, they would have made a terrifying sight for the defenders who, with few exceptions, would never have seen such beasts before. He banked on their shock value being enough to unnerve the besieged so the rest of his army would have a relatively easy task to force their way through the resultant gap. However, he had not reckoned on the cunning of Damis, who also had experience of elephants in war under Alexander:

> Indeed by pitting his native wit against the brute force of the elephants, Damis rendered their physical strength useless. He studded many great frames with sharp nails and buried them in shallow trenches, concealing the projecting points; over them he left a way into the city, placing none of the troops directly in front of it, but posting on the flanks a great many javelin throwers, bowmen and catapults.[3]

The Megalopolitans had laid an elephant trap of some sophistication and it was not long before it was tested:

> As Polyperchon was clearing the debris from the whole extent of the breach [in the original wall] and making an attack through it with all the elephants in a body, a most unexpected thing befell them. There being no resistance in front, the Indian mahouts did their part in urging them to rush into the city all together; but the animals as they charged violently, encountered the spike studded frames. Wounded in their feet by the spikes, their own weight causing the points to penetrate, they could neither go forward any farther nor turn back because it hurt them to move.[4]

With the huge beasts blocking the breach, the men behind them were unable to proceed and the Megalopolitans began to rain missiles down upon them, particularly aiming for the Indian drivers who were the only people able to control the elephants. When the leading animal collapsed, both from the pain of the wounds in his feet and the harassment of enemy missiles, his fellow beasts became demoralized. Chaos resulted with the elephants either crumpling in a heap or turning back and trampling over their own men. Polyperchon, deflated at the complete failure of what he was certain was a strategy that would win the day, had to call off the attack.

This was substantially the end of the siege and this reverse was compounded by news arriving of the destruction of his navy under Cleitus.[5] It all meant that Polyperchon found himself feeling very exposed amongst the hills of Arcadia. This was, in fact, the beginning of the end for the veteran general as a major player though he would erupt occasionally into the *Diadochi* world for years to come. He virtually called off the siege, taking most of his army and leaving only a token force around the bloodied but unbowed city of Megalopolis. The bubble was bursting, the morale within the ranks of the royal army was deeply affected and some of the mainland Greek cities defected to Cassander. Setbacks at Piraeus and Megalopolis set in motion an erosion of support that would dramatically change the balance of power in the Balkans and end with Antipater's son established on the Macedonian throne at Pella.

The second siege we know much about took place in 304 BC at Rhodes, after many years when Antigonus and his extraordinary son had been battling against Cassander, Ptolemy, Seleucus and Lysimachus, the other generals who had established themselves in the post-Alexandrine world. The siege is one of the great events of the age partly because it was a proxy battle between all the other rulers, sustained by the plucky islanders of Rhodes and the Antigonids, and partly because of the character of

Dem.etrius who led the besieging forces. The thread of military invention that ran through much of the fourth century bore extraordinary fruit under the young Antigonid. His efforts were limitlessly imaginative and occasionally absurd but his technical vision touched a chord with co ntemporaries who could not help admiring that aspect of his achievement even when deploring his lack of personal propriety. The siege of Rhodes was o ne of the epic contests of this epoch, and in it Demetrius would hit peaks of engineering ingenuity. Another factor was that the success of the defenders in repelling such an over-mighty enemy led directly to the building of the Colossus of Rhodes, one of the Seven Wonders of the Ancient World.

Demetrius assembled the expedition to bring the city into line at Loryma, on the Carian mainland, almost directly opposite Rhodes city, and for a time it seemed that the mere presence of the young conqueror with his ships, soldiers and siege engines would be enough to ensure success. The islanders sent envoys to explain that they had re-thought their position and were now prepared to join the alliance against Ptolemy as Antigonus required. But now even virtual capitulation was not sufficient. Demetrius had been put to considerable trouble to mobilize his armament and he was determined to ensure that if he disbanded it the Rhodians would not once more change their minds. Against just such a contingency, he demanded the islanders hand over 100 leading citizens as hostages and that he be allowed to enter Rhodes harbour with his fleet to collect them. This proved the last straw for the proud republic; they had agreed to all the required conditions but still these tyrants wanted more. The envoys withdrew and the island determined to resist the invader. There is something about these exchanges that does not ring true; giving hostages was normal practice and having conced ed the key demands it seems strange they should risk destruction ov er this issue. The likeliest explanation is that Rhodes had long since decided, on res sistance and the protracted negotiations had been purely to gain tirie to prepare the defences.

Demetrius descended with his 200 warships and 170 transports, 40,00 soldiers and pirate allies. This formidable armament arrived outside the por of Rhodes and, this was not all as it is also claimed, there were almos another 1,000 yachts and trading craft owned by maritim e entrepreneur eager to join in the looting of Rhodes. The citizens of the t own which ros up from the shore like a great amphitheatre were treated to a n extraordinar sight 'so that the whole space between the island and the opp osite shore wa seen to be filled with his vessels'.[6] After this attempt to strike fear into th hearts of the opposition, the invaders looked to set up a safe b ase. Round th coast a suitable landing place was found and a protected c amp built, fa enough to be out of missile range but near en ough to keep his victim i constant apprehension of a surprise attack. Then Demetrius ordered that a breakwater be built to ensure the enemy could not easily get at his boats and a triple palisade was erected to protect the camp against enemy sorties.

Control of the well-defended harbour was crucial to both sides as it would allow an effective blockade to be applied. Shipwrights roped cargo scows together and mounted towers and batteries of ballistae, protected by penthouses (sheds of hides, boards and padding to give protection to the men working the machines) on their decks. In front of these clumsy catamarans, a floating boom fixed with large spikes was built to deter the nimble Rhodian warships from ramming them. Other boats were armoured with thick wooden planks and filled with catapults and Cretan archers. The task force approached the port, intending to clear the defenders from the walls of the harbour with their missiles before the assault troops went in.

The Rhodians for their part also used ballistae and catapults placed in 'machines on the mole and three upon freighters near the boom of the small harbour'.[7] Other ships at anchor were also utilized for catapults. The two sides ultimately failed to engage with each other due to rough weather but in a night raid the Antigonids did win a small foothold on the mole that protected Rhodes harbour. Here, 500 feet from the main town defences, Demetrius constructed a siege fort with a garrison of 400 men as a base for further efforts. But the Rhodians dug in and began to throw up a series of jerry-built walls to isolate the fort. There was hard and bloody fighting for eight days, reminiscent of nothing so much as the Athenian siege of Syracuse in 415 BC. There, too, it had been hard work with walls thrown up to cut off the enemy and then counter walls built to intercept the other's line of building.

While the battle on the mole was pressed, a continuous attack was maintained on the rest of the waterfront area. Seaborne engines were brought up time and time again to try and drive the defenders off the walls around the port while the Rhodians used combustible missiles and even fire-ships to good effect. A surge on the eighth day got Demetrius' men onto a part of the harbour wall and it looked, for a time, as if from this bridgehead they would break into the town. But, the defenders, with their existence at stake, threw every soldier into the breach and drove them back. And, later the same day, when assault troops seemed about to establish themselves in another sector, desperate defence once more prevailed and the attackers lost heart when officers as well as men were pushed to their deaths onto the rocky seashore below.

After this, the Antigonids drew away to repair the damage to ships and engines and regroup. For a week Demetrius geed up their spirits before trying again. The second offensive was carelessly handled. They aimed to destroy the ships in the port and surprise the defenders on the walls. In fact, three Rhodian ships in the harbour got under way and inflicted great damage on the Antigonid fleet until numbers overcame them. The weather then intervened and some of Demetrius' engine-bearing vessels were wrecked by a sudden storm and, thus encouraged, the defenders attacked the Antigonids' fort on the mole, took it and captured the garrison. The loss of his one calculable success dispirited Demetrius and he prudently withdrew to the shelter of his artificial harbour.

This was to be the last onslaught by Demetrius in a miserable season in front of Rhodes' walls and his disappointment was further compounded by the sight of reinforcements sailing into the port he had so singularly failed to close; 650 (some of them Rhodian) mercenaries who had been sent by Ptolemy and other friends in Crete. Winter storms now threatened, putting a stop to any possibility of continuing the assault and the Antigonids resigned themselves to wintering on the island.

Failure both to capture the port and cut off the supply of reinforcements caused a change of tactic in 303 BC. Demetrius turned his attention away from the harbour to the land walls of the town. As soon as the weather allowed, soldiers built trenches and palisades, miners began the tunnels that would snake under the walls and his engineers uprooted every tree on the island to construct the machines that would directly assault Rhodes' defences. Epimachus of Athens was responsible for the building of the giant *helepolis* used against Rhodes. A smaller machine had been deployed against Salamis in Demetrius' siege of the Cypriot city in 307 BC (shortly before the naval battle where he routed Ptolemy). At Salamis:

> he constructed a device called the '*helepolis*' which had a length of forty-five cubits on each side and a height of ninety cubits. It was divided into nine storeys, and the whole was mounted on four solid wheels each eight cubits high ... On the lower levels of the *helepolis* he mounted all sorts of ballistae, the largest of them capable of hurling missiles weighing three talents; on the middle levels he placed the largest catapults, and on the highest his lightest catapults and a large number of ballistae; and he also stationed on the *helepolis* more than two hundred men to operate these engines in the proper manner.[8]

As a cubit is 1.5 feet approximately (though there are several possible different measures of cubit), the *helepolis* would have been 135 feet high, 68 feet square and its four wheels would have been 12 feet in diameter. This wooden Cyclops was destroyed by fire-bearing arrows from the city which was under the control of Menelaus, Ptolemy's brother, although Demetrius eventually captured the town.

Presumably learning from this experience, the *helepolis* used at Rhodes was certainly the largest ever constructed and, indeed, has never been surpassed. We have four different descriptions of the machine by Vitruvius, Plutarch (in his life of Demetrius), Diocles of Abdera (as recorded by Athenaeus Mechanicus) and Diodorus. Unfortunately, there are significant variations in measurement but the machine was most likely 150 feet high and 75 feet square at the base, thus bigger than its Salamis counterpart though not by that much. The *helepolis* was made of wood but its three exposed sides were protected by iron plates. This protected it from fire and the fate its predecessor had suffered at Salamis. In addition, the inside was covered by expanses of animal hide designed to protect the men within from ballista and catapult fire. The machine was on eight wheels, each 20 feet high (the one at Salamis had four wheels), and also had casters so it could allegedly be moved sideways as well as forwards and backwards.

How it was moved is a mystery and much ink has been spilt trying to solve it. To move such a huge machine would have required prodigious manpower and it has been suggested that up to 800 men would have been needed, exposing them to considerable risk from the firepower of the defenders. It has also been doubted whether there would have been enough room for this number of men to be accommodated even if some were inside the machine as well as outside. Another alternative has been mooted, that of the use of draught animals such as cattle. We know that they were used in other circumstances. Xenophon records that Cyrus, the Persian king, used just such a method:

> So Abradatas set to work, and this four-poled chariot of his gave Cyrus the idea of making a car with eight poles, drawn by eight yoke of oxen, to carry the lowest compartment of the battering engines, which stood, with its wheels, about twenty-seven feet from the ground. Cyrus felt that if he had a series of such towers brought into the field at a fair pace they would be of immense service to him, and inflict as much damage on the enemy. The towers were built with galleries and parapets, and each of them could carry twenty men.[9]

But the use of animals could easily be neutralized by the defenders killing them at a distance as the Goths found to their cost in 537 AD at the siege of Rome. They tried to pull a siege tower to the walls by the use of oxen, only to find that the Romans simply shot them whilst the machine was still some distance away, thus effectively extinguishing the threat. It is also the case that Cyrus' tower was not a siege tower, as such, but a tower used behind the main battle line to throw and catapult missiles at the enemy. In this case, the oxen would presumably have been led away (once they had brought the tower into position) to safety.

A third alternative, the use of winches and pulleys has been suggested. It appears that there was a winch in Poseidonius' machine built for Alexander in the 330s BC. If Epimachus' *helepolis* also had one it could, in theory, have been driven by some sort of continuous belt drive but doubt has been poured on this concept on the grounds that this method was probably not known until the Middle Ages with the invention of the spinning wheel and also, even if it existed, whether such a large machine could have been moved in this way is problematic. However, men could also, in theory, have run forward to position bolt anchor points in the ground and then attach ropes to them and run these back to be attached to the winch. Men inside the *helepolis* could then winch it forward to the anchor points, perhaps aided by men physically pushing the machine. But all these methods of propulsion remain pure conjecture.

Whatever mode of transport was used some points are clear. Animals and/or men involved in moving the machines were at high risk from the defenders and to move it must have been ponderous in the extreme, the machine probably not moving more than a few hundred feet a day. The notion of sideways movement alluded to in our sources seems even more unlikely.

The *helepolis* was divided (as with the one used at Salamis) into nine separate storeys reached by two internal staircases, one for ascending and one for descending, both of which went from the ground floor to the very top. Each storey had 'ports on the front, in size and shape fitted to the individual characteristics of the missiles that were to be shot forth'.[10] These ports, which had shutters, were protected by animal hides to absorb the blows of enemy missiles.

The lowest storey contained apparatus for throwing stones, in the middle storeys were catapults and on the highest levels further catapults and stone throwing machines were housed. The heaviest catapults were placed on the lower levels and at Salamis, Diodorus recounts that one catapult was capable of throwing missiles of 3 talents. Presumably similar-sized catapults were housed in Epimachus' construction at Rhodes but 3 talents are roughly 180 pounds in imperial measurements. If it wasn't for the other huge measurements involved in all the various other siege machinery it would be tempting to consider this a mistake in the sources, since these are truly huge balls and it is difficult to see how they could have been loaded, let alone fired. One also wonders about the potential for catastrophic mistakes as they were fired from a virtually enclosed space within the tower.[11]

It is thought that an incredible 3,600 men may have been needed to man the machine. The weight may have been over 160 tons. According to Vitruvius, Epimachus constructed at enormous expense, with the utmost care and exertion, an *helepolis* one hundred and thirty-five feet high and sixty feet broad. He strengthened it with hair and rawhide so that it could withstand the blow of a stone weighing three hundred and sixty pounds shot from a ballista; the machine itself weighed three hundred and sixty thousand pounds.[12]

The *helepolis* was not the only machine Demetrius had built; he had no less than eight so-called 'tortoises' for filling ditches. These were essentially movable sheds or 'penthouses' as Diodorus called them, which provided cover for men to fill in the enemy moat outside the walls. We even have a detailed design for them written by Vitruvius, admittedly 300 years later:

A tortoise intended for the filling of ditches, and thereby to make it possible to reach the wall is to be made as follows. Let a base, termed in Greek *eschara*, be constructed, with each of its sides twenty-one feet long, and with four crosspieces. Let these be held together by two others, two thirds of a foot thick and half a foot broad; let the crosspieces be about three feet and a half apart, and beneath and in the spaces between them set the trees, termed in Greek *hamaxopodes*, in which the axles of the wheels turn in iron hoops. Let the trees be provided with pivots, and also with holes through which levers are passed to make them turn, so that the tortoise can move forward or back or towards its right or left side, or if necessary obliquely, all by the turning of the trees.[13]

They were constructed with four sloping sides so enemy missiles would simply hit the fireproofed tortoise and roll off. They had wheels but how they moved, as in the case of the *helepolis*, is open to question. Being smaller they could have been simply pushed into action though how they were able to move sideways, as Vitruvius mentions, again is not known. Although the measurements of Demetrius' tortoise are not mentioned, other examples suggest they would have provided cover for up to fifty or sixty men to work in filling the ditches. Diodorus is vague in his description of them only saying that they provided cover for 'sappers' which might possibly imply they were also used to provide cover for men to undermine the walls, though this is not attested to elsewhere in ancient history.

Last but not least of Demetrius' remarkable and innovative machines were two ram tortoises: 'two enormous penthouses in which battering rams were mounted'.[14] He also had two similar machines at Salamis. Diodorus goes on to describe these rams as being 180 feet long, wrapped in iron and that no less than 1,000 men were used to move the tortoises. We have descriptions of ram tortoises built for Alexander by Diades and also a detailed description by Vitruvius and Athenaeus Mechanicus of one built by

Hegetor of Byzantium in the same era. A specific link between Hegetor and Demetrius has been suggested but is controversial.[15]

The ram tortoise from Vitruvius' description seems to have consisted of a tortoise like the ditch-filling tortoise, only bigger and with eight wheels. However, with the ram tortoise a central turret was needed to utilize the ram. The ram appears to have been suspended above the turret underneath an observation point. How the ram swung back and forth to hit the city walls again is pure conjecture. The ram was presumably suspended in a harness and controlled by ropes below on perhaps some sort of pulley system. As for the tortoise itself, Hegetor's and presumably Demetrius' had eight wheels. Just to compound the problems of interpretation several commentators have questioned whether a 180 feet ram would be at all practical.[16]

To shift these engineering marvels was a feat in itself and, to ensure they could be moved smoothly up to the city walls, a roadway was created so wide that it covered the distance between seven of the towers that studded the landward curtain wall of the city. This prodigious effort, alone, apparently took 30,000 labourers to accomplish, with the crews of the fleet being recruited for the task. The fears of the Rhodians could be imagined when they saw the *helepolis* ponderously moving down the levelled road towards them with four ditch-filling tortoises and one monstrous ram tortoise on either side. The Antigonids eventually manhandled their machines up to the walls and a general assault was ordered. While massed ballistae and catapults opened fire, the galleys simultaneously came out from behind their defensive boom and attacked the harbour once more. However, the Rhodians were not idle themselves and sent out nine ships to look for aid and which, in the event, sank some of Demetrius' galleys and plundered their stores and provisions, which somehow they got back to the city. They also captured a quadrireme which apparently had Demetrius' royal robes on it, painstakingly made or acquired for him by his wife Phila (Antipater's daughter and ex-wife of Craterus).

But at the walls, battering rams and soldiers with picks and bores soon began to make short work of the lower courses of stone. The main curtain wall was undermined to such an extent that the defenders found they could not keep open the walkway that ran the whole of its length. However, strengthened in their resolve by the arrival of more supply ships sent by Ptolemy, and food aid from both Cassander and Lysimachus, they counterattacked and drove back Demetrius' men and machines.

Despite the resultant loss of precious time, soon the contraptions were laboriously rolled back for a further assault. The already-weakened curtain wall now collapsed completely. Bloody battles were fought for the towers that remained standing and both sides suffered considerable casualties in the rubble of the breached and broken defences. When they finally broke through, Demetrius' forces found, to their chagrin, that the enemy had built another wall behind the first. The wooden beams and masonry from the houses that had stood close up to the original wall had been used to construct this second obstacle as well as using masonry from the theatre and various temples. The Rhodians promised to repay the gods with bigger and better ones if they could prevail against the Antigonids. Not content with this, they were now engaged on building a third wall in the event of the second not holding.

These makeshift defences were a real problem for the attackers. Demetrius' engines would have had great difficulty in being manoeuvred over the intervening rubble to reach the second line of defence. It was further compounded by the fact that the resourceful Rhodians had also dug a moat between the walls. Demetrius was, by now, almost at his wits' end. The blockade had not worked, a fact underlined by another defeat handed out at about this time to a corsair fleet off the coast of Caria. Demetrius' main pirate ally had been captured with his ships and escorted back to the port of Rhodes. Now the land attack had faltered in the face of the ingenuity and industry of the defenders. Even an attempt to bribe the commander of the guard (a mercenary from Miletus) failed.

The Rhodians further compounded Demetrius' problems by launching a night fire-missile assault on the *helepolis*. They dislodged some fire plates on the contraption which was only saved by Demetrius being able to get men to drag it out of missile range, though how this could have been done so quickly is again a mystery. Interestingly, Vitruvius has another more colourful version of events on how the machine was stopped in its tracks :

After a great amount of water, filth, and excrement had been poured out during the night, on the next day the *helepolis* moving up, before it could reach the wall, came to a stop in the swamp made by the moisture, and could not be moved forwards, nor later even backwards. And so Demetrius, when he saw that he had been baffled by the wisdom of Diognetus, withdrew with his fleet.[17]

This Diognetus was apparently a Rhodian architect, though he is not mentioned by Diodorus. Vitruvius goes on to say that the *helepolis* was eventually dragged into the city and set up in a public place in honour of Diognetus.

Demetrius determined on one final effort. He organized his best men for a risky, but potentially-decisive, night escalade. To attempt this surprise assault, 1,500 soldiers were picked and given instructions to establish a foothold in the city where the rest of the army could follow. Utilizing a breach in the battered walls, the stratagem nearly worked, as initially the

Rhodian guards were overpowered and the attackers managed to reach the theatre in the city itself. There they were halted and counterattacked by the recently-arrived reinforcements from Ptolemy. Trapped, their only hope was rescue by the main army, but Demetrius could not reach them and eventually all were killed or captured after heroic resistance.

Antigonus, at last, intervened and ordered his son to make peace with the brave islanders. Demetrius was reluctant, his personal prestige was bound up in the enterprise, but he did comply. To the very end, he never faltered in his obedience to his ageing autocratic father. The arrival of an Aetolian delegation served as the rationale, urging him to come to Greece to oppose Cassander. They were not the first people to plead for his intervention in Greece during the siege, but this latest arrival allowed the fact of his defeat to be shrouded as an act of policy. The peace terms agreed left no doubt about who had prevailed. The treaty between the republic and the Antigonids specifically excluded any duty on the island's people to take up arms against Ptolemy.

One wonders whether Demetrius' penchant for bigger and better machinery, which in the end seemed to undermine their functionality, was an aspect of his personality. Diodorus records that he was 'exceedingly ready in invention and devising many things beyond the art of the master builders' and the machines used at Rhodes seem almost ludicrous in their grandiose size and need for so many men to operate them.[18] A pertinent reminder of this is the fact that in the nearly 2,500 years since the siege of Rhodes, no larger machine has ever even been contemplated, much less constructed. Our modern day and age and its penchant for cod psychology would have had a field day with Demetrius and (like Alexander) his need, perhaps, to outdo his father. Furthermore, one can only speculate that his epithet, Poliorcetes (Besieger), may have been bestowed on him ironically, given the ultimate lack of success he actually had in this his most famous siege.

It was a rare enough event that a free city should fight off the ambitions of one of the Macedonian powers. But, this was only the opening turn for Rhodes as a great player in the east Mediterranean world. In centuries to come, they would both dominate trade at sea and contribute to sucking Rome into the Hellenistic orbit (they had already made a treaty with them in 306 BC); an intrusion that would eventually bring down catastrophe on the heads of the great dynasties that were riding so high at the end of the fourth century.

What is immediately apparent about these two detailed examples of the art of siege warfare in the era of the *Diadochi*, is that they both ended in failure. This despite, on both occasions, the attackers having great forces at their command; the resources first of a kingdom and second a powerful empire were thrown against two cities that were, if not insignificant, certainly not of the first rank. But, in both cases the attacker failed even though the Macedonians had made great strides in giving the offensive the advantage. New techniques and a new determination certainly seem evident throughout Alexander's career and beyond. At Tyre, a great mole was built to connect the mainland with the island city so towers and rams could be brought across to get at the walls; catapults were shipped onto triremes to get in range of the defenders. Later at Gaza, ramps were built to get to a city built high on its tell, and then batteries of catapults, towers and miners were brought up to bring down the walls. Not that these were easy victories, the defenders, in most cases, would break out to contest the day trying to set fire to the machines and put back the attackers' enterprises as far as they could. But, still, whether it was a classic escalade or some bizarre ruse, as when Alexander sent his specialist climbers to get above the defences of the Sogdian rock, success was usually the result.

But then, as always the dialectic, techniques of defence were advanced and when the protagonists of protection took up the cudgel they were able to use many of the same advances that the attackers had pioneered. There is even a suggestion that the art of siege warfare reached in the Hellenistic era was a kind of balance between the attacker and defender, that defence had caught up with attack.[19] That is to say that the initial impetus given by the introduction of torsion weapons and the use of great siege towers and sophisticated engineering techniques had been countered in defence by more advanced wall and gate design and the deployment of catapults and ballistae in defence, with the end result that the defenders could keep the attackers at a distance where they could have less impact.

Certainly the affairs of Megalopolis and Rhodes seem to bear this out. Huge resources were brought to bear but, even if it was frequently touch and go, the defences survived in a way they seldom seemed to do when Philip or Alexander were at the gates. And, other great sieges seem to give more support to this contention. The very first war of the post-Alexandrine world centred round the siege of Lamia, which after an initial attempt at assault resolved itself into a blockade that saw the army of Antipater trapped and enduring a winter in the one city in the region that stood by the Macedonian cause. Similarly at Pydna in 317/316 BC, it took a winter season cut off from supplies and support to bring the end for Olympias, hunkering down there with her freezing elephants. Again, though we know little of the details, Antigonus spent years on his siege of Tyre and, in the end, needed to build a navy to achieve the consummation he craved by starving the people into submission. So different from Alexander the Great who, though he too endured a long siege of Tyre, eventually ended it by bloody escalade.

Equally, after the turn of the century, Athens and Thebes stood up to a number of enemies and if not always with success, at least with a resolution that meant the process was extremely time-consuming for their assailant. In Demetrius' siege of Athens in 294 BC it is no happenstance that the one main event we hear of is Ptolemy's admiral and his mercenaries aiding the Athenians getting the harvest in to prepare for the siege. Indeed a most dramatic detail of the impact of blockade comes from this time:

> Among many examples of the extremities, to which they had been reduced, it happened that a father and son were sitting in a room and had abandoned all hope that they could survive. Suddenly a dead mouse fell from the ceiling and as soon as the two saw it, they sprang up and began to fight for the prize. It was at this time too, we are told, that the philosopher Epicurus kept his disciples alive with beans, counting out and distributing a ration for them each day.[20]

Yet this list of failed affairs or ones brought to conclusion by starvation is far from exhaustive and in a way tells a misleading story. In the twenty-plus years of war after Alexander's death (where we are privy to some good detail of what befell) the picture is not apiece with this contention at all. Cities large and small fell or changed allegiance with surprising rapidity, not in every case but enough to make us reconsider what is happening. Campaigns in the Peloponnese are very illustrative on this point. As often as not, towns in that region seem to fall at the arrival of armies outside their gates. In 314 BC, Alexander, son of Polyperchon, might be rebuffed at Elis but Aristodemus, with a mercenary army fighting for the Antigonid cause, had no trouble taking control at Patrae and Aegium on the southern shore of the Gulf of Corinth. Nor does Alexander have to spend much time to get back control of Dyme when he goes on the counterattack. And, then with equal felicity Aristodemus' mercenaries return and take the place back from Alexander's people. No doubt the thing would have gone on ad nauseam if Alexander had not been assassinated by disgruntled citizens of Sicyon.

The Peloponnese saw the likes of Cassander, Polyperchon, Alexander, Aristodemus and their agents shooting around like billiard balls from one town after another, starving them into surrender, taking them by escalade or, as often as not, being let in by disaffected citizens, who, currently not at the top of the communal pile, hoped for promotion of their ambitions with the sponsorship of the attacking force. Similar things occurred elsewhere. Antigonus came back from his great battles in the upper satrapies intent on ensuring control of the Levant and establishing himself as a great sea power. He took over two years to take Tyre, the great Phoenician port city on its island stronghold, but while it was going on Antigonus also sent off detachments to take Gaza and Joppa which fell with no such trouble at all. After that, the Antigonid machine descended on Anatolia. No rival there had an army that could face them so the campaigns became an itinerary of cities that fell through storm, treason or starvation. Arrhidaeus in Hellespontine Phrygia saw his friends and allies either go over to, or be taken over by, the Antigonid war machine that came at them by land and sea. Asander, satrap of Caria, fared the same, great cities whose pedigree in culture and science went back centuries were taken with apparent ease. Miletus, so important in her time, did not hold out long. Caunus, which Antigonus intended to use as a major naval base, fell to assault but we know no details. Often we hear that towns are sold by citizens and the garrisons repair to the citadel where they try to hold out. Yet none of this seems to delay Antigonus to any great extent, certainly not in the manner he had experienced at Tyre.

Again we have Seleucus in Cyprus in 315 BC as he cruises the coast of that island, on behalf of Ptolemy of Egypt, capturing city after city with no great apparent effort until the end of the season when Citium endures a siege that we do not actually know the outcome of. This preparedness to come to terms surely cannot be because of confident expectation of good treatment from someone who got his orders from the man in Alexandria, Ptolemy, who, a little later, ordered the complete extermination of the old city of Marion on the northern coast of Cyprus.

Then we have Demetrius, unsuppressed by his failure at Rhodes, cutting a swathe through the strongholds of the Peloponnese. He even rolled into the extraordinarily-defensible Acrocorinth. Sicyon had fallen just before and Orchomenus succumbed to an assault driven by Demetrius' bile that had been stimulated by being insulted by the garrison. Still, later, in the campaigns before Ipsus, strongholds like Abydos, Ephesus, Synnada and Sardis fell like ninepins to one side or the other as Lysimachus and Prepelaus first prised away Antigonid control and then Demetrius returned to reassert it.

But, what happened on these occasions had less to do with technology than the inclination and determination of the defenders. Very frequently our sources attest that citizens sold the pass and that, as often as not, their reward was to rough up their political opponents in frequently-lethal manner, even when they had fled to temples for protection. None of this was new. Communal rivalry was the lifeblood of these cities, big and small. Aristocrats contended with democratic opponents with words or swords, whichever was appropriate at the time. These local rivalries could be played on by any outsider who cared to. Alexander had favoured democrats in Asia Minor because the Persians had usually ruled through oligarchs, while his viceroy, Antipater, in Europe, based his own power on those same oligarchs who happily exiled democratic opponents to sustain their regimes. These kings could also change their minds if it suited them. Alexander did a volte-face in Greece at the end of his life; his Exiles Decree would have brought back into contention, if not power, the very people who had lost everything while Antipater ruled.

Polyperchon then carried on the process with his decree of Greek freedom that was meant to undermine the oligarchic regimes that would have supported the son, Cassander, as they had the father, Antipater. Antigonus, at his camp near Tyre, repeated the mantra and all the *Diadochi* would bang on about freedoms they would never really give their own subjects but were happy to decree elsewhere as long as it caused problems for their rivals. What this meant is that, in so many of these campaigns, particularly in the Peloponnese but also in Asia and elsewhere too, an attacker was let in by the local party that was out of power.

If the towns were garrisoned, the soldiers would often retreat to the citadel to try and hold out as they would usually not have the numbers to hold the walls when not seconded by the populace. But these attempts at resistance often ended quickly enough, with mercenaries seldom sufficiently committed to risk too much against an enemy that might soon turn into another employer. So the riven politics of these Greek communities made them vulnerable in a way that made it pretty irrelevant how powerful were the torsion catapults and how huge the towers and battering rams of the attacker.

The region and how it was placed between the rival kings could also have a major bearing on how sieges in this era played out. The political instability translated into a failure of will to resist occurred most particularly in the regular cockpits of war where rivals armies came and went repeatedly. Where at one time one dynast was up, and then the other, so local politicians could always hope that their sponsor would soon be along to shoulder them up the greasy pole again.

It was often very different in those places further out on the edge, where local elites mainly interfaced with just one of the great rulers. A particular example of interest is Lysimachus' relations with the Black Sea cities. There we do not have any great detail but what we do know indicates no lack of communal will to resist. No aggrieved partisans open the gates to the invader here; there is a determination to resist that borders on the heroic. They were not always successful but the presence of this truly patriotic spirit frequently translated into long drawn out sieges, often with neighbours, Hellenic and otherwise, offering succour against a regional power that was perceived as a threat by other potential victims in the area.

Thus the city of Callantia was repeatedly besieged by Lysimachus, who for many years was undistracted by wars with the other *Diadochi*. He could concentrate on these impertinent citizens, but still he found it no easy job to suppress them. It is, in fact, unclear when he was able to establish full control of the town and in the end it seems many of the inhabitants preferred a move to a new foundation under the sponsorship of Eumelus, king of Cimmerian Bosporus, as against submitting to Lysimachus.

Nor was it just the volatile politics of the citizen body that might undermine the spirit of defence. It could also be military leadership that had feet of clay. It is particularly noticeable in the invasion of Anatolia by Lysimachus in 302 BC that the generals left by Antigonus to protect his strongholds were very prone to changing sides for straight lucre and for promises of a good future in the new order. At Sardis, Phoenix gave over the town to the invader and at Synnada, Docimus (an old hand as a turncoat) was also only too happy to hand over the keys to the stronghold.

Humanity was always more important than technology and this remained true in the decades and centuries after as great sieges punctuated the history of the western world. In Greece, the great Attic capital seemed often at the centre; from the time shortly after our era when the Macedonians of Antigonus Gonatus took two years to force a heroic Athens to surrender in the climax of the Chremonidean War (when Sparta and Athens geed on by the Ptolemies had again challenged Macedonian power); to the long and awful siege of Athens by Sulla in 87/86 BC, in the First Mithridatic War, that finally ended in the merciless sacking of the venerable city. Or to the west in the Roman world, where again great sieges were the epics establishing and ruining reputations, whether the enemy were the Greeks of Syracuse and Capua, the African powers of Carthage, the Iberians of Numantia or even down to the Gauls of Vercingetorix at Alesia.

Chapter Eight

Naval Warfare

Plato described the Greeks as living 'like frogs round a pond'and the sea was always crucial to ancient life in the Mediterranean world.[1] Overland travel could be difficult and communications between communities that were frequently near or by the sea was best done by ships that progressed by hugging the coastline. In a world where warfare was endemic, control of the sea was important for supplying and reinforcing troops that were engaged in warfare.

The first attested sea battle seems only to have occurred around 1210 BC between Shuppululiuma II, the king of the Hittites, who defeated a Cypriot fleet. Naval battles were fairly rare and it was not till the Persian Wars of the fifth century that there were records of any substantial naval operations. The Greeks, in the Trojan War, famously launched a 'thousand ships' to regain Helen, but they were essentially transports and any naval combat would have simply consisted of crews engaging in hand-to-hand combat or using missiles from a distance.

What transformed naval warfare was the invention of the ram in the ninth century BC. The ram was a beam sheathed in bronze attached to the bow underneath the waterline. With this a ship could ram an enemy vessel. But even then it still needed the development of a ship that would make most use of this technology. The basic ship at this time was the *pentekontor* which was a simple, long, narrow, one-level ship used for transporting goods and people. These had long been in use; it is thought, for instance, that they may have been used in the Trojan War. They were fitted with twenty- five oars a side, thus holding at least fifty men. By about 700 BC a new type of ship, the bireme, had been invented. It was developed probably in Phoenicia and it added another bank of oars above the first. As a ship it had a long life being used, for example, in the Roman invasion of Britain by Julius Caesar in the first century BC. But it was only with the invention of the *trieres* (trireme) in the sixth century BC that naval warfare really came into its own. The trireme had, as the name suggests, three times the number of oars of the *pentekontor* but how they were arranged is, as in so much else of our era, disputed.

However, it is generally thought that the oars were arranged in three tiers with one man to an oar. Excavation of the harbour ship sheds at Piraeus near Athens in the 1890s enabled some intelligent estimates to be made of a trireme's length and depth. They are now thought to have been approximately 120 feet long, 18 feet wide and 8.5 feet deep. Unfortunately no wreck of a trireme has ever been found but a famous replica ship, the *Olympias*, was built in the 1980s and can still be seen at Athens' modern day harbour. Such a ship with its numerous oars could be both fast and extremely manoeuvrable. It survived in use until the fifth century AD. The triremes were made of wood with metal spikes to hold the wood together. The most common woods used were fir, cedar, and pine.

Naval tactics in classical Greece revolved around two manoeuvres. The first was the *diekplous* manoeuvre, which, translated, means 'break through and ram'; the oarsmen rowing very quickly into the hull of the enemy vessel. With a fleet of ships this required them to row at the enemy often in a straight line to break through and expose them to ramming. Such a manoeuvre was quite complicated with a whole fleet of ships and needed intense training to enable the right degree of co-operation to carry it out successfully. The other tactical manoeuvre was the *periplous*, which involved one fleet outflanking the other and ramming the enemy ships in the flanks. If carried out successfully it could decide the outcome of a battle in very little time. An easier manoeuvre than the *diekplous*, it still required a high level of skill to accomplish successfully. The most successful exponents of this and all naval warfare were, of course, the Athenians. Their triremes were manned by the poorer Athenian citizens (not slaves as is so often thought) and it is said with good reason that the skill they used in co-operating in naval tactics helped give rise to the idea of democracy, which they so assiduously practised.

Bigger boats than triremes had begun to be used by the middle of the fourth century, usually credited to Dionysius I of Syracuse which he developed for his war against Carthage. By the era of the *Diadochi* they were standard. The *tetreres* or 'four' (better known by the latin-derived term 'quadrireme') was the ship of the line, the *penteres* or 'five' (latinized as quinquereme) was the dreadnought and the *heptares* ('seven') and *dekares* ('ten') were the superships and carried the commander's flag. But all were larger than the kind of vessels that went at each other's throats at Salamis in 480 BC. And what this meant was that they could not only transport many more soldiers, but also catapults and other missile-throwing machines. Indeed they might even carry, if bound together, siege towers, rams and much else to threaten the defences of ports that had not had to face this kind of threat before.

The names refer to the numbers of oars but how they were arranged is a matter of some dispute, even more so than in the case of triremes. According to some commentators, the numbers used to describe galleys counted the number of rows of men on each side, and not the banks of oars. Thus, the quadrireme has been posited as being possibly reconstructed in three different ways. Firstly, one row of oars with four men on each oar, though this is felt to be unlikely as this would mean a very broad vessel. Secondly, oars on two levels with two men on each oar and finally oars at three levels with two men pulling the top oars and one each on the remaining two. The most obvious arrangement, given the name, of four banks of oars, is a physical impossibility. Similarly, the fives (quinqueremes) are thought to have had three rows of oars, with two men pulling each of the top two oars and one pulling the lower. Likewise, it is thought that the seven had one bank of four oarsmen and one bank of three whilst the tens had two banks of five. But though the technology is debated and the practicality wondered over, what is considered sure is that it would not have been practical to have had more than three layers of oars and probably no more than eight men rowing on each individual oar.

Much happened at sea in the era of Alexander's Successors. Many campaigns were fought (though for all but one the sources are scant indeed), many developments occurred which need describing but equally much remained the same. However big the battleships of Demetrius or Ptolemy became, they still remained rowing shells that must hug the coast, never seagoing cruisers that could stray far from sight of land. They would be beached most nights, though they might stay out for a few days if it was absolutely required. But, whether a trireme or *dekares* they were full to the brim with rowers and seamen and they just did not have the capacity to carry the supplies all these men needed, nor indeed the space to allow them to stretch and to sleep once the day's rowing was done. Water, especially, could never be carried in sufficient volume. A trireme would seldom carry fewer than 170 oarsmen, sailors and marines and bigger vessels proportionally more. A quinquereme would have usually carried at least 300 men and perhaps many more when a battle was anticipated. On an occasion before the Battle of Ipsus, Cassander's brother, Pleistarchus, is reported as travelling on a sixer and also that he was accompanied by 500 men; this would have been far more than normal, as essentially the ship was acting as a troop transport, but it still shows how crammed full these big galleys might become. So the great fleets that Demetrius launched might be manned by well over 60,000 men and they would have to beach at the end of the day somewhere near where there was fresh water for these myriads to slake their thirst.

Control of the coastline was always a crucial matter and island stepping stones were vital to any puissant commander of the sea who aimed to make his power more than just a mark in the shifting sand. Also because of this, one of the most commonly used of naval strategies was not open to the big maritime players of the period. Blockade was very difficult to achieve because staying at sea was so difficult, even in fair weather, never mind in foul. So, any blockade runner had just to wait until the enemy ships had beached for the night to get in or out. Few examples exist in ancient times where it was tried and none that were achieved without great difficulty. Pompey's fleet tried to cut off Caesar's army from supplies and reinforcements after he first crossed to Epirus to track down his enemies in the siege of Dyrrachium in 49/48 BC. The Pompeians were by far the dominant party at sea but they still could not really keep up the blockade for any length of time. Mark Antony managed to get the second half of the army over so Caesar was able to achieve some numerical parity to bring on the great battle he desired. And, if this subordinate had his troubles, the greatest damage was done by the weather rather than the galleys of his opponent's fleet.

The future rulers of the world Alexander took east in his conquering army were not naturally men of the sea. Yet, they knew their strategy whether it was practised on brown earth or blue water. Most of them were well-prepared and capable of leading navies as much as they were a land army. Some, like Seleucus for a number of years, had naval careers (though after this period he never wet his feet again) and Cleitus the White, before being snuffed out in the Thracian Chersonese, seemed to have specialized in maritime warfare, though he had also led cavalry under Alexander in the far eastern wars.[2] Medius, who hosted the party where Alexander fell fatally ill, served as an admiral for Antigonus for many years.[3]

Ptolemy always kept his eye on developments at sea and led his navies in person on a number of occasions. And of course, Demetrius' greatest claim to fame, apart from being the era's greatest besieger, was as a monarch of the seas. Cassander managed at least one victory at sea but Lysimachus and Antigonus of the major players never seem to have ventured on the element personally, though the latter poured mountains of resources into boosting his clout in the nautical arena.

At the very beginning of our period, in the Lamian War, it became apparent there were choke points that would crop up again and again in the maritime story of the Macedonian Empires. The crossing of Europe to Asia was just such a one. When the Greek navy laid its plans in 323/322 BC the Athenian admiral, Evetion, had at his disposal 200 triremes and 40 quadriremes, a formidable fleet manned by Athenian oarsmen, who for centuries had been some of the most expert sailors in the world of the eastern Mediterranean.[4] His strategy demanded the fleet be divided; the larger detachment sailed to the Hellespont to deny any passage to Macedonian reinforcements while the other detachment moved to bottle up the 110 triremes Antipater had brought to the Malian Gulf to support his land campaign.

The Greek leaders knew the war was bound to turn against them if the soldiers and resources of the Macedonian empire in Asia were allowed to cross over into Europe. The plan was initially pursued with some success, the fleet blockading the Malian Gulf ensured protection for the seaward flank of Leosthenes' army, and the Hellespontine task force, though unable to deny the crossing of Leonnatus, were soon in a good enough position to prevent any further reinforcements. However, in the spring of 322 BC, Cleitus brought up the Macedonian Asiatic fleet to try and clear the Greek navy from the Hellespont. The two armadas met in a great battle at Abydos where Evetion had 170 warships facing 240 under Cleitus. The Macedonians achieved a decisive victory. Having won the initiative, Cleitus followed the retreating enemy ships intending to eradicate them from the Aegean. He took the opportunity to attack the second fleet in the Malian Gulf and after dispersing them was able to take command of Antipater's fleet as well, in preparation for a final battle. The remnants of the Greek fleet had withdrawn south to the island of Amorgos in the southern part of the Cyclades archipelago, 60 miles south of Samos, in the hope that they could escape Macedonian attention and be able to recover their strength and regroup.[5] Unfortunately for the harassed and desperate Greek sailors, Cleitus was a determined and ruthless foe. He sailed to Amorgos and forced them to fight. The result was a foregone conclusion; with the Greeks outnumbered and in low spirits, only a few of their ships survived to limp back to Piraeus as the fleet was emphatically destroyed by the rampant Macedonian admiral.

Cleitus, not a man given to understatement (under Alexander he had always conducted any business whilst walking on purple cloths), reportedly celebrated his great victory by styling himself 'Poseidon, god of the sea', and thereafter carrying a trident. This sea fight ended an era as never again would Athens be a significant naval power. For nearly 200 years her fleet had been a major force in the Aegean, sometimes dominant, sometimes suffering decline but never to be discounted. The victory over Xerxes at Salamis had ushered in this era and the fifth century glory of Athens was based on thalassocracy. At Aegospotami, in 405 BC, Lysander of Sparta had inflicted a serious blow on Athenian control of the Hellenic seas but, even so, during the fourth century the shipyards of Piraeus could still put to sea a fleet of awesome power. It was this naval capability that persuaded both Philip and Alexander to make considerable concessions to ensure Athenian support in the war against Persia. But, after Amorgos, the citizens would never look out again on a harbour with an Athenian fleet that could hold its own against the other Hellenic naval powers.

The second great battle at the junction of Asia and Europe, in 317 BC, hugely compounded the problems Polyperchon had already acquired at the siege of Megalopolis, but for the self-proclaimed Poseidon it was to have fatal consequences. Cleitus was, by now, the ex-satrap of Lydia, having been ousted by Antigonus, and he had been sent by the guardian to block the Propontis with his fleet. Aided by the forces of Arrhidaeus, the ruler of Hellespontine Phrygia, his task was to ensure Antigonus could not send reinforcements to Cassander in his struggle to win Macedonia from Polyperchon. In response, Nicanor, Cassander's very capable commander at Piraeus, was despatched to rendezvous with Antigonus' fleet to try and open up the route.

A fierce naval battle ensued near Byzantium. Nicanor had about 130 ships but Cleitus probably outnumbered him.[6] He is described by Diodorus as taking the whole fleet, and as he had 240 ships only a few years before it is reasonable to suggest he still had most of these with him.[7] Initially he was successful, sinking seventeen and capturing almost forty ships, and Cassander's admiral was forced to flee with the remnants of his fleet across the Bosporus to Chalcedon. Lulled into a false sense of security by his apparently decisive victory, Cleitus displayed untypical carelessness which was to cost him dear. He assumed he had rid himself of all the enemies in the vicinity but did not reckon on the indefatigable Antigonus. The latter had arrived on the Asiatic shore facing Byzantium with his army and, utilizing vessels provided by allies in that city, he rapidly shipped over troops to attack Cleitus who had beached his fleet oblivious of any danger:

> All this had been arranged in one night. At dawn those on land began to discharge their javelins and arrows; the enemy some still asleep and others just wakened, having nothing to protect them suffered many wounds. Some were tearing off the stem cables, others were pulling up the gangways, others were raising the anchors; there was general noise and confusion. Antigonus signalled to the 60 ships also to go in to the attack and to ram the enemy ships, dashing enthusiastically through the waves. So it soon came about with one group attacking from the beach and the other from the sea that they conquered those who had previously been victorious.[8]

According to Diodorus, Nicanor also joined in with what was left of his fleet and he eliminated all of Cleitus' ships that had managed to get under way, except for the one boat that Cleitus, himself, was on.[9] His fleet destroyed and fearful of capture if he tried to flee by sea, Cleitus got back to shore on the

Thracian side, no doubt hoping to make his way overland back to Macedonia. But his luck was out and he was captured by soldiers of Lysimachus and promptly murdered.

The other choke point was that area where the second Greek squadron had waited in the Lamian War. This was Artemisium and the squadron placed there controlled the channel between the long island of Euboea and the mainland. The men posted there would have been well aware of the other fleet made up mostly of Athenian ships that had waited in trepidation for the overwhelming Persian enemy in 480 BC. But, this time, the outcome was to be very different. Unlike their forebears at that other Battle of Artemisium, who showed well against overwhelming odds, this time the Athenians and their allies fled after a short struggle, intending to try and recoup their strength far to the south.

In 313 BC the straits between the mainlands of Euboea again became a cockpit of considerable naval altercation. The Antigonids were clearly intent on testing Cassandrine power in the Balkans and he had to prepare very seriously against this threat. Cassander's position in Attica and the south was fairly securely held but his eastern flank had holes in it. The island of Euboea, which was likely to be the target of an Antigonid offensive, was largely in Cassander's pocket but the city of Oreus on the north coast was not towing the line. Cassander intended to secure it before it could become a breach which his enemy could penetrate. He mobilized what ships he could, thirty in all, and sailed south, passing close to the Thessalian coast where he descended on the northern coast of Euboea. Cassander was in no position for a patient policy and he was energetically preparing for an escalade when what Cassander must have feared transpired, an Antigonid fleet hove into sight. What he did not know was that this was not just one fleet but two. Telesphorus, Antigonus' nephew, on hearing of the activities in Euboea, had set sail from the Peloponnese with twenty ships. On his way he rendezvoused with a fleet of 100 vessels sent from the eastern Aegean, led by Alexander's old admiral Medius. Cassander was outnumbered many-fold and events were to show the enemy were equipped with the latest weapons of naval warfare. Early in the resulting engagement, fire pots were dropped or catapulted into Cassander's ships, four were burned out and the rest were in very great danger of catching fire too, an awful prospect for the wooden, highly-flammable craft of the period. Cassander had no option; when he saw the results of this uneven conflict, he pulled out his ships as best he could, packed up his army, raised the siege and ended the blockade. The attempt on Oreus was shelved and Medius was able to reinforce and supply the brave defenders.

But the course of maritime combat in this age was an unpredictable matter. Often, after a victory, the winners were lax in their precautions, overconfidence leaving them vulnerable. The Antigonids, on this occasion, relaxed their guard in the knowledge of their superior numbers and beached their warships with little thought for defence. Cassander, showing great resilience, called up reinforcements from Athens under the admiral, Thymochares, and counterattacked. The surprised enemy sailors rushed to defend their boats but not before Cassander's captains had sunk one and towed off three others as prizes, thus neatly compensating for his own losses in the earlier battle.

What is inescapable in these accounts is that the one crucial fact about ancient navies was how vulnerable they were when the boats were beached. Twice in this short period, good beginnings crumble into disaster, or at least defeat, when a fleet was caught high and dry on the beach. Cleitus and Medius had both won victories and each considered their opponent to be a busted flush. They did not take the kind of precautions they surely would have if they had known that an active enemy was at hand. On both occasions, these experienced and usually-competent admirals beached their ships and failed to put up proper defences to protect them. In the case of Cassander's attack we are not told that Medius' fleet was beached but merely that they 'were off their guard' but this is most likely to mean when they were beached, as ancient fleets did not stay under way unless preparing for battle or going somewhere.[10] Neither of these were the case here, but then again it does say three were seized with their crews whom, it could be argued, would unlikely to have been on board if the vessels were beached. The reference, however, is so brief that speculation, though inevitable, has little to work on. It is possible the crews had got on board to try and get out to sea so they could manoeuvre but were still caught by the attackers. Equally, it could be argued that as one ship was sunk they probably were at sea. But this is not decisive as we certainly hear on other occasions of ships being pulled off the beach to be sunk. And it just seems improbable that a squadron at sea with its crew on board and ready to react could be so surprised, particularly when the fleet that suffered defeat was still much larger than the force that attacked it.

But with Cleitus there is no question; both Polynaeus and Diodorus make it clear the attack took place on the unprepared, disembarked (and some probably sleeping) crews. Looking to baggage and prisoners taken in the previous encounter made getting Cleitus' ships underway even more difficult and we hear nothing of guard posts that should have been needed to be overcome during the land assault that was carried out by what seem to have been mainly Antigonid missile men. The attack from the sea was delivered by ships carrying 'many of his bravest infantry', presumably heavy infantry.[11] It seems Cleitus put up no palisade or ditch to protect his beached fleet though this was certainly a normal precaution when a fleet intended to stay put for any length of time.

Not that these two were the first to succumb in this way. On a more momentous occasion, almost a century before, much the same thing had occurred. The final efforts of a war-traumatized Athenian community had raised a fleet to face the Spartan, Lysander, and his Persian-funded navy. They did well until, at Aegospotami in 404 BC, opposite Lampsacus on the eastern side of the Hellespont, they let themselves be lulled into a false sense of security by Lysander's behaviour. He, by repeatedly offering battle then returning to harbour when it was refused, ensured that the Athenians would begin to assume that this would always happen. After this pantomime had been played out one more time, the Athenian leaders sent their men off to forage and Lysander attacked and caught them beached and completely off guard, destroying the last fleet Athens could muster in the Peloponnesian War.

Apart from the two choke points already explored, another region was crucial for any power wanting to dominate the east Mediterranean sea lanes. These were the islands of the southern Aegean. It is no surprise that when Antigonus began his ship building programme in 315 BC, as he besieged Tyre, his eyes were drawn there. When the Phoenician, Cilician, Hellespontine and Rhodian bottoms, that were the core of his navy, evolved into a potent fighting force he directed them west.

It was not, however, all plain sailing for his infant marine. One of his squadrons was picked off by the power most disturbed by his growing naval puissance. Polycleitus, Ptolemy's admiral, had been sent from Cyprus by Seleucus to help the cause in Greece but on finding Alexander, Polyperchon's son, had gone over to Cassander he had no real enemy to fight. At a loose end, he cruised the Anatolian coast from Pamphylia to Cilicia. Whilst there he heard Theodotus was taking some Rhodian built boats with Carian crews to join the main Antigonid navy. The new fleet was being escorted by an army under Perilaus who was marching along the coast, keeping up with the fleet. Polycleitus disembarked a considerable army and ambushed Perilaus. The army and its leader were captured and when the Rhodian ships went to try and help he led out his fleet from round a promontory where they had been hiding and captured the whole squadron which was caught unprepared and not drawn up for battle at all. With these spoils of war, Polycleitus returned first to Cyprus and afterwards home to the main base, at Pelusium, in Egypt.

Yet, despite this setback, Antigonus was still able to assemble a fleet of 240 ships, fully manned, whilst yet more were still under construction. He launched ten *dekares* ('tens'), three nines, ten fives and ninety quadriremes, the balance being made up of triremes and thirty smaller un-decked vessels;

a force that had much more than an even chance of wresting control of the seas from Ptolemy's men. Antigonus sent fifty ships to the Peloponnese and put his nephew, Dioscurides, in charge of the remainder, who was sent west, both to support his allies and agents in the attempt to secure the Aegean islands that were such crucial bases for the enemy's war fleets in the region.

By 314 BC, Dioscurides was flying the flag of his uncle to considerable effect in the Aegean. Large numbers of the island cities either came over to him or were captured by his marines. If he could establish the family in the Cyclades many benefits would accrue. Here, fleets based in the south Aegean could ensure safe passage between Asia and Greece. Armies could be shipped to the Peloponnese, Attica, Euboea or even Boeotia with ease to ensure opponents in Greece could never feel safe from Antigonid interference. Antigonid control of the southern islands also denied easy communications between dynasts in Europe and Africa who might want to gang up against them.

If the key points at the European crossing, Artemisia and control of the Cyclades, were crucial in controlling the western seas, further east another place was central to maritime hegemony. This was Cyprus and here took place the greatest sea battle of the whole era and fortunately one we have considerable evidence for. Ptolemy had struggled for years to impose his control on the island and Antigonus was no stranger to the place. He had campaigned there in the first civil war when it was controlled by Perdiccans, in one of the many fronts opened against that dynast. As Antigonus had for many years controlled Syria and Cilicia, the main coastlines near the island, he could always use influence, money and threats to undermine whatever his Lagid enemy achieved there. But when he had achieved at least parity with Ptolemy at sea, his ambitions became more all consuming. He had thought for years of invading the island but wars with powerful enemy coalitions and the eastern campaigns against Seleucus had kept him involved elsewhere.

But in 307 BC all things looked possible. Ptolemy had recently sailed all over the Aegean, even establishing a foothold at Corinth and Sicyon and showing that, whatever Antigonus had achieved, his rival still was in the game. To finally dispose of him Antigonus needed Demetrius' fleet and army. The old man ordered that his son should secure what he held in Greece and set sail to the island. Demetrius arrived in northern Cyprus with a force of 110 triremes and what Diodorus describes as 'fifty-three heavier transports and freighters of every kind sufficient for the strength of his cavalry and infantry', as well as 15,000 foot and 400 horse.[12] After securing a centre of operations around the captured towns of Urania and Carpasia, the invaders marched straight to attack Salamis, where Ptolemy's brother, Menelaus, had his headquarters. He fought a battle outside the walls but was defeated and soon Demetrius had his enemy bottled up behind the city defences and settled down to besiege the place.

Siege engines were constructed on the spot, either from local timber and iron or out of sections of dismantled machines used before in Greece, and shipped over for this new enterprise. Particularly noted outside the walls of Salamis was a *helepolis*, or city-taker, nine storeys high. This machine, with accompanying battering rams, wreaked havoc, clearing the walls of defenders and causing great cracks in the fabric of the defences. Menelaus' men managed to set most of these constructions alight with fire arrows during the course of one night but even this success could not hide the fact that time was running out for the garrison. The defenders had fought with skill and determination but without relief there could be only one final outcome, a complete eviction from Cyprus for the Ptolemaic party.

Word was sent to Ptolemy warning of the imminent loss of the island he had been working to dominate for years. He had poured in money, sent his best officers to subjugate the place and was perfectly prepared to brutalize the families of the petty local dynasties. All this in an effort to retain a territory that would be central to the ambitions of his house, right down to its extinction almost 300 years later. The wound that the Antigonids clearly wanted to inflict could not be contemplated; it would ring a death knell to any ambitions Ptolemy had to retain his influence in the waters of the eastern Mediterranean. More than this, the island was the last dependable source of timber left to the Lagids (a crucial resource without which no navy could be created or sustained), especially as the only other reliable stock was in the Levant which Antigonus, of course, already controlled.

Ptolemy realized he was not facing a peripheral threat, this was a vital contest and he decided he would have to deal with it himself. Every arsenal and port was scoured to mobilize a navy and army that might take on Demetrius to resurrect his fading dreams of thalassocracy. By the time he had called in all his reserves and recruited from allied cities on Cyprus, Ptolemy had a fleet that totalled 140 ships, the largest he had so far ever mobilized. Skirting the southern shore of the island, the great armada pushed on to the rescue of the garrison of Salamis. Slipping a messenger through the siege lines to Menelaus, Ptolemy relayed to his brother that an attack was to be mounted by the Egyptian fleet the next day and that Menelaus was ordered to support the offensive by leading his own sixty ships out from Salamis harbour to join him. Demetrius, far from blind to this threat, assigned ten quinqueremes to blockade the narrow exit from the port to the sea, a precaution of crucial importance in the day ahead. He also took advantage of his control of the countryside to deploy cavalry to patrol along the coast, so they could aid his mariners as much as possible in the coming encounter.

Though one tradition suggests Ptolemy had sailed at the dead of night and hoped to enter Salamis without a fight, there is no doubt he expected and prepared for a full-scale sea battle.[13] Masts and sails were stowed away soon after the fleet left Citium. Dawn broke early on this summer morning and it would soon have become oppressively hot for the sailors and marines whose journey was greatly increased by the need to round the promontory of Pedalium before the fleet turned north to approach Salamis. Somewhere along the coast south of the besieged city, possibly near Leucolla, they found the Antigonid fleet drawn up in battle order and eager for the fight.

There is considerable dispute about the size of Demetrius' fleet. Plutarch mentions 180 warships, Polynaeus has 170 whilst Diodorus reports him with 108 vessels. Clearly the similarity of the numbers involved with Plutarch and Diodorus suggests a commonality of source with one or the other misreading the original figure. It is likely on this occasion that Plutarch is correct, as earlier in the year, at Athens, Demetrius commanded a fleet of 250 and we hear of no disaster or act of policy that would have so far eroded his former strength.[14]

It was a huge war fleet that confronted Ptolemy and dotted along the arch of the Antigonid line were those broad high-sided sevens that were some of the largest warships yet seen in the eastern seas. At about 0.5 miles distance from each other, the two fleets paused to sacrifice to the gods and make the final arrangements for the proper alignment of their battle lines. The 140 warships of Ptolemy's fleet [15] were either quinqueremes or quadriremes and they spread out in line abreast with the supply ships (carrying the troops that could not be accommodated on the warships)[16] well to the rear. Their commander led the left-wing squadron where the largest craft were marshalled and where an even greater concentration of numbers may have been achieved by deploying a second line of warships in support.

Demetrius' forces were considerably more mixed in type and usefulness than his opponents. At least 110 of his warships were light triremes, while he also fielded sevens and sixes that carried more artillery and soldiers than anything Ptolemy had. The balance was made up of quadriremes and quinqueremes. Antigonus' son had much to fight for; this was his first opportunity for revenge against the man who had humbled him six years before at Gaza. No longer a young untried commander, but a general at the height of his power and reputation, and as the day would show, as an admiral he had considerably more initiative than his opponent. On the left of the Antigonid battle line he personally commanded the most powerful squadron. Here, there were seven sevens from the ports of Phoenicia and thirty Athenian quadriremes under the experienced Antigonid admiral, Medius. And, behind this front line were deployed in support ten sixes and ten fives. Together these fifty-seven warships comprised the biggest and best of the fleet crammed with ballistae and seasoned troops on the re-inforced decks above the oarsmen. It was with them that he intended to decide the encounter. The centre and right-hand squadrons were made up largely of triremes that, though maneuverable, would be at a disadvantage in the melee when the two fleets collided.

Ptolemy gave the order to attack all along his formation by trumpet blasts and flashing shields. His own flagship led the way at the head of a squadron of fives on the left of his line. The Antigonid vessels, opposed to him, were commanded by Hegesippus of Halicarnassus, and it is probable many of the seamen of Demetrius' fleet came from the same region as this admiral. The rugged coast of Caria and Lycia and the islands of the southwest of Asia Minor had for generations nurtured brave and skilful mariners; the chief pilot of the fleet came from Cos while one of the admirals in the centre of the line was a native of Samos. The lighter triremes that experienced the brunt of Ptolemy's assault were at a disadvantage as their sea-room was constricted between the shoreline to their right and the central squadron on their left, they simply did not have the room to manouevre that might have allowed them to cope with the larger and better-protected enemy vessels. The outcome in this part of the battle was not long in doubt, some of Hegesippus' ships could not take the shock of contact and sunk while Ptolemy's marines boarded and made prizes of many more. The details of the battle are not described but the logic of events indicates that, at the point of his greatest success, Ptolemy lost control of the direction of the battle. His captains may have got carried away by their victory and pursued the fleeing enemy too far or perhaps became involved in securing individual prizes. Whatever the reason, by the time Ptolemy had reorganized his squadron in preparation to build on his local advantage he found it was already too late.

Demetrius had raised his battle cry on the other wing and ordered his high-sided dreadnoughts forward at the same time as his opponent. Ballistae and archers on both sides had opened a withering fire well before the two lines clashed on this seaward flank of the battle and even in these preliminaries the Antigonid sixes and sevens showed a marked superiority. Once the lead ships engaged in a crunching of timbers and splintering of oars all became chaos. 'For in contests on land', writes Diodorus, 'valour is made clearly evident, since it is able to gain the upper hand, when nothing external and fortuitous interferes; but in naval battles there are many causes of various kinds, that contrary to reason, defeat those who would properly gain the victory through prowess.'[17] Naval warfare in this age was a lottery. But still there were factors that might give the edge to one side or the other. On this flank the advantage lay with Demetrius, once the two lines were mixed and locked together the greater number of marines on the bigger Antigonid vessels told to great effect.

Some larger craft had their oars swept away by the handier Egyptian boats, but even when elements of Demetrius' front line were incapacitated there was the second line in support to plug the gaps. It was a desperate affray in this part of the battle, many a boarder slipped and fell into the sea to drown as they tried to cross the rails onto an enemy vessel, and, at close quarters, the ballistae created mayhem with their heavy bolts delivered into the massed ranks of marines on the open decks. Demetrius, himself, was constantly in danger. His flagship, a seven, was naturally the target of attack by a number of enemy ships. Ptolemaic marines boarded his ship in such numbers as to put his life at risk, members of his bodyguard were cut down and he needed all his courage and skill to defend himself. Eventually, with his gilded body armour battered and dented by the ferocity of the blows aimed against him, Demetrius beat off the attackers and regained control of his flagship. Able to look around at the larger picture he saw the powerful left wing squadron he had led into battle had completely routed the enemy ships opposed to them. Ptolemaic craft around him were either sinking or being brought under control by his own men, while the bulk of his ships on this flank were intact and in good condition.

In the centre of the battle, an indecisive contest was in progress. Demetrius' commander in that sector was Marsyas, the historian and half-brother of Antigonus. He and his Samian colleagues had been handling their triremes with great skill. The enemy had heavier ships but had failed to take advantage of the edge their fours gave them when the two lines clashed. Nothing is known about this contest except that it was still undecided when Demetrius was able to intervene. The signal was given from Demetrius' flagship and his victorious captains turned their vessels inwards towards the coast and fell on the flank and rear of the centre of Ptolemy's fleet. The effect was immediate, with the awful threat of being driven onto the shore, the Lagid line crumbled and their will to resist failed in the crisis.

This was the scene of disaster that faced Ptolemy when he collected the ships of his squadron who though they had won the fight on their front had allowed the main conflict to be decided without them. Taking what seemed the only course open, Ptolemy gave the order to withdraw and save what was left of the fleet.

Demetrius had pulled off a brilliant victory, but it had been a very different affair from those achieved by the fleets outfitted by Athens over a hundred years before. Then, sleek triremes manned by skilled crews had been able to achieve victory by dexterous seamanship. But, at this Salamis, it had been different. Here there is no suggestion of the *diekplous* manoeuvre

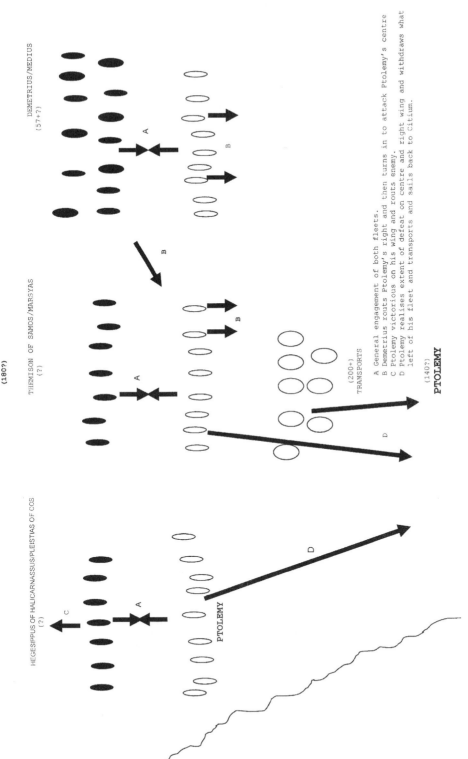

HEGESIPPUS OF HALICARNASSUS/PLEISTIAS OF COS
(?)

THEMISON OF SAMOS/MARSYAS
(?)

DEMETRIUS/MEDIUS
(57+?)

(180?)

(200+)
TRANSPORTS

(140?)

PTOLEMY

A General engagement of both fleets.
B Demetrius routs Ptolemy's right and then turns in to attack Ptolemy's centre
C Ptolemy victorious on his wing and routs enemy.
D Ptolemy realises extent of defeat on centre and right wing and withdraws what
  left of his fleet and transports and sails back to Citium.

Battle of Salamis, 306 BC.

with a line of boats ahead cutting through the enemy line to come up on their quarter. Nor the *periplous* where practiced crews would bring their boats around the end of the opposing line to attack the flank of the opponent. It has been suggested that Demetrius pulled off a form of *periplous* at Salamis but this seems very doubtful.[18] His captains did not manouevre round and attack the enemy flank; instead they used brute force to crush the enemy wing in front of them, which then allowed them to fall on the flank of Ptolemy's centre.

But whatever we call the tactical techniques used by the Antigonid seamen, the victory at Salamis was notable for the innovative use of the long-range weaponry that the new bigger galleys could carry. These catapults caused mayhem, even before the ships closed, when the archers and javelin men could then join in on a devastating barrage. The superships of Demetrius' fleet, his sevens and sixes had decided the day, not only because the larger vessels enabled much more effective missile fire but they were also able to carry far more marines equipped to fight hand-to-hand. Of course, they also gained advantage by boarding from their higher-sided craft. But, if these advantages counted for much, Demetrius had also been lucky. Apart from having a more powerful fleet qualitatively, with his sixes and sevens as opposed to Ptolemy's fours and fives, his men had been able to rest and await Ptolemy's navy who had been tired by the exertions of rowing through at least part of the night just in order to reach the battle.

In Salamis' harbour, another battle had taken place on the same day. Menelaus had striven hard to obey his brother's injunction to bring his ships into the battle but his captains had found their egress to the open sea blocked by the ten battleships Demetrius had left to counter just this eventuality. A stern fight took place at the harbour mouth with Antisthenes, Demetrius' admiral, holding his fives together against the onslaught of six times their number. This resistance could not last indefinitely as even in this confined space the ability of Menelaus' captains to replace damaged vessels and use relays of fresh marines to make their attacks meant their opponent's capacity to resist was gradually worn down. Eventually the defensive cordon was breached; the Antigonids found their position untenable and were forced to flee to the safety of the main camp of the army. Even so, their efforts had been sufficient to keep the sixty warships of the Salamis squadron out of the major battle and when Menelaus' admiral, Menoetius, eventually arrived on the scene Ptolemy's fleet was already defeated and in flight.

The flotilla returned to Salamis with the news and Menelaus realized, though his ships had won a victory, the war was lost. His position in Cyprus was impossible now that the Egyptian navy could be discounted as a factor of any significance. What allies he had left on the island were bound to transfer allegiance to Demetrius and, deprived of supplies from outside, he could neither pay nor feed the considerable army that was trapped in the city. The sources again differ but well over 10,000 foot and horse were incorporated into the Antigonid army when Salamis surrendered and Menelaus withdrew to Alexandria with what small part of his army he could pile onto the remaining boats, reflecting on the battered hopes of Ptolemaic ambition in the Cypriot seas.

For Ptolemy the day had been an unmitigated disaster. He had committed all his military resources and had lost. Diodorus reports that Ptolemy had lost over 100 of his supply ships with over 8,000 soldiers on board captured. This must have been particularly galling as these men had not even been able to participate in the battle before all had been lost. As for his actual war fleet, forty galleys were captured and a further eighty disabled and towed into Salamis harbour, leaving the Lagid only twenty to flee with. Plutarch recounts that his losses were even greater with only eight warships left to him. To compound Ptolemy's discomfort, Plutarch goes on to say that the vessels carrying his treasure, personal furniture and mistress had also been captured.[19] Demetrius' losses were minimal, twenty of his ships were disabled but all subsequently recommissioned.

Cyprus was lost and Ptolemy was left with not much more than he had when he first arrived in Egypt. He had beaten the youth Demetrius at Gaza but the man had turned the tables. If the defeated looked to saving what they could, the victors had thoughts on grander things. A charming story told by Plutarch has it that Antigonus was waiting for news of the naval battle when it was heard that his old and trusted agent Aristodemus of Miletus was approaching. The old marshal was in his palace in a ferment of anxiety over the fortunes of his son and fleet. Aristodemus had come by swift trireme from Salamis to ensure he was first with news of victory and intended to milk the occasion for all it was worth in the expectation that his commander's relief would be matched by the generosity of the messenger's reward. He refused to tell those who came to meet him what he knew and made his way from the boat to the palace on ageing legs and in so doing caused his master an agony of frustration. The potentate became so agitated that he rushed to meet him at the door where, at last, he was released from his ordeal by the tidings of his son's victory. His joy, though, did not prevent him exacting a small revenge on the self-important old retainer who was informed that as he had delayed in getting his message to Antigonus, likewise would his reward be delayed.

Antigonus had good reason to worry, Demetrius had been commanding the cream of the navy he had spent so long creating and one battle, or even a freak storm, could have ruined that endeavour overnight. His anxiety would have been great when news had come that Ptolemy was coming in full force to face his son. Like Xerxes, at the other Salamis over 150 years earlier, he could only sit and wait, but, unlike the Persian, he was unable to observe the combat firsthand. At times, he must have regretted the decision not to command the fleet himself but even he, at the age of 75, probably balked at starting a new career on an unfamiliar element.

After this second Salamis there was no real rival able to contest the seaways with the Antigonids. Not till near the end of the first generation of *Diadochi* would this thalassocracy be disputed. But sea power was never quite absolute. Ancient galleys were just not as robust as later sailing ships; they did not last as long. Large numbers of oarsmen could not be kept permanently mobilized and paid. The hardware, itself, was fragile; the boats would not stay seaworthy for long if not very well looked after. They had to be hauled out of water as much as possible to keep them dry, light and fast and free from worm, rot and seaweed. They were also kept in ship sheds, if possible, out of the sailing season which in the Mediterranean usually only lasted from April till November. When peace arrived, the motivation to maintain and repair fell away. Certainly Athens and Carthage famously had military ports well-equipped to keep their fleets in a state of high preparedness, but in neither case did these preparations eventually ensure against the demise of their maritime supremacy.

And, in the later years of the *Diadochi*, if the Antigonids were the great sea power they were not the only ones. Rhodes, puny in comparison, still remained significant enough to irritate the pirates of the region. The policing role they efficiently undertook (we do not hear of either the Antigonids or the Lagids undertaking this), meant the freebooters were happy to join Demetrius when he attacked that city in 304 BC. Ptolemy still had some ships that had survived the debacle of Salamis and his senior maritime officers would nurture this remnant until changing fortunes allowed it to become the core around which later expansion would occur.

We know nothing of Lysimachus's naval resources; certainly in the 313 BC campaign, when Antigonus sent a squadron to help his enemies, there is no indication Lysimachus had any ships to oppose it. This might seem surprising as the Greek cities of the Black Sea coast and the Thracian Chersonese would probably have had something in the way of navies, we certainly know Heraclea had some ships at her disposal. But, surely, he could either not get them to fight in any numbers for him or they were not first-rate forces that could stand up in battle against the fleets deployed by the foremost dynasts.[20] After Ipsus, Demetrius could raid Lysimachus' coastline with impunity, even putting his new capital of Lysimacheia at risk, indicating that the Thracian ruler's naval means were very slim indeed. His only hope was that Ptolemy might show up to help but that pragmatic ruler was not about to risk what was left of his navy to help a distant ally whose interests might not always match his own.[21]

All Lysimachus could do was wait until Demetrius had vented his bile, as, despite the disaster at Ipsus, he was still unstoppable at sea. Indeed only when Demetrius' adventures completely ended deep in Asia in 286/285 BC did Lysimachus even begin to gain a navy. Some of the fleet Demetrius left at Miletus went over to him when his men entered the city and forced the Antigonid admirals to sign up with one or other of the remaining sovereigns who could offer them employment. How many ships came over to him we don't know (some went to Pyrrhus) and no details of any activity are left to us before Lysimachus exited the stage at the Battle of Corupedium in 281 BC.[22] After his demise his fleet ended up in the hands of Ptolemy Ceraunus, where ironically it was used victoriously against Demetrius' son, Antigonus Gonatus, in 280 BC.

Cassander never was a major naval player. He could mobilize fleets on occasions; invading Salamis near Athens in the time of Polyperchon, he put up a fight against Medius, and when he campaigned in the Adriatic against the Illyrians and islanders from Leucas and Corfu he must have had ships. But, it is unlikely that they were numerous or very powerful and after 312 BC there is no record of any naval adventures begun by the ruler at Pella.

Seleucus, after his stint as a maritime functionary in Ptolemy's pay, never took to the waves again as far as we know. He certainly had his window on the sea, port towns near Antioch where he must have deployed some ships, but we hear of nothing and it is doubtful they were much more than coastguard vessels. Certainly, when Demetrius entertained him on his great thirteener during the negotiations over Seleucus' marriage to his daughter, Seleucus did not reciprocate with meetings on an equivalent vessel of his own.

In the end, it was the two who had fought at the great set-piece at Salamis that were always the major contenders: the Antigonids on the up when father and son put huge resources into their shipbuilding programmes; Ptolemy, able to hold his own until the disaster at Cyprus made this no longer a credible strategy, then recovering over the decades as the Antigonids fell gradually from the pinnacles they had climbed.

However, the future of naval dominance after all the old men had died was to be a fragmented one. No power completely ruled the east Mediterranean waves in the generation after the *Diadochi* in the way the Antigonids had done. The Lagids were still sufficiently powerful in the 270s BC that they could attack Antiochus I in Asia Minor. The Seleucids, the Macedonian Antigonids, the Rhodians and the kingdom of Pergamum all would send out fleets and fight set-piece battles. But, in general, the effect was a sort of balance; it might even be claimed that as they fought each other to a standstill, they allowed Rome to intrude in a way that would eventually ensure the eclipse of them all. Rome, bloodily apprenticed at sea against the

Carthaginians, and in 190 BC they fought the Seleucids at Myonessus, in tandem with the Rhodians. A new force was arriving that would change everything.

The ever-practical Romans did not follow the Hellenes down a road of naval gigantism though the powers around the east Mediterranean continued with super ships. Ptolemy IV even built a forty, a monster apparently over 400 feet long and requiring 4,000 oarsmen, and there are reports of ships with libraries in them, though almost certainly none of these were meant for use in battle. The Romans utilized triremes and quinqueremes as the mainstay of their fleets though they also used fours and occasionally a six, and at the Battle of Actium in 31 BC Mark Antony even kept his flag on a ten. But, they did not just downsize their ships of the line; they found a way to transfer their strength in terrestrial fighting skills to the sea. Not for them the subtle manoeuvres of the *diekplous* or the *periplous*, instead they introduced the *corvus*, a hinged boarding platform attached to the bow of the ship which they could drop onto an enemy deck. Fighting a land-style war on the waves, they changed combat at sea as they changed so much else in the centuries after Alexander's death.

Chapter Nine

Border Wars

Apart from the giant tussling that shaped the world of Hellenistic kings, there were also smaller dramas played out; smaller but none the less interesting for that. As with much concerning the *Diadochi,* what we have to go on is of mixed quality. Inevitably, the centrist bias of our root sources is pretty profound but there are conflicts on the edges where we find a considerable amount on the record. None get the attention or have their details passed down in the way the great Antigonus-Eumenes battles or some of Demetrius' campaigns do, yet still there is plenty of interest. Also, impinging as these events do on folk of the wider world, it is often different and introduces peoples who are not encountered in the main story. North, west, east and south of the Successor realms we are told about border wars where the dynasts faced very different problems from the ones they were used to when warring with each other. And what is also apparent in these encounters is how often they came up short.

All of the *Diadochi* had their encounters with peoples of the periphery, whether it was Seleucus with Indians from the Punjab and steppe tribes of central Asia, Ptolemy in Cyrenaica with Greek settlers or indigenous Libyan tribesmen, or Cassander who spent much of his efforts shoring up his Illyrian, Epirote and Arcananian marches. Then there was Lysimachus, who had to fight for the right to survive, against first the indigenous kings of Thrace and then the Getae and Scythians who frequently threatened his borders. Even Antigonus and Demetrius involved themselves in campaigns against the Nabataean Arabs and the peoples round the Dead Sea that are quite well documented.[1]

The earliest of these conflicts occurred in an area well known to the Classical world but involving some peoples who were regarded as the most uncivilized of the neighbours of the Hellenistic states, events taking place in some tough terrain where warriors from as far afield as Carthage would, on occasions, feel they had an interest.

Ptolemy, who was the man involved, did nothing to instigate what developed in his very dusty backyard, but when others had brewed the stew he showed he was not averse to expanding the frontiers of his new satrapy. The direction his interest was drawn was westwards towards Cyrene, almost halfway to Carthage, 500 miles west of the delta where the desert coast begins to turn south and a fist of land was fertile between the highlands and the sea. In 631 BC, the city of Cyrene itself had been founded by settlers from the Aegean island of Thera, driven by drought from their homeland. Many who came later were Peloponnesians, people tough and warlike enough to beat off at least one invasion from Egypt in 570 BC. They lived well, growing grain and rearing sheep and horses, but internal tension between the colonists was enough to ensure that groups soon left to found other communities, like Barca, which was inland and 60 miles further west.

The independent communities in this region had not been conquered by Alexander (though they had certainly accepted his tutelage and perhaps paid a tribute) and before Ptolemy's arrival as their neighbour, no salutary foreign oppression had suppressed those tendencies to communal squabbling they had brought with them from mainland Greece. The years before Ptolemy came to Egypt had been particularly riven with internal strife, a situation aggravated by the arrival of a rootless warlord eager to profit from the political vacuum attendant on Alexander's death.

Thibron was a Spartan mercenary captain, who had accompanied the dishonest treasurer Harpalus when he fled from Alexander to Athens in 324 BC. After they had been refused entry there, these fugitives took themselves, and the 5,000 veteran mercenaries they had picked up in Asia, on to Crete via the Peloponnese. During their stay on the island, Thibron and his brother officers decided that Harpalus was an albatross around their necks. He would never be forgiven by Alexander, whom he had cheated twice over, and nobody was likely to befriend them for fear of reprisals from the man who effectively ruled the world. Harpalus was assassinated by the very men he had hired to protect him, while the ruthless Spartan took control of both the army, now totalling 7,000 men, and the remaining fortune of his victim.

Amongst the army on Crete were a number of Cyrenean exiles who persuaded their comrades that their old homeland on the North African coast would be an ideal spot for this rootless band to establish themselves. In 324/323 BC, these freebooters landed on the coast near Cyrene city and, guided by local men, approached the place. The citizen soldiers (presumably hoplites bearing *aspis* and spear but also including war chariots, the use of which they must have learned from the local Libyan tribes) proved no match for Thibron's men and the Cyrenean army was defeated outside the walls. Many were cut down or made prisoner but the rump managed to get back and man the defences before their enemy could enter the town gates. In the scramble, control of the harbour was lost. Cut off from the sea and badly shaken by defeat, the city fathers were quickly forced to come to terms and pay off these pirates.

It cost the Cyreneans dear to ransom a temporary security: 500 talents and half the chariots they possessed were promised, but, for the moment, their tormentors left and Thibron led his mercenaries, as a sort of mobile protection racket, in a tour of the other major towns in the region. This descent on Africa brought some considerable profits but then the newcomers fell out over the division of spoils and one of Thibron's Cretan officers, called Mnasicles, deserted the ranks. He returned to Cyrene city and stirred up the citizens against his old commander. A call to arms against the men who had recently humiliated them touched an eager chord amongst the Cyreneans, especially as the ransom had only been partly paid; 440 talents were still due, and reneging on the agreement meant the townsfolk could keep what was still owed.

A considerable war developed between Thibron, his friends at Barca and Hesperis on one side (they were eager to support any enemy of their local rival) and on the other the Cyreneans, Libyan tribesmen and even Carthaginian elements who they had called to their assistance. Thibron hoped that the professional experience of his hard core of mercenaries would quickly win the war for him. He first marched back to the port of Cyrene to establish his headquarters from where he could sort out these treacherous backsliders. Then he moved to besiege the city itself. But he could not encircle the place before the Cyreneans sent out a considerable force to ravage the lands of Barca and Hesperis. The mercenary general responded and marched off to save his new friends but in so doing left the port undefended, so Mnasicles was able to lead the garrison in Cyrene city against it and recaptured the harbour. The Cretan was making himself popular in the city as his enterprise meant the citizens retrieved the goods which had been thought to be lost when it was captured.

After a small crisis of confidence, the hard man Thibron recovered his nerve and went back on the offensive. He besieged and took a city called Tauchira, a community something under 100 miles west down the coast from Cyrene and presumably their ally. But he was far from having it all his own way; because he had lost his port facilities at Cyrene, his fleet had had to be beached on the open strand. Then the crews, who could not get food from their stores, went off to forage and were ambushed by Libyans. More than this, those who escaped capture departed in their ships but were caught in a storm that either sank them or left them high and dry on shores as far apart as Cyprus and Egypt.

Thibron sent back to the Peloponnese for more mercenaries. There his recruiting sergeants found many who had heard what good pickings were to be had in North Africa. Approximately 2,500 unemployed soldiers were picked up but before these reinforcements had arrived the Cyreneans had acted. They had trounced the men Thibron had with him and driven them away from the city. But the newcomers were eager and their enthusiasm reinvigorated the dispirited gangsters they found when they arrived. Thibron determined to renew the campaign against targets whose riches made them still very tempting.

With his reinforced army, Thibron again approached Cyrene city to find his enemies had not been idle during the meantime, but had recruited allies and mercenaries from the local Libyans and from Carthage. A huge battle was fought outside the walls with 30,000 claimed on the Cyrenean side, but they were not enough and Thibron's men cut through the enemy's massed ranks, dispersed them all and set about besieging both the port and the city itself. Mnasicles still had the citizens' confidence and he and some others were swiftly elected to replace the generals who had died in the battle. Up to this point, the Cyrenean war had been a local affair but events were now to involve the wider world. The struggle with Thibron had exacerbated stress in Cyrene's social fabric and this, intensified by the shortage of food due to the siege, meant a coup occurred that deprived the wealthy citizens of the control they previously exercised. Many of these opulent Cyreneans slipped out of the city, fearing their lives as well as their political power and property might be at risk. Some found refuge with Thibron while others made a longer journey into exile in Egypt where they implored their powerful neighbour to intervene.

These events found Ptolemy well established in his new satrapy and also very flush having taken 8,000 talents from his deputy, Cleomenes, who he had just eliminated. He was not currently threatened by any rivals, all of whom had plenty to do in establishing themselves in their several domains. No one else had much of an interest in these western regions, so, if he could overcome the local factions he could expect to enjoy exploitation of the area uncontested. A force was sent west under Ophellas, a Macedonian general, who the future would show harboured unchecked ambitions of his own.

Alarmed as news filtered in that Ophellas was fast marching down to Cyrene, Thibron raised his siege, sent in ambassadors and made common cause with the 'democratic' leadership of Cyrene. This rapprochement was facilitated when the mercenary general murdered all the Cyrenean exiles in his camp, who represented the only substantial domestic opposition still in the area. Those now in power at Cyrene understood Egyptian interference represented a threat far more fundamental than that posed by Thibron's followers. There would be little room for mercy if the oligarchs who came in the train of the Egyptian army regained control of their city. The popular government had already shown it was capable of mobilizing considerable forces, but Ophellas also had a powerful army and, perhaps, now some who had sent aid before were reluctant to be seen to be opposing the powerful ruler of Egypt. Whatever, Ophellas overthrew Thibron's mercenaries and local allies with some ease. The Spartan adventurer was captured and crucified while Cyrene and the other towns were taken or came to terms.

After his general's success, Ptolemy made the long journey west in person. And, when he got there, what is significant is that his handling of Cyrenean affairs showed great sensitivity to world opinion. The cities he had conquered had long been independent and overtly advertising their subjection would dent his reputation in Greece where he sought to make friends. The public relations conundrum was overcome with some panache by Ptolemy's (still extant) new constitution.[2] At first glance it seems an unexceptional *polis* form of government with citizen bodies, councils of elders and some election by lot. In the shattered and unpredictable world at the turn of 322/321 BC it was well worth an appearance of appeasing the sensibilities of potential allies. However, the Lagid reserved certain vital functions for himself. He was to be permanent *strategos*, control the election of elders and whether exiles should be re-admitted to the citizen body. And, crucially, though there is no mention in the constitution, Ophellas was left with a garrison to ensure Ptolemaic rule.

Ptolemy's interfering on his western march was never central to his foreign policy, indeed, in some senses, it caused him more trouble than it was worth, involving him in both the stress of an ambitious viceroy intriguing, and it rubbed him up against the interests of the great city of Carthage. But, for Cassander, his marcher lands were far more central to his thinking. For the man at Pella, his relations with Illyrians, Epirotes and Acarnanians were central to the direction of his whole political strategy.

In the years since Cassander grasped the reins of power in Philip and Alexander's old kingdom, activity to the south and east had been incessant. Often his involvement there had been a forced policy, proactive in response to the conduct of his mighty rivals. But, while his efforts had been largely directed to building security on the shifting sands of Peloponnesian, Euboean and Boeotian politics (which had been far from universally successful), survival and retention had been the keynote, not expansion and construction. The Aegean and Mediterranean fronts were fraught with danger but in another direction Cassander had seen opportunity beckon. To the west, along the Ionian littoral, Macedonia's neighbours were, by and large, weak, culturally 'backward' and politically divided.

The coast that looked across the straits of Otranto to the heel of the Italian peninsular made a harsh rampart with few of the easy entrances or the tolerable hinterlands of the Aegean flank of Greece. The islands that lie off this coast, though, are large and by nature destined as important staging posts of trade and power. Most notably Corfu (Corcyra), though now a holiday playground, had been, in a past that was recent to Cassander's contemporaries, the spark that ignited the Peloponnesian War in 431 BC. The main interruption in this stern coastline was the bay of Ambracia (better known by its Roman name, Actium) directly across from the Malian Gulf on the eastern side, indenting like a belt pulled in tight around the waist of central Greece. A natural base with a small but fertile hinterland, this place would have its greatest day in history when Agrippa won the Roman Empire for his seasick commander in 31 BC. The Gulf marked the northern frontier of the Acarnanians who, in 314 BC, Cassander had visited to organize resistance against Aetolia. With these people firm allies, he was able to intervene further in the west. He ferried his army over to Leucas, the large island that flanked the coast of Acarnania. The islanders had little option but to join the cause of the powerful intruder. Directly north of the Gulf of Actium lay Epirus and there, since the war with Olympias (when Aeacides, her cousin, was deposed) a faction favourable to Cassander had been in power. Further up were the lands of the Illyrians, historic enemies of the Macedonians. Along the coastline, where geography had allowed, the Greeks had planted cities but this was only a thin crust over a 'barbarian' interior where tribal kings tolerated the benefits this presence brought. It was towards these towns that the Macedonians now sailed on a fleet quickly recruited from Cassander's allies.

Apollonia had been originally founded by the Corinthians and it had prospered on commerce with the Illyrian hinterland and from its position on the trade route into the Adriatic. The citizenry were ill-prepared for the sudden arrival of a Macedonian warlord and the city, whose defences were more geared to repel Illyrian raids than an attack by a modern Hellenistic army, fell at the first assault. Cassander pressed on eastwards into the heart of Illyria, along the route the Via Egnatia would follow in Roman times. The king in this part of the country was Glaucias, who had had a rough experience of Macedonian arms two decades before, when he had been part of the Illyrian coalition that a young Alexander had routed in preparation for the invasion of Asia. Time had not dimmed his belligerence and he mobilized his army to face this new intruder. The Illyrian reaction shows that, since the death of Antipater, internecine Macedonian strife had allowed an assertion of independence that had been largely suppressed in the days of Philip and Alexander.

Glaucias fielded numerous skirmishers, javelineers, slingers and bowmen as well as the spear-and-shield-bearing core of the national army. But none of these wore anything but the lightest armour and even the nobles would have sported only a helmet and fought as javelin-armed light cavalry. This essentially-tribal agglomeration of warriors was sufficiently organized for the raiding parties that were their normal tool of aggression both on land

and sea, but were incapable of the steady and disciplined fighting that characterized the Hellenic army they now had to face. The outcome was the same as almost every contest between Illyrians and Macedonians since the defeat and death of Perdiccas III in 359 BC, with Glaucias beaten and forced to come to terms with Cassander.

Aspects of this agreement throw light on Cassander's long term policy in the west, 'he made a treaty with the king according to which Glaucias was not to wage war on Cassander's allies', a clause that primarily concerned Epirus.[3] Though Neoptolemus II was on the throne (initially under the tutelage of Cassander's general Lyciscus) the situation was by no means stable.[4] The deposed Aeacides still had substantial support, but if his faction was to have any chance of success it would be to Illyria they would look for aid. Glaucias had already shown a preparedness to become involved when he gave refuge to the infant Pyrrhus, Aeacides' son; and it was against just this that Cassander hoped to insure. Binding oaths were not all the Macedonian ruler utilized in his campaign to curb the Illyrian threat. He garrisoned Epidamnus (another Greek city on the coast) as he had Apollonia before.[5] From the straits of Otranto to the Gulf of Corinth, Cassander had planted strongholds or ensured his friends were in power and as he marched east to Pella at the end of the campaigning season of 314 BC, he reasserted Macedonian control of the direct land route from Pella to the Adriatic.

If the Antigonids frustrated Cassander's ambitions to the east, on the western march distance and terrain was almost as great a hindrance. Macedonian viceroys might prop up the governments of his friends in Acarnania and Epirus and isolated garrisons occupy key stations, but limited means dogged efforts to defend what had been achieved. In the very next year, a minor power was able to make a great dent in Macedonia's western wall. The rulers of Corfu had deeply resented the intrusion of a new power into their backyard. They had previously sustained a local prominence that, though occasionally threatened by Greek or Italian navies, had been durable. King Glaucias was contacted to isolate Cassander's Illyrian garrisons from the landward side while forces from Corfu landed from the sea. At both Apollonia and Epidamnus the Macedonian garrisons were ejected.

If this erosion of his power was galling enough for Cassander, it was not the greatest threat his western policy was subject to in 313 BC. Epirus, the keystone of the regional alliances, wobbled in its Macedonian allegiance. The context of these events was that Ptolemaeus, Antigonus' nephew, was rampant in Euboea and Macedonia was under threat from a direct invasion by Antigonus. Able to give little personal attention to events in the west, Cassander at least had good fortune in his lieutenant on the spot. The histories of these Macedonian potentates were very much family affairs. It was from the extended family that dependable senior officers were drawn, that counsel was taken and wholehearted support expected. Alexander's generals were establishing dynasties long before they took on the diadem of monarchy. They might wrap themselves in the ideological trappings of the sophisticated politics of the Greek cities but at heart they remained familial heads whose trust and ambition rested in sons, daughters, close relatives and established retainers. Antigonus had his talented sons and nephews, Lysimachus and Seleucus became dependent on their sons while Cassander, though he gave independent commands to talented supporters on a number of occasions, relied on his brothers to share the responsibilities of campaigning.[6]

One of these siblings was called Philip and had served in Asia as a royal page (Justin claims him as an accomplice in the king's poisoning). He is interesting not just for his activities in 313 BC but for the fact that his son, Antipater, ended up as king of Macedonia for forty-five days in 279 BC, immediately after the last of the Successors had perished. Philip had been given a command against the Aetolians whose antipathy to the Macedonians had only been fuelled by the arrival of Ptolemaeus and his formidable force. Philip had not been granted many troops by Cassander and it was expected that the Acarnanians would help remedy the shortfall; a test of the solidity of the alliance that Cassander had so recently forged. They were instructed to march out from their new cities and join Philip in the push east against Aetolia. However, news from Epirus forestalled these plans. Aeacides had returned to try and reclaim his throne. It is not clear where he had been during his exile but it is known that he had linked up with Polyperchon when they were both at their lowest ebb and had sought refuge in Aetolia. It is probable that he remained there fighting with his hosts and planning his eventual return. Years of border warfare would have bound adventurous Aetolians to him to supplement his loyal band of Epirote retainers. With these followers, he entered Epirus where time had been a great healer of his reputation.

Large numbers of Epirotes flocked to his standard eager to oust their pro-Macedonian rulers. Prospects seemed extremely favourable, as also an army from Aetolia was on its way to support their protégé. Aid given in the calculation that an alliance between Aetolia and Epirus would be sufficient to defeat Cassander; an objective neither could hope to achieve independently. Philip was well aware of this danger and forced-marched north to catch Aeacides before the full Aetolian army could reinforce him. In this, he succeeded and in the battle that followed he defeated Aeacides who fled with as many of his men as he could rally. He was able to fall back on the Aetolian forces which had arrived just in time to see their candidate lose. Philip, showing energy and enterprise, allowed Aeacides no respite and attacked the Aetolians' position almost immediately. In open battle, the

Macedonians again showed their marked superiority and Philip won his second victory where Aeacides perished. Whatever judgements might be made about the political and military abilities of this member of the Molossian line, there was no doubting his valour and spirit; qualities his son, Pyrrhus, would inherit in full measure.

Philip was not content to rest on his laurels but pushed on in pursuit, driving the enemy back into Aetolia itself. He was now in a position to fulfil his original aim of invading Aetolia. The inhabitants, shaken by their recent reverses, had reverted to their traditional tactics to which their mountainous country and unsettled life was so suited. They fled (as they had before Craterus in 321 BC) from their undefended villages and hid with families and flocks in inaccessible mountain caves and forest retreats while Philip wreaked havoc and destruction on the rest of the countryside before the end of the campaigning season forced his retreat. What is puzzling is that after this outstanding campaign Philip is never heard of again. The usual speculation is that Cassander had him killed as Philip's successes aroused his jealousy, like Nicanor before him. Yet Cassander, in his present precarious position, needed all the capable commanders he could muster and the demise of Philip almost certainly has a more prosaic explanation. Whatever happened to him, he had done his brother a fine service in an otherwise bleak year.

Success in Epirus seemed inevitably ephemeral. While an active Macedonian ruler was too powerful to enable a hostile dynasty to take hold of the Molossian throne, the corollary was that an Epirote monarch who was too pliant to the administration in Pella could expect local resistance around an anti-Macedonian theme. The government that Philip had saved from Aeacides now felt the iron grip of this imperative. Far from being able to take advantage of his death, they contrived to lose control to Aeacides' elder brother, Alcetas. This man had been exiled years earlier by his father for his uncontrollable temper and events were to show that the father knew the son for Alcetas appears to have been mentally unbalanced. His psychological state did not concern Cassander but the fact that he shared his dead brother's hatred of Macedon certainly did. It looked like Philip's impressive military achievements of the previous year would be in vain.

Lyciscus, the ex-viceroy of Epirus, had since been acting for Cassander in Acarnania but now he was ordered to return. Marching rapidly with his own army and Arcananian allies he reached Cassopia in southern Epirus and set up his headquarters. From there, he encouraged the opponents of Alcetas, offering a refuge and rallying point. The new Epirote monarch immediately responded with all the armed might at his disposal. The royal guards and household troops were alerted and led out on the road to Cassopia, while Alcetas' two sons were left behind to call out the national levy. This precipitate and risky offensive with a skeleton force was typical of the mercurial and unstable nature of the man but there was also policy in it. He felt himself strong enough, if not to overwhelm Lyciscus, at least to bottle him up until the arrival of reinforcements gave him decisive numerical superiority. In this he may have been right had it not been for the temper of his troops. Their monarch's aberrant cruelty during his short reign had already alienated the loyalty of many of his men and when he neared Cassopia the army suffered wholesale desertion. Humiliated, Alcetas could only flee to find refuge in the mountains. Lyciscus followed up and trapped his quarry in the lakeside city of Eurymenae and began a siege. But the tables turned when the Macedonians heard the Epirote levy led by the king's sons was nearby. A bloody battle followed, the siege was raised and Alcetas from a fugitive became again a force to be reckoned with at the head of a victorious army. However, these combatants were tenacious characters and Lyciscus, though beaten off, only paused to send for reinforcements before returning to the fray and eventually managed to drive the king, his sons and the battered Epirote army out of Eurymenae and deeper into the mountains.

Cassander, on hearing of Lyciscus' initial defeat, intervened personally, leading the rest of the Macedonian army into this troublesome state but he soon became aware that his general had turned the situation around. Assessing at first hand, Cassander felt that the time and effort required to subdue Epirus would not be well-spent and decided to come to terms. The army was needed elsewhere and Cassander calculated that Alcetas would cause so many internal problems that he would pose no real threat to Macedonia.

Cassander now turned his attention to Illyria again but he seems to have been unusually lacklustre at this time, having even less luck than he had enjoyed against the Epirotes. Indeed, he suffered the indignity of being driven off by the citizens of Apollonia, after hard fighting, and, with winter drawing on, was forced to withdraw to Macedonia. His army was patently neither strong nor numerous enough, indicative of the severe manpower shortage he was suffering. The final insult came when he was safely back at home and heard that his garrison on the island of Leucas had also been evicted by the Corcyraeans who had taken advantage of a local insurrection to prise out the Macedonian interlopers.

In two years, the son of Antipater had seen the edifice he had constructed so painstakingly on this flank of his kingdom crumble in front of his eyes. His western policy was in tatters; Ptolemaeus and his Aetolian and Boeotian allies were rampant in central Greece. So, when peace proposals arrived from Antigonus in 311 BC, Cassander grabbed at them with both hands. The years after the peace of 311 BC did not see any major campaigns on Cassander's western quarter. Epirus seemed quiet, he never tried to involve himself in the Adriatic islands again and the Illyrians are not mentioned apart from one of their tribes, the Autariatae. Cassander apparently resettled them after a dispute with the Paeonians; an act not repaid with any great loyalty, as nine years later they deserted to the Antigonid side at the Battle of Ipsus! There are also elusive hints in our sources about a Celtic raiding party he had to rebuff near the Haemus mountains; a harbinger of things to come after he was long dead.[7] But, for the main part, Cassander had plenty on his plate dealing with the Antigonids on his doorstep and he did not live long enough after Ipsus (he died in 297 BC) to push any ambitions he might have had over his barbarian borders. Even though this kind of involvement would for Macedonian rulers, both before and after him, be just as much of a historic imperative as any need to interfere in mainland Greece itself.

Cassander's long term foes, the Antigonids, were the archetypal central power of the post-Alexandrine world. Their capital of Antigonia sat on the fulcrum where the Levant hinged with Anatolia and their concerns were centred on the east Mediterranean. And, though they might head east (to campaign first against Eumenes and then to Babylonia when Seleucus took back his old realm), the coastline from Abydos to Gaza, which enclosed the seaward side of the regions, was where their real interests lay. Yet, even they, on one well attested occasion, found themselves involved in a fight on the fringes where it seemed their great projects were not crucially involved.

In 311 BC, Antigonus had been determined not to lose time in rectifying the problems raised by Demetrius' defeat at the Battle of Gaza. His veteran army soon accomplished the recovery of his Levantine holdings and with Ptolemy refusing to face him in Phoenicia or Coele-Syria he prepared to follow into Egypt.[8] Before doing so, he chose to try to subdue the inhabitants of the nearby desert country. Alexander had cast greedy eyes on the apparently-forbidding peninsula of Arabia inhabited by these people and their like, but he had not been the first. The Egyptians, nearly 2,000 years before the Macedonian's birth, had taken copper and turquoise from the Arabians who lived near their borders. Assyrian armies had frequently campaigned against the oasis states of northern Arabia. The details of their conquests are vividly detailed on the self-aggrandizing sculpture made for their kings yet they never completely subdued them and Nineveh could not depend on controlling the spice trade that made the conquest of these desert wastes worthwhile. Two factors made the road tolls of this region one of the most lucrative sources of income in the ancient world. In what is now the Yemen, in the southwest of Arabia, great amounts of frankincense were grown. Here, a sedentary, civilized community utilized the benefits that nature had bestowed on that one corner of the arid peninsula to grow this most sought-after of balms. The caravans that took this treasure to the Mediterranean markets crossed the northern deserts and those who controlled these routes grew rich on the backs of the commerce. Nor was it just home-grown spices that came this way but also products from India and even further east. The enterprising inhabitants had controlled this sea borne trade for centuries and the exotic spices they unloaded at the quays of their ports followed the same route as the frankincense to the great markets of the west.

The nomads who had come to control the trade route southeast of the Dead Sea were known as the Nabataeans, who had migrated from the north in the early sixth century BC. At this time they were a loose federation of clans and had not yet settled at Petra, the amazing 'red rose' city that would be the royal seat of the Nabataean kings. The zenith of their fortunes was to be in the first century AD when their power stretched to Damascus, having received a portion of Seleucid territory in reward for being loyal clients of Rome. For them, the Nabataeans were a useful buffer against Parthia and a powerful military support in the region. In 70 AD they provided thousands of troops for Titus in the siege of Jerusalem. During this period the merchants and caravanners of Petra grew more and more prosperous through servicing the huge expanding market of the Roman Empire. Perhaps it was the very opulence of these merchant princes of the spice trade that caused their downfall when Trajan found them too attractive a prize to leave unconquered as he passed this way on his great eastern campaigns against the Parthians.

The ancestors of these rich middlemen lived on the desert flank of Antigonus' likely route if he wanted to march directly on Egypt and he probably felt it would be useful to neutralize them to protect the communications of an army of invasion. His solution to the problem of possible attack by mobile Arab raiders against his inland flank was bellicose from the start. A swift and awesome example of his power was intended to intimidate into submission these 'simple', mainly-pastoral people, who were thought to only number 10,000 altogether. Good intelligence meant he knew the date when the nomads met their sedentary brethren in a commercial fair at the great rock where Petra later stood. With them they would bring the herds and spice consignments on which their livelihood depended. Three days before the event began, Antigonus despatched a strong detachment under an officer, called Athenaeus, from his camp in Idumaea. They surprised the Arabs at midnight after a secret march and rounded up huge amounts of spice, silver, sheep, goats and camels as well as 500 talents of silver. But, in response, the Nabataeans gathered all available warriors to the number of 8,000.[9] They fell on the Antigonid raiders' camp while the men were asleep, killing all, either in their beds or with javelins as they struggled to get in battle order; fifty horsemen alone managed to extricate themselves and take back news of the disaster.

The attempt to eliminate the power of the Nabataeans had signally failed and only served to stir them up. They posted strong pickets against further inroads on the borders of this arid area, where any attempt to invade with a large body of men and animals was extremely difficult. But Antigonus was determined and prepared to wait till their guard had dropped. Disciplined observation proved impossible to sustain for a people who needed to keep on the move with their flocks and when the Macedonians thought the watchmen had withdrawn they prepared to act. Young Demetrius was sent, this time, with a mobile army of 4,000 cavalry and the same number of light infantry. He, too, tried to surprise the enemy, even providing iron rations so his men would not need to cook on the march, but they found their intended victims warned by signal fires and well-defended on the same great rock, now reinforced by man-made defences. All-out assaults failed and Antigonus' son was persuaded into treating with them, apparently by that old chestnut of emphasizing what little the Arabs had in comparison with the men who were trying to despoil them.

He left with forage and hostages, provided by the Arabs who had nothing to gain by a continuing conflict that disrupted crucial trade. The Antigonids made their return journey almost certainly by the same route from Petra that the later Roman road followed, directly north across the desert, reaching the Dead Sea after 34 miles. There, Demetrius camped and his officers made a detailed investigation of this rich and exotic region. Asphalt had been gathered for generations from the lake by local people who traded it in Egypt for use in embalming. The palms grown in the irrigated valleys nearby were also sold for great gain in the Levantine markets. These new sources of potential revenue were all that Demetrius could offer to compensate for the second failure against the independent desert tribes on his return to the headquarters in Idumaea.

Antigonus had wasted time, men had been lost and morale shaken. But, if much had gone wrong, he intended the whole campaign should not end without profit. The bitumen harvest of the Dead Sea in his control would mean not only personal gain but the bleeding of Egyptian wealth to the detriment of his rival. Hieronymus of Cardia, Eumenes' old confidant and future historian, was sent to organize the exploitation of this golden goose but found the task far from a lucrative sinecure. Local resistance emerged to the tune of 6,000 bowmen who shot down his followers and drove them off the lake; a third debacle that convinced Antigonus that his propensity for giving himself bloody noses in the Jordanian desert was unintelligent. His behaviour is in some ways difficult to understand, a hefty bribe would no doubt have brought round his 'barbarous' neighbours even after the first attack. The desire to control the spice routes explains much but there remains a suspicion that Antigonus miscalculated and, once committed, his prestige did not allow a withdrawal.

The equipment and organization of these people who gave the Antigonids such trouble is little detailed. Almost all Arab soldiers mentioned in ancient sources are described as missilemen, either javelineers or bowmen. Horses were apparently very rare amongst them and richer folk would have ridden camels, dismounting on most occasions to fight. However in 547 BC, the king of Lydia's highly-reputed cavalry had been upset by his Persian enemies fielding soldiers on camels, so it is clear fighting aboard the beasts had its advantages. The bow they used was described by Herodotus as long and, certainly, Hieronymus could vouch for its effectiveness from close, personal experience. The Antigonids found these skirmishers very difficult to combat on ground of their own choosing.

What is noticeable in so many of these small wars is the trouble the *Diadochi* could have with apparently puny, 'uncivilized' and poverty-stricken peoples. The fact was that on the great powers' borders there thrived communities who though thought backward were potent and indeed, in some senses, they were potent because they were 'backward'. No military specialization prevented instant mobilization, each man, and even, on occasions, woman, was a warrior and natural skill in unconventional warfare gave some 'Colonel Blimps' of the established powers much to make them scratch their heads when they confronted these folk in arms.

Chapter Ten

Conclusion

The years between 323 and 281 BC had been a time of civil war, not perhaps brother against brother, but, at least, cousin against cousin; the Macedonian nation had not been an entity long enough to make it the former. There were strangers involved in these family affairs, whether they were urban Greeks or men from the parts of Asia that the Macedonian Empire had absorbed, but they were, apart from one spectacular exception, not often at the very centre of things. In these kin-contests it was not unusual for the parties to look to compromise before coming to blows but such interaction was often fraught with suspicion, and when no common ground could be found ties were rent apart and gave the prospect of particularly-bloody carnage. This was a traumatic process that, with changeable contestants, ensured years of slaughter before there emerged the kind of dynastic polities that were able to rub up against each other in a more normal, less cataclysmic way.

There was little enough ideology in all this, only occasional genuflections in the direction of Greek city rights that were equally abused by all and equally used by each as a stick to beat the other when it suited. The only rationale for most was the age-old one of 'I am the rightful ruler here.' This was an eventual offspring of the understanding that the Macedonian world empire would not necessarily survive as an absolutely unitary entity. It took some years before we recognize any imperative towards regional particularism but this, in the long term, was arguably the crucial transmogrification that characterized our period. In the beginning, at Babylon, and in the years of the First Macedonian Civil War the participants were, barring odd exceptions, fighting to control a whole empire that Alexander would have recognized. Only after grinding years, where permanent warfare seemed to becoming institutionalized, did the leading men begin to adjust their thinking to new realities. They began to conceive of the unitary Macedonian Empire breaking down; an assessment that allowed the emergence of regional states in the territories that had been under Alexander's sway. And, these became for the ruling élites, the kings and generals, who tenanted them the very entities they went in to bat for. A plenum, a full range of threats meant these rulers evolved from squabbling underlings into principals, some of whom made such a success that their houses lasted for very respectable lengths of time and in the case of the Ptolemies made a claim to dynastic longevity that had seldom been seen before.

A recent historian memorably likens these Macedonian conquerors to the kind of mountain clan chieftains who followed Bonnie Prince Charlie in the '45 and imagines them setting up fiefdoms all over mainland Europe and even beyond.[1] This is an apt comparison that helps us keep in mind that these were men from the fringes with only a veneer of 'civilization', yet who made a real sea change in the world. In one sense, almost ending the Classical era which we are so familiar with, but also spreading the spirit of Greek civilization over half the known world. There had been deep influences before, Greek sailors had navigated the Indus for Darius and architects and craftsmen had contributed to Persepolis, but it was the achievement of these Macedonian hill chiefs to really establish a hugely extended world of the *koine*. And it was in the talent they possessed and the formidable and intelligent application of Greek thinking in the area of military affairs rather than any other, that the Macedonian kings and the *Diadochi* showed themselves truly the heirs of the civilization that flourished to the south of their own homeland.

The group that led armies and guided states in these years were of a very high martial calibre indeed. Seleucus, Ptolemy, Antigonus, Cassander and Lysimachus; all the big figures who survived were very competent military commanders. They all had, to a considerable degree, the physical, intellectual, personal and professional skills needed to lead great armies to success in combat. They were all possessed of robust health that allowed them to campaign over great distances well into advanced years with few debilitating illnesses ever being mentioned. Only Demetrius is noticed as having ailments that affected any of his projects. Once, when king of Macedonia, Demetrius incapacitation encouraged Pyrrhus to intervene and, near the end in the hills of Asia, when looking like he might make a miraculous escape, Plutarch reports he was forced to his bed for forty days. Obviously it is possible others suffered from illnesses that our sources see fit not to mention but the fact of their general longevity suggest rude heath characterised these men of action. They all knew how to retain the loyalty of demanding and difficult followers, most were generous, a key to keeping followers satisfied, though if Demetrius is to be believed Lysimachus fell down here.[2] They knew how important it was to attend to things personally when it really mattered; Antigonus visited his men bearing gifts on occasions when they were experiencing a crisis of morale. Some had the common touch, some did not. Antigonus and his son certainly did and Seleucus, we know, persuaded his men to continue on against the odds by his personal oratory. Lysimachus and Cassander seem far less humane but we should never forget that our ultimate source worked for a family firm that saw these two as some of their most dastardly competitors. With Ptolemy, again we get the impression of his being just the personality to be catnip to his Hellenistic followers, but then this impression may have come flooding from the nib of his very own stylus.

Most had the ability to put themselves in their enemies' shoes to know how best to plan counter-strategies, guessing where the enemy might put his strongest troops so they could be countered by their best; Eumenes at Gabene springs to mind here. Like Alexander, they knew the worth of a good ruse, of duping the enemy to gain advantage. Alexander did it before the Hydaspes, so he could cross that river to confront Porus; Lysimachus in Anatolia in 302 BC and Eumenes, before both Paraetacene and Gabene, misled the enemy by lighting fires to give the impression a whole army was present or employed deserters to spread incorrect information so he could steal a march on his opponent. They were strategically sophisticated and could be tactically innovative. It is seldom that they lurch about with little or no plan. Most of the heirs of Alexander had clear goals and clear plans to accomplish them.

They were all, by and large, brave and tireless, almost all of them led from the front. This was an essential quality of a Hellenistic warlord modelling themselves, as they did, on the absurdly-brave Alexander himself. The only one we know of who seemed to balk at this role at the head of his soldiers was Cassander, and even with him we know he led from the front on a number of occasions. It was typical of their hill baron background the tendency to lead at the head of their men in battle. A frontier lord usually fights in this style; this is the nature of his condition, almost the whole point of his existence and how he builds up a group of loyal warriors around his often-rickety seat of power. The Macedonian kings and the *Diadochi* took this ethos with them, as the world they inhabited grew to a point where pure calculation made this less of a sensible choice. It is very difficult to find examples of where they stayed back to direct matters, feeding in reserves, and keeping tight control of all aspects of the battle. They were unlike Xerxes looking on from his throne at Salamis in 480 BC, in order to be able to reward courage and punish cowardice, and again unlike Roman consular leaders who also had an oversight ethos of leadership (though, it should be said, they frequently showed ferocious courage when they were younger subordinate officers).

This fighting like a hero was the norm; Alexander was no aberration in this. Antigonus, when well over 60, led his charging horsemen in most of his battles. Only at the final fight did he stay back a little with the infantry phalanx but by that time at the age of 80 he could reasonably have expected to have done his bit in the heat of battle. Seleucus and Lysimachus, according to one account, actually fought hand-to-hand at Corupedium, when both of them were well over 70 years of age. Eumenes famously duelling with Neoptolemus and Pyrrhus with Demetrius' general, this was what was expected. It is noticeable that Marcellus in the third century BC was only the third Roman commander-in-chief in several centuries to defeat an enemy commander-in-chief in combat and strip him of his war gear. Our men could provide three examples of such adrenalin-pumped leadership in just three decades.

One result of this was that, though sophisticated practitioners of the military art, none of them tended to make much use of tactical reserves. Alexander seldom practised this tactic in the sophisticated sense of keeping units back to counter defeat and feed success. Certainly he deployed a second infantry line on occasions, particularly at Gaugamela, where support units behind the wings were deployed. In this very special situation, where massively outnumbered and expecting to be outflanked, he needed his army to form almost into an all-round defensive formation when this occurred. In the battles we are able to describe there are few, if any, examples of this. Only at Ipsus, where it is possible the elephants were held back to be used when necessary, do we have a plausible example. On other occasions, commanders kept troops in hand to be thrown in at the appropriate time, like Antigonus at Paraetacene, when his attack saved the day, but this was just good timing in committing his front-line right wing, it was not the use of a tactical reserve. Equally they might move their men around early in the battle; Eumenes did this at Paraetacene, taking horse from his left wing, Ptolemy did it at Gaza, moving troops from one wing to another but, because they would usually themselves be very soon involved at the head of their own retainers in the fight, it was pointless to have a reserve as they would not have the oversight or be in a position to commit it at the right time.

Despite the qualities of these men, there was still room to ascribe to their careers those themes beloved of Greek chroniclers, particularly hubris. They were far from infallible and not immune to the arrogance that sometimes leads the powerful headlong to disaster. Lysimachus was one, with his failure to appreciate the quality of his Getae enemies and so he foundered, chasing a chimera across the steppe just as Darius the Great's Persians had done when they tried to conquer Scythia 200 years before. Antigonus, famous for failing to take advice, almost came badly unstuck against the Cossaeans. Then there was his son, Demetrius, who, refusing to pander to the expectation of Macedonian petitioners, found himself bundled off his throne in double-quick time. Even Cassander, who was usually pre-eminent as a patient organizer, made such flawed dynastic arrangements for his succession that the kingdom of Macedonia was very soon completely lost to his family.

But there were others apart from those who fought these great battles, perhaps not premiership contenders but still leaders whose names are familiar from Alexander's years and after. Many of these bit-part players showed terrific talent in the military field. Leosthenes, early on in the Lamian War; Alexander, son of Polyperchon; Ptolemaeus, nephew of Antigonus; and Agathocles, son of Lysimachus, had careers that showed them in a favourable light before falling at the hands of enemy missiles, intriguers, false friends or a parent who took the god Kronos for a model. Even Pithon the great intriguer is discovered as a very competent and successful officer and at the end Ptolemy the Thunderbolt, if the most dangerous man of the era to have around, still was clearly charismatic, energetic and talented. Perhaps if he had not bumped into a Gallic horde in a particularly aggressive groove he would have established a state in Macedonia that history would remember with some applause. And, of course, the most famous of the second generation of Successors, Demetrius Poliorcetes and Pyrrhus of Epirus, exhibited extraordinary and much-lauded gifts that were regarded by many as only matched by concomitant failings of character and temperament.

But, like any group of predominantly blue-blooded military types from all ages, there was very far from any guarantee of intelligence. Dunderheads are common enough in the uniform wearers of any period and the Successor epoch was no different. It is something to do with an aristocratic background and a military education that always leads to the construction of some of these chinless fools. Leonnatus was very much of this mould; incompetent intriguing and ultimately-fatal recklessness in battle were his forte. Others, like Pleistarchus, Cassander's brother, seemed pretty much to make a hash of everything they laid their hands on: captured in Caria, outwitted in Chalcis, shipwrecked before Ipsus and swiftly losing the kingdom of Cilicia he had been given in the carve up after the battle. Arrhidaeus was another; clearly he must have been a senior figure to be given the task of overseeing the construction of Alexander's funeral carriage and he was lucky enough to be in the right place when Perdiccas was snuffed out in Egypt. But, when tested as co-regent with Pithon, he was completely out of his depth and though, after this derisory performance, he still received the satrapy of Hellespontine Phrygia as his portion at Triparadeisus, he quickly made a useless fist of defending it against Antigonus. Polyperchon might also with some justification be placed somewhere here; though competent enough as a soldier, he seemed to fold when he had the top job handed to him on a plate by Antipater.

In a class of his own was Eumenes, the provincial Greek who over a decisive period showed himself the most considerable military genius of them all. He was a man whose career may have ended in defeat and death; not at the hands of an opponent, but from the treachery of his own side. He duped and tactically bested the very cream of the Macedonian generals. He faced both triumph and disaster with resolution and, despite the disadvantage of his birth, kept together a coalition army led by deeply treacherous officers through a campaign of triumphs that was only undone at the end. The only criticisms that can be made are that he allowed his health to be compromised when leading his men towards the first of the two great battles against Antigonus. But with the reputation his Macedonian comrades had for drinking perhaps this was forgivable. The other failure that fate did not forgive, however, was his last one, where he failed to provide adequate defence for his baggage train at Gabene, allowing Antigonus' light horse to capture it and eventually swap it for his own head. If he had followed Alexander's example at Gaugamela and left an adequate camp guard, the upshot of the great central war of the *Diadochi* epoch might have been very different.

That this first generation of Successors generally shines so bright is no fluke; there is some Darwinism here. They had to compete hard from the beginning to survive at the high table of dynastic politics. When after decades and even centuries had passed, the combination of having power handed on a plate down the royal line and years of inbreeding meant there appeared the kind of defectives we are more familiar with amongst modern era royal families. This is particularly the case with the court at Alexandria though there were some pretty spectacular disasters amongst Seleucus' descendants too. However, Macedonia only lasted less than a century-and-a-half from the end of the *Diadochi*, not a sufficient period to brew up a truly messy regal gene pool.

Enough is known about the background of the first Successors to understand something of the world they came from and how it shaped them. Most were from Macedonia, a marcher state, the kind of polity that not infrequently have been the progenitors of empire. Constant border warfare makes such people strong and skilful in war. They have lands on their borders that, after conquest, can be exploited with particular efficiency. The crushed populace are not protected from bone-deep exploitation by hallowed custom, forms of common law and long-held practice that put some sort of brake on oppression in old established communities in the homeland. So it is possible to build a martial and well-funded realm and as a bonus there is always available, to bolster the home levy, the very warlike peoples whose rivalry kept the marcher peoples on their toes in the first place. China was first unified by the ruler of a state whose sinews had been tempered by centuries of conflict with the tribes of inner Asia. Spain's great empire was bred of border conflict with the Moors, who had conquered most of the Iberian Peninsula in the eighth century AD. The Hapsburgs began as marcher lords on the edge of the German world and Russia, crushed by the Mongols and for centuries exposed to the depredations of their remnants, such as the Golden Horde, earned her imperial spurs in Eurasia before she began to impinge on the world of the West.

Coming from such a place, the *Diadochi* were military men. Many were the sons of almost-independent local dynasts who Philip II had brought to his court, both to include their families in the national project and tame the centrifugal tendencies their background had nurtured. This gave the king a hold over potentially-troublesome local warlords and gained him followers who were brave and skilful fighters. It also surely explains much about the reactions of these men who were only a generation away from a time when Macedonia had little tradition of a strong centre, nor any history of powerful loyalty to the ruling dynasty. The effect of all this and the implications for their policy choices could be glimpsed when they were left leaderless and rudderless. Men from a long-established state with time-hallowed institutions would have tried harder to find a legitimate leader and then given that person their backing. With these great officers, though they created a formula to keep the Macedonian Empire in one piece for a short time, the imperative to carve out personal holdings did not take many years to emerge. This was very different from when comparable imperial entities, whether Achaemenid, Sassanian or Roman, experienced the traumas of internecine warfare. In these polities, where legitimacy at the core was longer established, it was usually this centre that was the prize of civil conflict. The resources of the periphery, financial and military, would be utilized but always to take control at the heart of things, whether it be Darius the Great establishing himself where before the direct descendants of Cyrus had ruled, or Sulla crashing his way back to Rome on the tail of his legions whose loyalty he had won in a successful war against Mithridates. These Macedonians were different and soon enough were creating states at the edge of empire that have few parallels in the history of these other empires.

Comparison can be a helpful tool of analysis when what is, at first, difficult to understand or sparsely evidenced is compared with an equivalent period that is well sourced. But with the *Diadochi* it is difficult to find another example where men followed a charismatic leader in founding a great empire and then fell out and fought over the carcass of what they had helped bring into being. Julius Caesar certainly gained a great domain but, on his death, his followers did not split the Roman Empire in the way Alexander's Successors did. The later Roman Empire seems more to fit the bill with various local usurpers, Emperors and Caesars fighting to win and hold their patches. Yet, even these divisions were not usually institutionalized, though after Theodosius the Great, at the end of the fourth century AD, the Roman Empire split into west and east, never to rejoin again. Perhaps the closest parallel is found when we look at the Dark Ages and the great Frankish Empire of Charlemagne in the ninth century AD. Aiming to recreate its Roman forebear, it was, nonetheless, very soon divided between the various lines of its progenitor's offspring. But even this does not really throw much light on the process that occurred in the years following Alexander's death as the two societies where these events played out were so different in nature.

With the sources petering out, the Battle of Ipsus almost shuts down any discussion of the military history of Alexander the Great's immediate Successors. After this epochal contest there really are no more detailed accounts of either full campaigns or individual battles. The *Diadochi* continued to clash for two more decades but we have no information about the size or composition of their armies or of the tactical evolutions that occurred during these encounters. Certainly we know something about the general outline of their actions and sometimes we even get details of particular episodes. We hear of the occasion when Seleucus, only accompanied by his guard and eight elephants, outflanks and accepts the surrender of the rump of Demetrius' army after they had traversed Anatolia, herded there by Lysimachus' son Agathocles. We get a few details on the conditions in Athens under siege by Demetrius in 296 BC but we can learn virtually nothing of the military details of the encounter. None of this allows us to analyze the conflicts as we can for some of those that were fought before 301 BC.

But while the sources are scanty for the period 301 to 281 BC, this is also the case for many periods of ancient history. Paucity of detailed military information is far from unusual, which should make us be particularly appreciative of the considerable amount that is left to us on the *Diadochi* before the turn of the century. After this there is only an outline and the sources on military matters virtually run dry for over half a century after the death of Seleucus, in 281 BC, before any details of fighting in the Hellenistic world are available again. Only when Polybius takes up the baton with his close-to-contemporaneous account, towards the end of the second century BC, can we begin again to understand what is happening in the martial story of the Hellenistic world. Even so, if the decades before are pretty bereft for those interested in military developments, they are still crucial as these years saw the very long reigns of Antigonus Gonatas, Ptolemy Philadelphus and Antiochus I. Decades long, almost Augustan in their extravagant longevity and like the Roman Empire, with its sickly, un-heroic but long-lived ruler, these endurance kings ensured the Hellenistic world, after the trauma and bloodletting of the *Diadochi* years, had a comparative period of stability. Time was allowed for the three great Hellenistic kingdoms to establish themselves. It was not that these were years of peace but it was usually border conflicts on a much smaller scale than before. So with this breathing space, the Antigonid, Ptolemaic and Seleucid establishments had time to embed their dynasties into the regions they ruled. With the result that the dynastic achievements of Alexander's Successors were etched into the fabric of southeast Europe and the Middle East before the Romans came to snuff them out.

Notes

Abbreviations

ABSA   *Annual of the British School at Athens*
GRBS   *Greek, Roman and Byzantine Studies*
JHS   *Journal of Hellenic Studies*

Introduction
1. For a recent version of this view see R Lane Fox, *The Classical World* (Allen Lane, 2005).
2. Plutarch, *Pyrrhus*, translated by I Scott-Kilvert and published in *The Age of Alexander* (London, 1973), 7.

Chapter 1: Soldiers and Armies
1. Cornelius Nepos, *Iphicrates*, translated by Rev. J S Watson in *Lives of the great Commanders* (London, 1886), 3.
2. See A B Bosworth, *The Legacy of Alexander* (Oxford, 2002), pp 71–2.
3. *Ibid*, p 72 ff contends that they would really have been less than this. He suggests that 7,000 would have remained based on the numbers and ratio of Asiatic troops Alexander had intended to mix together in new pike and missile armed phalanx, in order to utilize his recently recruited Iranian troops. However, the result may still be 10,000 if we assume the 3,000 hypaspists were not intended to be mixed but kept inviolate as might be expected of the royal guard. But as even Bosworth accepts, the sources and consequent figures for troops are all highly suspect.
4. Diodorus Siculus, *Universal History IX*, translated by R M Geer (London and Cambridge, Massachusetts, 1947), 19.14.5.
5. *Ibid*, 19.27.6.
6. *Ibid*, 19.29.3.
7. One piece of evidence that indicates they on occasions did carry the *sarissa* is that when killing Cleitus, the Black, Alexander took a *sarissa* held by his guard, who would surely have been one of the hypaspists.
8. See R A Lock, 'The Origins of the Argyraspids', in *Historia* 26 (1977), pp 373–378. Most other scholars reject this view, see, for instance, E M Anson, 'Alexander's

Hypaspists and the Argyraspids', in *Historia* 30 (1981) pp 117–20 and W M Heckel, *The Marshalls of Alexander's Empire* (London, 1992) pp 307–8.

9. For a useful discussion of this conundrum see A B Bosworth, *The Legacy of Alexander*, in particular pp 83–4.
10. Polybius, *The Rise of the Roman Empire*, translated by I Scott-Kilvert (London, 1979) 18.31.
11. Arrian, *The Campaigns of Alexander*, translated by A De Selincourt (London, 1958), 2.11.
12. Diodorus Siculus, *Universal History IX*, 19.19.4.
13. Diodorus Siculus, *Universal History VIII*, translated by C.B. Welles (London and Cambridge, Massachusetts, 1963), 17.17.4.
14. Quintus Curtius Rufus, *The History of Alexander*, translated by J Yardley (London, 1984), 8.14.28.
15. Diodorus Siculus, *Universal History IX*, 18.71.5–6.
16. Diodorus Siculus, *Universal History X*, translated by R. M. Geer (London and Cambridge, Massachusetts, 1954), 19.83.3.
17. The issue of the decline of Macedonian cavalry is discussed at length in P Sidnell, *Warhorse* (London, 2006) p127 ff.
18. Diodorus Siculus, *Universal History IX*, 18.15.2.
19. Some Thessalian cavalry accompanied Pyrrhus' army when he went to the aid of Tarentum, against Rome, in the years immediately after the death of the last *Diadochi*.
20. Asclepiodotus, *Tactica*, translated by the Illinois Greek Club, (London and Cambridge, Massachusetts, 1923), 7.3.
21. Arrian, *The Campaigns of Alexander*, 5.12.
22. It has been suggested that the elephants were still in the process of being trained for military action when Alexander died. See for example, L Ueda-Sarson, 'Alexander's War Elephants', in *Slingshot* 227 (2003) pp 19–22.
23. Diodorus Siculus, *Universal History IX*, 18.27.1
24. Plutarch, *Eumenes*, translated by B Perrin in *Parallel Lives VIII* (London and Cambridge, Massachusetts, 1919) 14.4.
25. Cited in Pliny, *Natural History*, 8.5.5. Surus is conjectured to mean the 'Syrian' which implies the animal was an Indian elephant rather than the African ones the Carthaginians would normally have used.
26. Livy, *Rome and Italy*, 9.19 translated by B Radice (London, 1982), 9.19.
27. *Ibid*, 9.18
28. Sumptuary laws were enacted in Athens by Demetrius of Phalerum with the inevitable resulting condemnation of him for spending large amounts on putting up his own statues all over the city. 'Austerity for others but not for us' became a well-known motif in Rome, a little later, when her successes had brought the wealth and art of Greece and the East flooding into her coffers.

Chapter 2: Lamian War

1. Diodorus Siculus *Universal History IX*, 18.12 notes that the Macedonians were short of soldiers because of the numbers sent out to Alexander in Asia. However, in that case, 13,000 Macedonian infantry seems an unlikely figure. A B Bosworth, *The Legacy of Alexander*, pp 77, suggests that the figure of 13,000 Macedonian infantry is defective and should actually read 13,000 mercenaries and 3,000 Macedonians. For a full discussion of the problem of Macedonian troop figures at the death of Alexander, see Bosworth *Legacy of Alexander*, chapter 3, p 64 ff.

2. Diodorus Siculus, *Universal History IX*, 18.12.4.

3. *Ibid*, 18.13.4. What this national business was is not explained. Quite possibly they invaded Acarnania with whom they were in almost constant conflict over the next few years.

4. A B Bosworth, *Conquest and Empire-The Reign of Alexander the Great* (Cambridge University Press, 1988), pp 293–4, denies that Leosthenes was elected Athenian general in 324, arguing that it was a different Leosthenes. This argument seems somewhat tenuous.

5. Jason of Pherae and Onomarchus of Phocis were the most notable examples of this, both raising large mercenary armies. Jason, a Thessalian, recruited a massive army but was assassinated in 370 BC before his plans could come to fruition. Onomarchus gained notoriety by plundering the temple at Delphi. His mercenary army conquered Locris, seized Thermopylae and invaded Boeotia. He defeated Philip twice in 353 BC before losing to him in the following year and being killed in the battle.

6. Hypereides, *Funeral Oration 10*, translated by J.O. Burtt in *Minor Attic Orators, II, Lycurgus, Dinarchus, Demades, Hypereides* (London and Cambridge, Massachusetts, 1954).

7. Diodorus Siculus, *Universal History IX*, 18.15.2.

8. *Ibid*, 18.15.4.

9. See Naval Warfare Chapter.

10. Diodorus Siculus, *Universal History IX*, 18.15.7.

11. Antipater's original army had only 600 cavalry while Leonnatus and Craterus brought over 1,500 each. Taking into account the losses sustained in two defeats and a winter's siege this would probably leave around 3,000 horse. There remains the strong possibility that Diodorus has garbled his figures.

12. Diodorus Siculus, *Universal History IX*, 18.17.2.

13. *Ibid*, 18.17.4.

14. There is a marked similarity in the brief description of Crannon with the preceding battle involving Leonnatus. The suspicion lingers that Diodorus has muddled them up.

15. Plutarch, *Phocion*, 26, attributes the defeat at Crannon to inexperienced leadership and Antipater bribing certain partners of the allied cause. The latter charge may have some substance but the former cannot be substantiated and seems to have been used by Plutarch in order to point up the qualities of Phocion.

Chapter 3: Eumenes' War

1. Why he needed this reinforcement is not made clear, but presumably the regiments he had raised to take to the war in Armenia had been demobilized in the meantime.
2. Plutarch, *Eumenes*, 6.3.
3. P. Green, *Alexander to Actium* (London 1991), p.14.
4. Cornelius Nepos, *Eumenes*, 3.
5. Plutarch, *Eumenes*, 11.1–2.
6. PSI XII 1284: This quote comes from a papyrus fragment discovered at Oxyrhyncus in the early part of the twentieth century. Identified as a fragment of Arrian, it has been put in proper historical context by A B Bosworth, 'Eumenes, Neoptolemus and PSI XII, 1284, in *GRBS* 19 (1978), pp 227–37.
7. One of Antipater's recent envoys to Leonnatus in Asia had been Hecataeus, the tyrant of Cardia, a close friend and confidant of the regent. One of his earlier tasks had been the arrest and subsequent execution of Attalus after Alexander's accession. Well-grounded in the lively and dangerous intrigues of his home city, he was a consummate political operator. Eumenes had long hated Hecataeus and had importuned Alexander, unsuccessfully, to have him replaced.
8. For this story see Plutarch, *Eumenes*, 2.
9. While there is every reason to believe that Craterus was popular with the rank and file Macedonians, our sources tend to overstate it. Ultimately dependent on the eye witness accounts of Eumenes' fellow Cardian, Hieronymus, this alleged popularity was used to point up Eumenes' cleverness. Uncritical acceptance of Hieronymus is all too often the case. He had his biases, too, as pointed out by J Hornblower, *Hieronymus of Cardia* (Oxford, 1981).
10. Plutarch, *Eumenes*, 6.5.
11. Diodorus Siculus, *Universal History IX*, 18.29.4.
12. For a full discussion of the vexed issue of how many Macedonian soldiers there were at the time of Alexander's death and where they were see A B Bosworth, *The Legacy of Alexander*, pp 64–97. As for the 4,000 veterans left by Craterus in Cilicia when he went over to aid Antipater in the Lamian War it is perfectly possible, as we suggest, that they fought for Neoptolemus and then transferred their allegiance to Eumenes.
13. Plutarch, *Eumenes*, 7.1–2. Pharnabazus had a very interesting past. Son of Artabazus, one of Darius' nobles, he was the brother of Barsine, Alexander's mistress. After the death of Memnon, he took command of the naval war in the Aegean, until captured in 332 BC. He later escaped but seems to have been forgiven and welcomed (like his father) by the Macedonians. Phoenix is hitherto unknown.
14. Plutarch, *Eumenes*, 6.3–4.
15. For this story see Plutarch, *Eumenes*, 13, and for its context see B Bennett and M Roberts, *The Wars of Alexander's Successors* Vol. 1 (Barnsley, 2008), p 62.
16. See Plutarch, *Demetrius*, 46.
17. Plutarch, *Eumenes*, 7.4–6.

18. Plutarch, *Eumenes*, 7.3.
19. As related in Plutarch, *Eumenes*, 7.4. He may well be the Gorgias who Olympias tried unsuccessfully to help evade the Macedonian draft and who arrived as a page at Alexander's court in 331 BC. Though there is another, possibly different, Gorgias who was a *taxiarch* in 328 BC, and according to the ever-unreliable Justin, was sent home with Craterus in 324 BC. Perhaps he remained in Cilicia and enrolled in Eumenes' army. For further details, see W Heckel, *The Marshals of Alexander's Empire*, especially p 327.
20. According to Plutarch, *Eumenes*, 7.8, Eumenes found Craterus still alive and mourned over him as he lay dying. This seems a highly-romanticized account.

Chapter 4: Gabene and Paraetacene
1. For details see J Hornblower, *Hieronymus of Cardia*.
2. There is, however, an anecdote in Polynaeus, *Stratagems*, 5.35, which tells of Nearchus capturing Telmessus, on the Lycian coast, from an old acquaintance, Antipatrides. If true, the incident most probably relates to the Antigonid campaign against Alcetas in Pisidia.
3. Diodorus Siculus, *Universal History IX*, 19.19.6.
4. *Ibid*, 19.22.2–3.
5. *Ibid*, 19.24.3.
6. A B Bosworth, *Legacy of Alexander*, p 126 suggests Eumenes may have been poisoned, drawing a parallel to similar rumours re Alexander's death.
7. Diodorus Siculus, *Universal History IX*, 19.29.1.
8. *Ibid*, 19.29.2.
9. *Ibid*, 19.29.4.
10. According to the very fragmentary Arrian, *Events after Alexander*, F.135, Amphimachus was the 'king's brother'. Philip Arrhidaeus' mother was a woman called Philinna from Larissa. As A B Bosworth, *Legacy of Alexander*, p 113, points out, it is by no means impossible that she had been married before and was the mother of Amphimachus as well.
11. Diodorus Siculus, *Universal History IX*, 19.27.6.
12. *Ibid*, 19.28.1.
13. *Ibid*, 19.28.3
14. *Ibid*, 19.28.4
15. Where these elephants were really deployed is discussed at length by A M Devine in his article 'Diodorus' Account of the Battle of Paraitacene', in *Ancient World* 12 (1985), pp 75–86. He contends that that the word used by Diodorus could be interpreted to mean that the elephants were used as just a flank guard and were not in front of Eudamus' wing at all. Devine believes that, if the elephants were curved round acting as defence both in front and round the side, this would have made their formation unworkable. Whatever the linguistics, he appears to make assumptions that are not warranted. Firstly, it seems that Eudamus' wing was

already anchored on high ground and so would not need all the elephants as well to make it safe and thus deprive the rest of the wing of the support of these beasts. Equally, his contention that a bent line would not be practical does not seem to hold water; single beasts with their infantry guards could manoeuvre in a curved line, without necessarily exposing a flank, especially as the enemy troops that might threaten them were the very horsemen whose steeds were afraid of coming near elephants at all. However, one point in favour of his argument could be that it explains why Antigonus could so easily get at the space between Eudamus' wing and the infantry because there would have been no elephants in his way as they were all on the far left acting as a flank guard. And this would also apply at Gabene where Devine in his subsequent article: 'Diodorus' Account of the Battle of Gabiene' in *Ancient World* 12 (1985), pp 87–96, again contends the animals act just as a flank guard and so, therefore, would not have impeded Antigonus getting at Peucestas and forcing him and so many of his followers to flee. But none of this explains why Eumenes, at Paraetacene, with more elephants would forgo having a guard of elephants in front of his weak left wing when this was exactly the work the beasts were intended for.

16. As with the arithmetic of Antigonus' army there is also a problem with Eumenes' host. When we add together each detachment it totals 11 more elephants and 200 more cavalry than Diodorus claims as his total. But, this is not a huge discrepancy and perhaps needs little explanation above the normal muddle due to attrition or troop accounting.

17. Diodorus Siculus, *Universal History IX*, 19.30.2.

18. *Ibid*, 19.30.10.

19. *Ibid*, 19.31.2 suggests as much; 'they were moving from column into line.'

20. *Ibid*, 19.31.4.

21. According to Polynaeus, *Stratagems*, 4.6.10, Antigonus detained the heralds to try and conceal the number of casualties he had sustained.

22. Diodorus Siculus, *Universal History IX*, 19.33.1.

23. A B Bosworth, *Legacy of Alexander*, p 144.

24. Plutarch, *Eumenes*, 15.7.

25. However, most historians reject this characteristic of Parmenion considering that it is merely a literary device to spotlight Alexander's superior judgement.

26. Alexander had created a corps of Iranian Companions (including Medes) shortly before his death.

27. Diodorus Siculus, *Universal History IX*, 19.42.1–2.

28. *Ibid*, 19.42.5.

29. *Ibid*, 19.42.5.

30. *Ibid*, 19.42.6.

31. *Ibid*, 19.40.3.

32. Plutarch, *Eumenes*, 16.4.

33. See Chapter 1: Soldiers and Armies.

34. Philip, himself, had had a chequered career, receiving Sogdia and Bactria at Babylon. In 323 BC at Triparadeisus he was apparently transferred to command in Parthia. However, Philotas is named as satrap of Parthia, when Pithon aimed at taking the province over, before Antigonus ever arrived east of the Tigris. Philip, perhaps, never had any great local support and had only been restored to some office after the arrival of Eumenes. He later served Antigonus. But, it should be noted that there were at least five officers named Philip under Alexander, so our identification is tentative. For an alternative view see R A Billows, *Antigonos the One-Eyed and the Creation of the Hellenistic State* (Berkeley, 1990), p 422, who considers the above mentioned Philotas to be an error, by Diodorus, for Philip.

35. Diodorus Siculus, *Universal History IX*, 19.43.3.

36. *Ibid*, 19.43.5.

37. J Hornblower, *Hieronymus of Cardia*, points out how Peucestas' behaviour during these campaigns is at odds with his faultless and brave demeanour under Alexander. It is more than possible that Hieronymus decided to blacken his character in order to glorify Eumenes.

Chapter 5: Battle of Gaza

1. See Chapter 4: Gabene and Paraetacene, note 34, – if it is the same Philip!

2. Diodorus Siculus, *Universal History X* 19.85.2.

3. *Ibid*, 19.80.2.

4. *Ibid*, 19.80.5.

5. Of course, it could be that Diodorus (or more correctly his source, Hieronymus, who was in the pay of the Antigonids) is building up Ptolemy and his reputation for rhetorical effect.

6. Diodorus Siculus, *Universal History X*, 19.81.2–3.

7. See Chapter 1: Soldiers and Armies.

8. Diodorus Siculus, *Universal History X*, 19.82.3.

9. *Ibid*, 19.83.5.

10. *Ibid*, 19.84.2–3.

11. *Ibid*, 19.85.3.

12. Plutarch (*Demetrius* 5), who has the briefest of descriptions of the battle, states that 5,000 men were killed and 8,000 more taken prisoner.

13. According to Diodorus, Universal *History X*, 19.86.2, even though Andronicus insulted Ptolemy, when he was captured by the Lagid he was treated kindly and 'advanced in honour' as 'one of his friends'.

Chapter 6: Battle of Ipsus

1. Diodorus Siculus, *Universal History X*, 20.109.1.

2. *Ibid*, 20.112.1.

3. *Ibid*, 20.112.3.

4. Polynaeus, *Stratagems*, 4.12.7, suggests that Lysimachus massacred 5,000 Autariatae immediately after the loss of the baggage train, which raises the problem of how the 2,000 who deserted survived. For discussion of the historicity of this incident see R A Billows, *Antigonos the One-Eyed*, p 180, and H S Lund, *Lysimachus* (London & New York, 1992), p 76ff.
5. Plutarch, *Demetrius*, 28.
6. *Ibid*, 29.
7. In 1987 a British army officer, Tony Clunn, whilst metal detecting, found 162 silver Roman coins, none younger than the reign of Augustus. He also found three sling shots of lead; these finds enabled him, with archaeologists, to pinpoint the exact site of battle.
8. See Chapter 1: Soldiers and Armies.
9. Diodorus Siculus, *Universal History XI*, translated by F R Walton (London and Cambridge, Massachusetts, 1954), 21.1.2.
10. W W Tarn, *Hellenistic Military and Naval Developments* (Cambridge, 1930) p 69ff.
11. B Bar-Kochva, *The Seleucid Army* (Cambridge, 1976) pp 105–110.

Chapter 7: Siege Warfare
1. Plutarch, *Demetrius*, 21.
2. Polynaeus, *Stratagems*, 4.14.1, translated for the authors by B Polack.
3. Diodorus Siculus, *Universal History IX*, 18.71.2–3.
4. *Ibid*, 18.71.3–4.
5. See Chapter 8: Naval Warfare.
6. Diodorus Siculus, *Universal History X*, 20.83.1.
7. *Ibid*, 20.85.4.
8. *Ibid*, 20.48.2–4.
9. Xenophon, *Cyropaedia*, translated by H G Dakyns (London, 1911), VI. 1. 52–53.
10. Diodorus Siculus, *Universal History X*, 20.91.5.
11. For details of this machine and its conjectural mechanism see DB Campbell, *Greek and Roman Artillery 399 BC–AD 363* (Oxford, 2003), pp 45. See also his other excellent books *Greek and Roman Siege Machinery 399 BC–AD 363* (Oxford, 2003) and *Besieged: Siege Warfare in the Ancient World* (Oxford, 2006) for other details on siege machinery and warfare which we are indebted to.
12. Vitruvius, *De Architectura*, translated by M H Morgan (Harvard University Press, 1914), 10.16.4.
13. Vitruvius, *De Architectura*, 10.14.1.
14. Diodorus Siculus, *Universal History X*, 20.95.1.
15. R A Billows, *Antigonos the One-Eyed*, pp 388–9, explicitly mentions Hegetor as designing tortoises for the siege of Rhodes, but the evidence for this is not clear.
16. See for instance, Diodorus Siculus, *Universal History X*, translated by R M Geer (London and Cambridge, Massachusetts, 1954), note 1, p 395.
17. Vitruvius, *De Architectura*, 10.16.7.

18. Diodorus Siculus, *Universal History X*, 20 92 2.
19. An idea first mooted in F E Adcock, *The Greek and Macedonian Art of War* (Berkeley, 1967).
20. Plutarch, *Demetrius*, 34.

Chapter 8: Naval Warfare

1. Plato, *Phaedo*, 109b.
2. He is usually called Cleitus the White to differentiate him from Cleitus the Black (who Alexander killed in a drunken brawl). He commanded an infantry battalion in India but later became a cavalry hipparch, serving as such at Sangala and Malli. He was sent home with Craterus and Polyperchon but was probably instructed to help in the construction of the fleet in Cilicia. There is no evidence that he was ever an admiral of Perdiccas (and subsequent defector) as is often suggested.
3. Ironically, perhaps the most famous of Alexander's admirals, Nearchus, never seems to have ventured on the seas after his master's death. Nearchus had been in charge of the fleet which went down the Indus in 324 BC and was then deputed by Alexander to remain in command of the fleet for the voyage to the Persian Gulf. Nearchus recorded the details of this harrowing journey (extant in Arrian's *Indica*) eventually reuniting with Alexander in Susa shortly before the king's death. But, after Babylon, Nearchus never returned to the sea, remaining as an officer of Antigonus and Demetrius (he allegedly tried to intercede to save Eumenes' life). Yet perhaps this is no real mystery as in the *Indica* there are clear signs of tension between Nearchus and an Onescritus, who may well have had real naval responsibility for the voyage. Nearchus' responsibilities may have been more financial than naval.
4. This number of ships was set out to be built in an Athenian decree in an attempt to regain their thalassocracy. In the original Diodorus manuscript it actually states 200 fours and 40 triremes, but one of his translators (P Wesseling in 1746) regarded this as unlikely given that Athens only had 50 fours in 325/324 BC and accordingly transposed the text! The emendation has been followed by all subsequent translators. For discussion of this see J S Morrison, 'Athenian Seapower in 323/2 BC: Dream and Reality' in *JHS*, 107 (1987), pp 89–90; and N G Ashton, 'The *Naumachia* near Amorgos in 322 B.C.', in *ABSA*, 72 (1977), p 5.
5. The course of the naval battles so vital to the ultimate Macedonian success is unfortunately little understood. Diodorus' account is brief and confused and it is unsure whether there were two, three or even four battles which took place. See, Diodorus Siculus, *Universal History IX*, 18.15.8–9 and note, N G Ashton, *ibid*, pp 1–11 and also his 'How Many Penteris?', in *GRBS*, 20 (1979), pp 327–42. And, for widely different interpretations, see J S Morrison, *ibid*, pp 88–97, N G L Hammond and F W Wallbank, *History of Macedonia*, vol. 3 (Oxford, 1988) pp 113–22 and W Heckel, *The Marshals of Alexander's Empire* (Routledge, 1992), pp 373–77.

6. According to Polynaeus, *Stratagems*, 4.6.8.
7. Diodorus Siculus, *Universal History IX*, 18.72.2.
8. Polynaeus, *Stratagems*, 4.6.8.
9. Diodorus Siculus, *Universal History IX*, 18.72.8.
10. Diodorus Siculus, *Universal History X*, 19.75 8.
11. Diodorus Siculus, *Universal History IX*, 18 72 7.
12. Diodorus Siculus, *Universal History X*, 20.47.1.
13. Mentioned in Diodorus Siculus, *Universal History X*, 20.50.5.
14. Plutarch, *Demetrius*, 16; Polynaeus, *Stratagems*, 4.7.7; and Diodorus Siculus, *Universal History X*, 20.50.2, respectively. It is also the case that Diodorus, himself, says earlier that Demetrius had arrived on the island with more than 110 triremes (see above) but now says that he has only 108 and then goes on to enumerate various sevens and fours within this 108! Clearly these are not reconcilable but the discrepancy can be explained by assuming that the transports and freighters mentioned in Diodorus, 20.47.1, were not transports as such, but in fact warships. If this is accepted, the amended Diodorus figure of 180 can be accepted. For a full discussion of the fleet strengths at Salamis see M Cary, *A History of the Greek World From 323 to 146* BC (London, 1951), Appendix 4, pp 385–6; and H Hauben, 'Fleet Strength at the Battle of Salamis (306 B.C.)' in *Chiron*, 6 (1976), pp 1–5.
15. This is from Diodorus Siculus, *Universal History X*, 20.49.2. Once more Plutarch, *Demetrius*, 16, gives a different figure of 150.
16. According to Diodorus Siculus, *Universal History X*, 20.49.2, Ptolemy had over 200 transports carrying over 10,000 infantry.
17. Diodorus Siculus, *Universal History X*, 20.51.5.
18. For different views see H Hauben, 'Fleet Strength at the Battle of Salamis (306 B.C.)', p 5 and especially K Williams, *Alexandria and the Sea: Maritime Origins and Underwater Exploration* (Sharp Books, 2004) pp 34–40.
19. The mistress, an Athenian called Lamia, was renowned as a flute player and had apparently already been not only the mistress of Ptolemy, but of Demetrius of Phalerum before him. The other Demetrius, despite being many years her junior, apparently also became besotted with her and she subsequently bore him a daughter, Phila. Plutarch recounts this affair in great detail in *Demetrius*, 27.
20. There is a charming, if somewhat unlikely, story in Plutarch, *Demetrius*, 20.4, about Lysimachus and Demetrius. Whilst trying to raise Demetrius' siege of Soli in Cilicia, Lysimachus apparently sent a note to Demetrius to ask whether he could see his siege train and fleet. After Demetrius agreed, Lysimachus saw them (no doubt with much envy), allegedly expressed his admiration, and went away again!
21. However, there was one ship that we know Lysimachus did have. That was his flag ship the *Leontophorus* attested to in a fragment of Memnon. Apparently built at Heraclea, it was an eight and famous for its sheer size and splendour. Leontophorus means lion slayer and thus is in keeping with Lysimachus' constant use of the lion motif. It required, or so we are told, no less than 1,200 oarsmen to row it and could

hold up to 1,200 marines. Such a monster almost puts the gigantism of Demetrius to shame. The ship is still attested as in service when Ptolemy Ceraunus took over Lysimachus' fleet.

22. Pyrrhus had a huge flagship which saw service and which apparently saved his life in 280 BC during his invasion of Italy, with a tempest sinking all his other ships. The flagship ended up in the hands of the Carthaginian Hannibal and she was used against the Romans at Mylae in 260 BC. It has been plausibly argued by R S Rice, 'The Peregrinations of the Queen: Technology Transfer in the Hellenistic World (http://ccat.sas.upenn.edu/rrice/queen.html' 1996) in a fascinating article that this ship must have been one of Demetrius' original fleet.

Chapter 9: Border Wars

1. For details of the campaigns involving Seleucus and, in particular, Lysimachus see B Bennett and M Roberts *The Wars of Alexander's Successors 323–281 BC. Volume 1: Commanders and Campaigns* and the chapters on Seleucus and Lysimachus.

2. See P Harding, *From the end of the Peloponnesian War to the battle of Ipsus*, Translated Documents of Greece and Rome, No 2 (Cambridge, 1985), pp 159–61 (No.125).

3. Diodorus Siculus, *Universal History X*, 19.67.7.

4. This period in Epirus is very confusing. Lyciscus was sent by Cassander as 'regent and general' of the Epirote alliance. He seems to have been regent for Neoptolemus II. This king's identity is much disputed but he was probably the son of Alexander of Epirus and Cleopatra (sister of Alexander the Great). Olympias had formerly been his guardian while she ruled jointly with Aeacides. Neoptolemus survived the vicissitudes of Epirote politics (possibly ruling as joint king with Alcetas) until he was murdered by Pyrrhus circa 297 BC. See P Garoufalias, *Pyrrhus King of Epirus* (London, 1979), pp 187–92; and N G L Hammond and F W Walbank, *History of Macedonia*, Vol. 3, pp 154–6.

5. Polynaeus, *Stratagems*, 4.11.4, describes Cassander capturing Epidamnus by an unlikely ruse. He allegedly set on fire villages nearby and hid the rest of his forces. The people of Epidamnus, thinking he had left, came out and resumed their farming, enabling Cassander to seize the town.

6. See W L Adams 'The Dynamics of Internal Macedonian Politics in the time of Cassander', in *Ancient Macedonia*, 3, (1983), pp 2–30.

7. Briefly mentioned by both Pliny and Seneca, the context and date of the incident are both unclear.

8. There is no actual evidence that Antigonus intended to invade Egypt but it is difficult to see the campaign against the Nabataeans in any other context.

9. So presumably 10,000 was too low an estimate of their total population (both figures are from Diodorus Siculus) or otherwise they had allies posted nearby.

Conclusion

1. J Keegan, *The Mask of Command* (London, 1987), p 13.
2. According to Plutarch, *Demetrius*, 25, Demetrius was scornful of all the *Diadochi* (apart from his father, of course). However, he reserved particular bile for Lysimachus whom he termed a treasurer. Apart from the obvious accusation of meanness, it had the added implication and insult that Lysimachus was a eunuch, as eunuchs traditionally filled the post of treasurer.

Bibliography

Ancient Sources

Arrian, *The Campaigns of Alexander*, translated by A De Selincourt (London, 1958).

Asclepiodotus, *Tactica*, translated by the Illinois Greek Club, (London and Cambridge, Massachusetts, 1923).

Diodorus Siculus, *Universal History VIII*, translated by C.B. Welles (London and Cambridge, Massachusetts, 1963).

Diodorus Siculus, *Universal History IX*, translated by R. M. Geer (London and Cambridge, Massachusetts, 1947).

Diodorus Siculus, *Universal History X*, translated by R. M. Geer (London and Cambridge, Massachusetts, 1954).

Diodorus Siculus, *Universal History XI*, translated by F. R. Walton (London and Cambridge, Massachusetts, 1957).

Hypereides, *Funeral Oration 10* translated by J.O. Burtt in *Minor Attic Orators, II, Lycurgus, Dinarchus, Demades, Hypereides.* (London and Cambridge, Massachusetts, 1954).

Livy, *Rome and Italy*, translated by B. Radice (London, 1982).

Plutarch, *Demetrius*, translated by I. Scott-Kilvert and included in *The Age of Alexander* (London, 1973).

Plutarch, *Eumenes* translated by B. Perrin and included in *Parallel Lives VIII* (London and Cambridge, Massachusetts, 1919).

Plutarch, *Pyrrhus*, translated by I. Scott-Kilvert and included in *The Age of Alexander* (London, 1973).

Polynaeus, *Stratagems*, translated for the authors by B. Polack.

Polybius, *The Rise of the Roman Empire*, translated by I. Scott-Kilvert (London, 1979).

Quintus Curtius Rufus, *The History of Alexander*, translated by J. Yardley (London, 1984).

Vitruvius, *De Architectura*, translated by M.H. Morgan (Harvard University Press, 1914).

Xenophon, *Cyropaedia*, translated by H.G. Dakyns (London, 1911).

Modern Authors

Adams, W L, 'The Dynamics of Internal Macedonian Politics in the time of Cassander' in *Ancient Macedonia*, 3 (1983) pp 2–30.

Adcock, F E, *The Greek and Macedonian Art of War* (Berkeley, 1967).

Anglim S, Jestice P G, Rice R S, Rusch S M and Serrati J, *Fighting Techniques of the Ancient World 3000 BC–AD 500* (Staplehurst, 2005).

Anson, E M, 'Alexander's Hypaspists and the Argyraspids' in *Historia*, 30 (1981) pp 117–20.

Ashton, N G,'The *Naumachia* near Amorgos in 322 B.C.' in *ABSA*, 72 (1977) pp 1–11.

Ashton, N G, 'How Many Penteris' in *GRBS*, 20 (1979) pp 327–42.

Ashton, N G, 'The Lamian War a False Start' in *Historia*, 30 (1983) pp 117–120.

Bar-Kochva, B, *The Seleucid Army* (Cambridge, 1976).

Bennett, B, and Roberts, M, *The Wars of Alexander's Successors 323–281 BC Volume 1: Commanders and Campaigns* (Barnsley, 2008).

Billows, R A, *Antigonos the One-Eyed and the Creation of the Hellenistic State* (Berkeley, 1990).

Bosworth, A B, 'Eumenes, Neoptolemus and PSI 12.1284' in *GRBS*, 19 (1978) pp 227–37.

Bosworth, A B, *Conquest and Empire-The Reign of Alexander the Great* (Cambridge, 1988).

Bosworth, A B, *The Legacy of Alexander* (Oxford, 2002).

Bugh, G R (ed.) *The Cambridge Companion to the Hellenistic World* (Cambridge, 2006).

Campbell, D B, *Greek and Roman Artillery 399 BC–AD 363* (Oxford, 2003).

Campbell, D B, *Greek and Roman Siege Machinery 399 BC–AD 363* (Oxford, 2003).

Campbell, D B, *Besieged: Siege Warfare in the Ancient World* (Osprey Publishing, 2006).

Cary, M, *A History of the Greek World from 323 to 146 BC* (London, 1951).

Devine, A M, 'Diodorus' Account of the Battle of Paraitacene' in *Ancient World*, 12 (1985) pp 75–86.

Devine, A M, 'Diodorus' Account of the Battle of Gabiene' in *Ancient World*, 12 (1985) pp 87–96.

Garoufalias, P, *Pyrrhus King of Epirus* (London, 1979).

Gardiner, R (ed.) *The Age of the Galley; Mediterranean Oared Vessels since Pre Classical Times-Conway's History of the Ship* (London, 1995).

Green, P, *Alexander to Actium* (London, 1991).

Hammond, N G L and Walbank, F W, *History of Macedonia vol.3* (Oxford, 1988).

Harding, P, *From the end of the Peloponnesian War to the battle of Ipsus*, Translated Documents of Greece and Rome, No 2 (Cambridge, 1985).

Hauben, H, 'Fleet Strength at the Battle of Salamis (306 B.C.)'in *Chiron*, 6 (1976) pp 1–5.

Heckel, W, *The Marshals of Alexander's Empire* (London & New York, 1992).

Hornblower, J, *Hieronymus of Cardia* (Oxford, 1981).

Keegan, J, *The Mask of Command* (London, 1987).

Lane Fox, R, *The Classical World* (London, 2005).

Lock, R A, 'The Origins of the Argyraspids' in *Historia*, 26 (1977), pp 373–378.

Lund, H S, *Lysimachus* (London & New York, 1992).

Morrison, J S, 'Athenian Seapower in 323/2 BC: Dream and Reality' in *JHS*, 107 (1987), pp 88–97.

Rice, R S, The Peregrinations of the Queen: Technology Transfer in the Hellenistic World (http://ccat.sas.upenn.edu/rrice/queen.html, 1996).

Sidnell, P, *Warhorse, Cavalry in Ancient Warfare* (London, 2006).

Tarn, W W, *Hellenistic Military and Naval Developments* (Cambridge, 1930).

Ueda-Sarson, L, 'Alexander's War Elephants' in *Slingshot*, 227 (2003), pp 19–22.

Warry, J, *Warfare in the Classical World* (London, 1980).

Williams, K, *Alexandria and the Sea: Maritime Origins and Underwater Exploration* (Tampa, 2004).

Index

Abdera, 125

Abradatas, 125

Abydos, 101, 133, 141, 167

Acarnania, xviii, 14, 19,161–5

Achaea, 14, 39

Achilles, xv

Acrocorinth, 133

Actium, Battle of 31 BC, 156, 162

Adriatic, 23, 155, 162–3, 167

Aeacides, 32, 162–5

Aegean, 45, 55–6, 60, 92, 101, 141, 143, 145–6, 158, 161

Aegium, 132

Aegospotami, Battle of 405/404 BC, 141, 145

Aelian, 1, 2

Aemilius Paullus, 10

Aeneas Tacticus, 2, 116

Aeolia, 101

Aetolia, xvi, 15, 27, 29, 32, 39, 43, 130, 162, 164–6

Agathocles, 175, 178

Agis III, 11

Agrianians, 14

Agrippa, 162

Ajax, 22

Alcetas, brother of Perdiccas, 42, 44–5, 55, 79

Alcetas, of Epirus, 165–6

Alesia, Battle of 52 BC, 102, 135

Alexander, of Epirus, 24

Alexander, the Great, xiii–xviii, 1–2, 4–28, 30–1, 35–6, 40–1, 43–5, 48–52,54–7, 59, 61, 63–6, 74, 76–8, 84, 89–91, 93–94, 99–100, 102–3, 107–8, 110, 113, 115, 117, 119–20, 126–7,130–133, 139–41, 143, 156, 158, 161, 162, 164, 167, 171, 173–178

Alexander, son of Polyperchon, 118, 132, 145, 175

Alexander Sarcophagus, 8

Alexander Severus, 2–3

Alexandria, 41, 44, 91, 117, 133, 153, 176

Alps, 115

Ambracia, 162

Amastris, 103

Amorgos, Battle of 322 BC, 141–2

Amphimachus, 65

Amphipolis, 16

Amyntas, 3

Androbazus, 85

Andronicus, 90, 94–5, 97, 100

Antigenes, 9, 62, 66, 84, 86

Antigonia, 107, 167

Antigonus Gonatus, 55, 135, 155, 178

Antigonus Monopthalmus, xv, xvii, xviii, 5, 7–8, 13, 15–16, 18–21, 25, 45–6, 50–1, 55–65, 68, 71, 73–79, 81, 83–6, 88–90, 93–97, 99, 101–103,106–13, 117, 121–2, 130–5, 140, 142–3, 145–8, 150, 153–5, 157, 163–4, 166–70, 172–176, 178

Antioch, 155

Antiochus, the Great, 3, 22–6, 92,111

Antiochus I, son of Seleucus, 22, 109–12, 155, 178

Antipater, xvii, 6, 9, 11, 16, 28–33, 35–37, 39–9, 54–5, 64, 84, 100, 104, 118–19, 121, 128, 131, 133–4, 141, 162, 164, 166, 175

Antiphilus, 30, 32–3, 35–37, 39

Antisthenes, 152

Apamea Celaenae, 103

Apollonia, 16, 162–3, 166

Apulia, 24

Arabia, 167

Arachosia, 56, 61, 65

Arcadia, 10, 15, 118–21

Aria, 56, 65, 85

Ariarathes, 44

Aristodemus, 132, 153

Aristotle, xvii

Armenia, 42–4, 74

Arrhidaeus, 79, 133, 142, 175

Arrian, 2, 19, 91

Artabazus, 50

Artemisium, 143

Asander, xvii, 45, 133

Asclepiodotus, 2, 13, 22

Asculum, Battle of, 279 BC, 111

Assyria, 115, 167

Athena, 48

Athenaeus, Antigonid officer, 168

Athenaeus Mechanicus, 125, 127

Athens, xiv, 3, 27, 39, 51, 117–18, 124, 131–2, 135, 138, 141, 144–5, 148, 150, 154–5,158, 178

Attica, 118,143,146

Autariatae, 104, 106,167

Azotus, 97

Babylon, xvi, xvii, 6, 24, 26, 28, 41, 43, 49, 56, 59–60, 73, 90, 94, 116, 119, 170

Babylonia, 6, 60, 73, 92, 100, 103, 106, 167

Bactria, 1, 6, 12, 19, 20, 41

Balkan Wars, 115

Beas mutiny, xvi

Barca, 158, 159

Bessus, 93

Bithynia, 103

Black Sea, xviii, 60, 103–5, 134, 154

Boeotia, 16, 28, 32, 99, 146, 161, 166

Boeotus, 90, 97

Bosporus, 104–5, 135, 142

Bottiaea, 16

Britain, 136

Brutus, 102

Bucephalus, 64

Byzantium, 89, 104–5, 116–17, 128,142

Cadusian, 100

Callantia, 134

Callisthenes, xvii

Camel Fort, Battle of, 321 BC, 9, 93

Campania, 24

Cannae, Battle of 216 BC, 20

Cape Taenarum, 27

Cappadocia, xviii, 41–2, 44, 46–8, 50, 51, 61, 66, 79, 100

Capua, 135

Caracalla, 2–3

Cardia, xv, 42–3, 46–8, 50, 54, 60–1, 68, 71, 75, 81, 88

Caria, 45,122,129,133,145,149,175

Carmania, 56, 66

Carpasia, 146

Carthage, 10, 135, 138, 154, 156, 158, 160–1

Cassander, xiv, xvii, xviii, 21, 61, 89, 100, 104–6,118–19, 121, 128, 130, 132, 134, 139–40, 142–5, 155–7,161–7, 172–5

Cassius, 102

Cassopia, 165, 166

Caunus, 132

Celts, xvi

Cephalon, 65

Ceteus, 73
Chaeronea, Battle of, 338 BC, 4, 39, 99
Chalcedon, 104, 142
Chalcis, 175
Chandragupta Maurya, 100, 111
Chariots, 1, 84, 109, 158, 159
Charlemagne, 178
China, 115, 176
Chremonidean War, 135
Cicero, xiv
Cilicia, 6, 35, 46, 49, 60, 90, 96, 100, 145–6, 175
Citium, 133, 148
Cleitus, xvii, 35, 79, 121, 140–2, 144, 145
Cleomenes, 25, 92,160
Cleopatra, 45
Coele-Syria, 90, 92, 107, 167
Colossus of Rhodes, 122
Coprates River, 57, 58, 71
Corfu, 155,161,163
Corinth, 13, 28, 27, 39, 56,118–19, 132–3, 148, 162–3
Cornelius Nepos, 3, 42
Corupedium, Battle of, 281 BC, 155, 173
Cos, 149
Cossaeans, 16, 59, 73, 174
Crannon, Battle of, 322 BC, 36, 38–9
Craterus, xvii, xviii, 6, 16, 20, 28, 35–6, 39, 41–50, 52, 54, 100, 107, 128, 165
Crates, 51
Crete, 14, 124, 158
Crimea, 115
Cyinda, 9, 25
Cynoscephalae, Battle of, 197 BC, 12
Cyprus, 100, 133, 145–7, 152–3,155, 159
Cyrene, xv, 93,158–61
Cyrus, 79, 125, 177

Daae, 19
Damascus, 168
Damis, xv, 94, 119–20
Danube River, xvi, 25

Darius I, 79, 172, 174, 177
Darius III, xv–xvi, 12–13, 18, 21, 24, 27, 48, 65–6, 74, 77–8, 84, 91, 100, 110
Dasht-e-Kavir, 74
Davout, 115
Dead Sea, 157, 168–9
Delphi, 30
Demeter, 48
Demetrius of Phalerum, xiv
Demetrius Poliorcetes, xv–xvi, 5, 15, 21, 51, 55, 65, 68, 78, 89–90, 92–97, 99, 100, 104–113, 117, 122–125, 127–130, 132–3, 139–40, 146–50, 152–157, 167, 169, 171–2, 174–5,178
Diades, 117, 127
Diocles, 125
Diodorus Siculus, xv, 6, 7–9, 12, 14–15, 18, 21, 25, 32, 36, 41, 49, 55, 61–3, 66, 68, 71, 73, 79, 81, 83, 92, 95, 97, 105, 107, 110, 125–7, 129–30, 142, 144,146, 148–9, 153
Diognetus, 129
Dionysius of Syracuse, 117, 138
Dioscurides, 146
Docimus, 135
Dorylaeum, 101, 106
Drangiana, 56, 65
Dutch, 1
Dyme, 132
Dyrrachium, Siege of, 49/48 BC, 102, 140

Ecbatana, 18, 43, 58, 60, 65, 116
Egypt, xviii, 3, 9, 42, 62, 90–92, 95, 100, 106–7, 115, 133, 145, 147, 150, 152–3, 158–1, 167–9, 175
Elephants, xiii, xv, xvi, 1, 9, 14–15, 21–3, 56, 59, 61, 63–6, 68, 74–5, 79, 81, 83–86, 93–4, 96–7, 107–12, 118, 120–1, 131, 174, 178
Elis, 14, 55, 132
Epaminondas, 3, 37, 99
Ephesus, 100, 104, 133

Epicurus, 132
Epidamnus, 163
Epimachus, 117, 124, 126
Epirus, xvii, xviii, 24, 48, 113, 140,
    162–6, 175
Ethiopia, 94
Etruria, 24
Euboea, 143, 146, 161, 163
Eudamus, 22, 56, 65, 68, 71, 85
Eumelus, 135
Eumenes, xv, xvii, xviii, 5, 7–10, 16–17,
    20–3, 37, 41–52, 54–66, 68, 71, 73–6,
    78–9, 81, 83–87, 89–90, 94–5, 97, 99,
    100, 103, 107, 110, 156, 167, 169,
    173–4,175
Euphrates River, xvi
Eumelus, 135
Eurydice, 3
Eurymenae, 166
Evetion, 140, 141

Gabene, Battle of 317 BC, xv, 8, 9,12, 21,
    22, 55, 62, 73–4, 80–1, 85–8, 90, 94,
    97, 110, 173, 176
Gamarga, 73
Ganges River, xvi
Gaugamela, Battle of, 331 BC, 16, 18, 19,
    21, 37, 66, 77, 84, 174, 176
Gauls, 22, 24,135
Gaza, 43, 90, 92, 131–2,167
Gaza, Battle of, 312 BC, 5, 15, 63, 88, 89,
    91–2, 96–100, 148, 153, 174
Genoa, 115
Getae, xviii, 156, 174
Glaucias, 162–3
Golden Horde, 177
Gordium, 6, 18
Gorgias, 52
Goths, 125
Granicus, Battle of, 334 BC, 16, 37, 77

Hadrian, xiv
Haemus Mountains, 167

Halicarnassus, 19, 116, 117, 149
Hamburg, 115
Hannibal, 2, 22, 94
Hannibal Barca, 24
Hapsburgs, 176
Harpalus, 25, 158
Hegesippus, 149
Hegetor, 117, 128
Helen, 137
Hellespont, 1, 6, 12, 25, 31, 33, 41–2,
    45–6, 54, 81, 104, 106, 141, 145
Hellespontine Phrygia, 56, 100, 104, 133,
    142, 175
Hephaistion, 48, 59
Heraclea on the Black Sea, 103–4, 154
Heracles, 59
Herodotus, xiv, 170
Hesperis, 159
Hieronymus of Cardia, xv, 55, 85, 97,
    107, 169–70
Hindu Kush, 65, 85
Homer, xvi, 20, 52
Hydaspes, Battle of, 326 BC, xvi, 15, 19,
    21, 43, 173
Hypereides, 30

Idumaea, 168–9
Illyria, xvi, xviii, 14, 49, 104,106, 155,
    161–3, 166–7
India, xv, xvi, xviii, 1, 9, 19–23, 43, 56,
    60, 73, 85, 90, 93–4,100, 111, 115–6,
    121, 155, 168
Indus River, 25, 65, 172
Ionia, 99, 161
Iphicrates, 3
Ipsus, Battle of, 301 BC, xviii, 1–2, 15,
    22–4, 99–100, 103, 107, 111, 133, 139,
    154–5, 167, 174–5, 178
Isauria, 41
Issus, Battle of, 333 BC, 11, 16, 37, 77
Isthmus of Corinth, 118–19
Italy, 12, 22–4, 63

Jason of Pherae, 30
Jerusalem, 168
Joppa, 90, 132
Jordan, 169
Julius Caesar, 2, 137, 177
Justin, 164

Lamia, 29–32, 35, 131
Lamian War, xviii, 6, 12–13, 17, 25, 27,
    29–33, 35, 43, 46, 49, 119, 131, 140,
    143, 175
Lampsacus, 104, 145
Langarus, 14
Larissa, 36
Leonnatus, xvii, 12, 20, 31–5, 49, 100,
    141, 175
Leosthenes, 27–32, 40, 141, 175
Leucas, 155
Leucolla, 148
Leuctra, Battle of, 371 BC, 3, 37, 99
Libya, xviii, 157–160
Livy, 23–6
Locris, 27, 32
Loryma, 122
Lucania, 24
Lucknow, 115
Lysanias, 63, 78
Lycia, 7, 8, 64, 83, 93, 105, 149
Lydia, 45, 56, 63, 78, 142, 170
Lysander, 141, 145
Lysimacheia, 154
Lysimachus, xvii, xviii, 20, 89, 100,
    102–6, 109–11, 121, 128,133–5, 140,
    143, 154–5, 157, 164, 172–5, 178
Lysiscus, 163, 165–6

Macedonia, xvi–xviii, 1–8, 10–21, 23–33,
    35–7, 39–41, 43–50, 54, 57, 59–64, 66,
    76–8, 83–6, 90–3, 95, 104, 106, 111,
    113, 116–17, 119, 122,130–1, 135,
    140–3, 155, 160–7, 171–7
Machiavelli, 1

Magnesia, Battle of, 190 BC, 12–13, 22,
    111
Malian Gulf, 28–29, 141, 162
Mantinea, Battle of, 362 BC, 3
Marcellus, 174
Marion, 133
Marcus Valerius Corvus, 23
Marengo, 115
Mark Anthony, 140, 156
Marmara, 104
Marsyas, 150
Massena, 115
Maurice of Nassau, 1
Media, 17, 19–20, 24, 41, 56, 58, 60–1,
    63–4, 66, 73–5, 78–9, 81, 89–91, 103,
    111
Median Gates, 59
Medius, 140, 143–4, 148, 155
Megalopolis, xv, 4, 10, 11, 15, 95,
    118–121, 131, 142
Megalopolis, Battle of, 331 BC, 4, 11
Megara, 118
Meleager, 119
Melitia, 32, 35
Memnon, 78
Memphis, 91
Menander, 45
Menelaus, 124, 146–7, 152–3
Menoetius, 152
Menon, 31–3, 35, 39
Mesopotamia, 1, 9, 49, 57, 63, 65–6,
    85,100
Methone, Siege of, 354 BC, 115
Miletus, 129, 133, 153, 155
Mithridates, 79
Mithridates VI of Pontus, 177
Mithrines, 44
Mnasicles, 159–60
Mongols, 176
Moors, 176
Motya, Siege of, 397 BC, 117
Myonessus, Battle of 190 BC, 156

Nabataea, 168, 169
Napoleon, 105, 115
Naseby, Battle of 1645 AD, 20
Nearchus, 59, 76, 89
Neoptolemus, xvi, xviii, 20, 42–52, 83, 100, 174
Neoptolemus II of Epirus, 163
Nero, 2, 3
Nicaea, 78, 85
Nicanor, 142, 165
Nile River, 9, 54
Nineveh, 167
Nora, 45, 81
Numantia, 10, 102, 135

Octavius (Augustus), 102
Odessus, 105
Odysseus, xv
Odrysians, 14, 19
Olympias, 21, 43, 48, 56, 61, 131, 162
Olympias, trireme, 138
Onomarchus, 30
Ophellas, 160–1
Orchomenus, 133
Oreus, 143
Orontes, Persian satrap, 44
Otranto, Straits of, 161, 163

Paeonia, 14, 19, 167
Palestine, 92, 100
Pamphylia, 7, 8, 64, 83, 93, 105, 145
Pammanes, 3
Pantauchus, xvi
Paphlagonia, 42, 50
Paraetacene, Battle of, 317 BC, xv, 5, 7, 9, 17–19, 22, 55, 66–8, 72–3, 75–6, 78–9, 81, 83, 85, 90, 94, 99, 173–4
Parium, 104
Parmenion, 6, 17, 18, 43, 77
Parapamisidae, 65
Parthia, 2, 18–19, 63, 78, 168
Pasitigris River, 16, 57

Patrae, 132
Patroclus, 22
Pedalium, 148
Peking, 115
Pella, xviii, 7, 31, 35, 39, 48, 55, 117–8, 121, 155, 161, 163, 165
Peloponnese, xvii
Peloponnesian War, 3, 116, 145, 162
Pelusium, 91, 145
Peneius River, 36, 39
Perdiccas, xvii, xviii, 3, 6, 9, 25, 41–45, 47, 49, 54, 62, 91–3, 119, 163, 175
Perdiccas III, 163
Pergamum, 155
Perilaus, 145
Perinthus, 116
Persepolis, 9, 16, 60, 116, 172
Perseus, 26
Persia, xvii, 6–7, 9–10, 12, 16–17, 19–20, 24, 30, 33, 35, 44, 51, 55, 57–61, 66, 77–9, 81, 85, 92–3, 100, 108, 110–11, 125, 133, 136, 142–43, 145, 154, 170, 174
Persian Gates, 43
Persian Wars, xiv, 137
Petersburg, 115
Petra, 168–9
Peucestas, xvii, 7, 9–10, 16, 56–57, 60–62, 66, 75, 79, 81, 83, 85–6
Pharaohs, xvii, 115
Pharnabazus, 50
Pharsalus, 17, 32
Phila, 128
Philip Arrhidaeus, 65
Philip II of Macedon, xvi, xvii, 1, 3–6, 8, 17, 25, 30, 36, 42–3, 47–8, 54, 61, 74, 77, 84, 90–1, 99, 102, 115–17, 119, 131, 141, 161–2, 177
Philip V of Macedon, 26
Philip, officer of Antiochus III, 22
Philip, officer of Eumenes, 83, 85, 90
Philip, brother of Cassander, 164–5

Philippi, Battle of, 42 BC, 102

Philotas, 43

Phocis, 27, 30, 32

Phoenicia, 60, 92, 132, 136, 145, 148, 167

Phoenix, 50, 135

Phrygia, xvii, 45–6, 63, 78

Piraeus, 116, 118, 120–1, 138, 141–2

Pisidia, 42, 44–5, 56

Pithon, Antigonid officer, 89–90, 95, 97

Pithon, satrap of Media, xvii, 12, 41, 54, 56, 60, 62–65, 68, 71, 73, 75–79, 85–6, 89, 175

Plato, 136

Plataea, 28, 32, 116

Pleistarchus, 104–6, 109, 139, 175

Pliny the Elder, 22

Plutarch, xiv, xvi, 21, 39, 40, 42, 48, 50–2, 107, 117, 125, 148, 153, 172

Polybius, xiv, 2, 6, 10–12, 178

Polycleitus, 145

Polyidus, 116

Polynaeus, 144, 148

Polyperchon, xvii, 15, 21, 49, 56, 61, 118–21, 132, 134, 142, 145, 155, 164, 175

Polytimetus River, 19

Pompey, 102, 140

Porus, xvi, 19, 43, 78, 93, 173

Poseidon, 141, 142

Poseidonius, 117, 126

Potidaea, 116

Prepelaus, 100, 106, 109, 133

Propontis, 42, 142

Ptolemaeus, nephew of Antigonus, 163–4, 166, 175

Ptolemy Soter, xv, xvii, xviii, 5, 9, 15, 25, 41, 48, 62, 90–7, 99–101, 106–7, 113, 121–2, 124, 128, 130, 132–3, 139–40, 145–50, 152–6, 158, 160–1, 167, 172–4

Ptolemy II, 178

Ptolemy IV, 13, 156

Ptolemy Ceraunus, 155, 175

Punjab, xvii, xviii, 156

Pydna, 131

Pydna, Battle of, 168 BC, 11–12, 26

Pyrrhus, xvi, 12, 22–3, 26, 32, 102, 111, 113, 155, 163, 165, 172–5

Quintus Curtius, 6, 15

Rameses II, 92

Raphia, Battle of, 217 BC, 13, 20, 22, 92, 94

Rhodes, 68, 100, 117–18, 121–6, 129–31, 133, 154

Rocroi, Battle of, 1643 AD, 20

Rome, xiv, 1, 11, 23–25, 51, 125, 130, 155, 168, 177

Sacred Band, 99

Sakae, 63

Salamis, Cyprus, Battle of, 306 BC, 100, 148–55

Salamis, Cyprus, Siege of, 307 BC, 124–7, 146–8, 152–3

Salamis, Athens, 155

Salamis, Athens, Battle of, 480 BC, 138, 141, 153, 173

Samnium, 24

Samos, 141, 149

Sardis, 44, 101, 133, 135

Sassanian, 18,178

Scipio Aemilianus, 10

Scipio Africanus, 2, 23

Scythia, xviii, 17, 19, 20, 63, 78, 105, 157, 178

Seleucus, xvii–xviii, 1, 20, 43, 56, 90–3, 95–6, 100–1, 103, 106, 109–13, 121, 133, 140, 145–6, 155, 157, 164, 167, 172–3, 176, 178

Sevastapol, 115

Shuppiluliuma II, 137

Sibyrtius, 61, 65

Sicyon, 132–3,146

Sidon, 100
Silver Shields, 2–3, 5, 8–10, 50, 56, 61, 66, 68, 76, 83–6, 97
Sippas, 28, 31
Sogdia, 1, 19–20, 41, 64, 116
Sogdian Rock, 131
Spain, 176
Sparta, 3, 11, 13, 39, 99, 116, 118, 135, 141, 145, 158, 161
Stasander, 65, 85
Sulla, 135, 177
Surus, 22
Susa, 7, 9, 57, 116
Susiane, 10, 55–6, 58
Synnada, 101, 106, 133, 135
Syracuse, 116–17, 123, 135, 138
Syria, 60, 90, 101–2, 146, 167

Tarentines, 63–5, 75, 78, 81, 95
Tauchira, 159
Taurus Mountains, 35, 42, 48, 89
Taxila, 48
Telesphorus, 143
Tenedos, 50
Teutamus, 66, 86
Teutoburgerwald, Battle of, 9 AD, 107
Thebes, xvi, 3, 37, 39, 116, 131
Theodosius, 177
Thera, 158
Thermopylae, 27–8, 35, 55
Thessaly, 17, 28, 31–2, 35–7, 39, 104, 117
Thibron, 158–61

Thrace, 3, 19, 31, 35, 104–6, 157
Thracian Chersonnese, xvii, 45, 140, 154
Thymochares, 144
Tlepolemus, 66
Tigris River, 57, 59
Titus, Roman Emperor, 168
Titus Manlius Torquatus, 23
Trajan, 2, 168
Triballians, 14
Triparadeisus, 9, 55, 89,175
Troy, 116
Trojan War, 22, 137
Tuthmose III, 92
Tyre, 90, 100, 116–17, 131–4, 145

Umbria, 24
Urania, 146

Vercingetorix, 135
Vergina, 55
Via Egnatia, 162
Virginia, 115
Vitruvius, 125–9

William Louis of Nassau, 1

Xenophon, 2, 20, 51, 60, 125
Xerxes, 141, 153, 173

Zagros Mountains, 59
Zama, Battle of, 202 BC, 23
Zeus, 107